Teaching with Children's Books

Teaching with Children's Books

Paths to Literature-Based Instruction

Edited by

Marilou R. Sorensen
University of Utah

Barbara A. Lehman
The Ohio State University at Mansfield

National Council of Teachers of English
1111 W. Kenyon Road, Urbana, IL 61801

Grateful acknowledgment is made to the following publishers for permission to reprint the selections indicated. "Stories I Ain't Told Nobody Yet" from *Stories I Ain't Told Nobody Yet* by Jo Carson, copyright © 1989. Published by permission of Orchard Books, New York. "I'd Like to Be a Lighthouse" copyright © 1926 by Doubleday, a division of Bantam Doubleday Dell Publishing Group, Inc., from *Taxis and Toadstools* by Rachel Field. Used by permission of Doubleday, a division of Bantam Doubleday Dell Publishing Group, Inc. Excerpt from *Yellow Bird and Me.* Copyright © 1986 by Joyce Hansen. Reprinted by permission of Clarion Books/Houghton Mifflin Co. All rights reserved.

Manuscript Editor: Jane M. Curran

Production Editor: Peter Feely

Cover Design: Pat Mayer

Interior Design: Doug Burnett

NCTE Stock Number 52929-3050

Library of Congress Cataloging-in-Publication Data

Teaching with children's books : paths to literature-based instruction /
  edited by Marilou R. Sorensen, Barbara A. Lehman.
     p. cm.
   Includes bibliographical references and indexes.
   ISBN 0-8141-5292-9 (pbk.)
    1. Literature—Study and teaching (Elementary)
2. Interdisciplinary approach in education. 3. Reading (Elementary)
I. Sorensen, Marilou R. II. Lehman, Barbara A. III. National
Council of Teachers of English.
LB1575.T42 1995   94-43698
372.6044—dc20   CIP

Contents

IV. Modeling

V. Teaching

Acknowledgments

Teaching with Children's Books exists because of the vision of NCTE to organize the Committee on Literature-Based Language Arts Instruction in Elementary Schools. The Executive Board continued to support this committee through the change in focus to "elementary and middle school" and through several national workshops that endorsed the initial function: *to review theory and research on literature-based language arts instruction; to explore the implications of such theory and research for building guidelines for using literature as a base for curriculum; to propose for publication helpful ideas, suggestions, and aids for teachers in literature-based curriculum.*

Particularly, we thank Michael Spooner, former senior executive editor at NCTE, whose helpful suggestions and patience were positive reinforcement through the writing process. To reviewers who assisted, we are also grateful: Evelyn Freeman, Patricia Scharer, Sue DiPuccio, Todd Shelton, and Vicki Smith.

The committee members either were contributing authors to this collection or gave endless support throughout the project. The friendships of this group will last throughout our lives. Our thanks go to:

Kathryn L. Gould-Anderson, California State University at Chico

Kathleen T. Isaacs, Park School, Brooklandville, Maryland

Fran Jennings, Arlington Independent School District, Arlington, Texas

Jill May, Purdue University, West Lafayette, Indiana

Jean McCabe, Grand Haven Schools, Grand Haven, Michigan

Sister Mary Moore, Coker College, Hartsville, South Carolina

Glenna Sloan, Queens College, New York

Agnes Stahlschmidt, Myers Ganoung Elementary School, Tucson, Arizona

Introduction

There have been volumes written about the values and uses of literature as a basis of teaching: enjoyment, developing lifelong readers, understanding cultural diversity, recognizing and interpreting literary works, and modeling positive writing styles. But the most fundamental asset is that literature provides the spoken and written story of human experience, the record of past and present, a paradigm on which to record the future.

Meek, Warlow, and Barton (1978) contend that children's conception of the world is rooted in the literature they read. In her May Hill Arbuthnot Honor Lecture, author Margaret Mahy (1989) says that literature allows us "first to give form to, and then to take possession of, a variety of truths both literal and figurative" (p. 32).

What are the literal and figurative truths of literature? When children read an assignment from a basal reader, they might accept the "correct" answers that publishers provide, someone's interpretation and understanding of the story.

Not so with literal and figurative truths of literature as Mahy perceives it. Teachers and students are the link to literary understandings. They are what makes the meaning. It is through their interpretations—their questions and their perceptions—that literature becomes an object to hold to the light in order to view its prismatic hues in today's sunshine. The beauty of that interpretation, both literal and figurative, is the realization that tomorrow's sunshine may bring different insights and hues. That possibility for transformation is what Bruner (1966) calls surprise: "an act that produces effective surprise . . . which is the hallmark of a creative enterprise" (p. 18). Literature in the classroom should be a creative enterprise for both teacher and student.

Very early, children learn to equate pleasure and surprise with literature. As they read a story or poetry, they delight in the sound of its language and imagery. As they hear a piece of nonfiction, they find joy in the satisfaction of curiosity and learning. What a disappointment that as they receive "formal" instruction, they struggle to understand what the writer intended. This disappointment is because children do not merely construct their "universe" from text. They watch the historic walk on the moon and then reevaluate their understanding by using a nonfiction book, perhaps to help explore their own space. They feel the tug and pull of growing up and then relate to protagonists who have also struggled with personal identity.

Students find no pleasure in trying to make meaning from contrived dialogue, all the time realizing that their responses must be what "the teacher expects." On the other hand, through literature, teachers and students explore the meanings as well as the devices that writers use to make that meaning: how words are combined to make text, how one story relates to other stories, and the background knowledge that is already theirs. They may even write *about* literature as a way to search for the meaning or create a poem that expands their thinking.

Readers have unique and individual interpretations of literary works. Just as a person atop the Sears Tower views Chicago differently from another person who is standing on the sidewalk, readers take literature and mold it to fit their own vistas. "Every group of readers gives every story many different shapes based on original patterns. . . . Our sense of what a story is changes even as we talk and think about it, and every time we read it" (Chambers, 1970, p. 61).

Why use literature in our teaching? Because it can never be a closed system, a sequence of prescribed events and answers. It is a dynamic duo: the text and the reader. From these two comes the essence from which meaning is made.

The path that teachers take in literature-based curricula is an exciting one. No two teachers tread this path in the same way, at the same pace, psychologically or academically, or with the same needs, interests, or knowledge.

Some see the movement to using trade books in the curriculum as a recent revolution. Actually, literature as reading instruction has been a phenomenon from the time that *McGuffey Readers* used stories to teach the value of good manners and *The New England Primers* taught phonics skills. With the advent of standardized teaching, however, the practice of using "real" pieces of literature was shifted to controlled vocabulary stories in basal readers that matched the notion of mastering sequenced skills. Even then, literature played a part in many teachers' lives as they balanced the staid curriculum with stories of adventure, humor, and fantasy.

Just as literature-based teaching is not a new idea, it is not, or never was, a "set" of methods or strategies that can be packaged and sold as a "kit." But the goals and intentions *are* very clear and have changed somewhat to accommodate contemporary literature for the reader of today.

The pathway to using literature in the classroom is a series of steps: understanding, considering, preparing, modeling, teaching, collaborating, assessing, and supporting. In each of these steps we have invited teachers, researchers, and administrators to present their perceptions of and research on striding toward literature-based teaching. Their views, strategies, and opinions may be varied, but the convergent path is clear in all of them:

- teachers *are* thinking about the way children learn
- teachers *are* thinking about their knowledge of literature
- teachers *are* thinking about the best ways to develop literature-based instruction

Teaching with Children's Books began as the fabric of discussion for the NCTE Committee on Literature-Based Language Arts Instruction in Elementary and Middle Schools, which pondered the concerns of researchers, administrators, consultants, librarians, and teachers and their role in using literature in the classroom.

As with many open forums, more questions surfaced about our direction than there were answers. Initially we struggled with the terminology *literature-based teaching* and *teaching with literature.* But we agreed that our function as a committee was to be wider than clarifying terms. We wanted to *know* what the practices were.

We found out that many teachers use literature as part of their teaching; some use it almost exclusively. Questions about *how* to move into literature-based programs abounded; the variation of the needs was apparent.

We also found out about teachers who were hesitant to give up the assurance of published sequenced skills contained in packaged programs. Some even admitted that they "sneaked" literature in between the mandated skills sheets. Concerns about "taking risks" and "professional empowerment" regarding choice of curriculum were not unusual.

Questions about networking, about convincing administrators of the need for literature, and about assessment abounded, ranging from "How do I start?" to the philosophical theories of learning and literary analysis.

Teaching with Children's Books in no way attempts to answer all of the questions and concerns regarding using literature in the classroom. That would be an impossible task. Every person has a unique set of reasons to try *or* not to try teaching with literature. Every classroom, district, and state has sets of parameters that encourage *or* limit the use of literature.

What we hope is that this text will become a way to organize groups to think about, talk about, and question the practice of teaching with story. If something in the book validates your present practice of teaching with trade books, we will be delighted. If a decision is made to try and link reading/writing and story, we applaud your efforts. If questions surface that cause you to examine your present classroom practices, then our efforts in collecting these writings will have been worth it.

Above all, we hope *Teaching with Children's Books* will be a way to network what *is* being done, what *could* be accomplished, and what *will* be ongoing with literature in the classroom.

References

Bruner, J. S. (1966). *On knowing: Essays for the left hand*. Cambridge, MA: Harvard University Press.

Chambers, D. W. (1970). *Storytelling and creative drama*. Dubuque, IA: William C. Brown.

Mahy, M. (1989). *A dissolving ghost: Possible operations of truth in children's books and the lives of children*. May Hill Arbuthnot Honor Lecture. Presented 23 April, University of Pittsburgh.

Meek, M., Warlow, A., & Barton, G. (Eds.). (1978). Interchapter. In *The cool web: The pattern of children's reading* (pp. 73–75). New York: Atheneum.

I Understanding

Questions of Definition

Glenna Sloan
Queens College, City University of New York

Exactly what is meant by *literature-based* teaching and learning? What theory underlies the practice of literature-based instruction? What are the distinguishing characteristics of this instructional approach? These and related questions of definition are explored in this chapter.

Literature-Based Teaching and Learning

In the simplest terms, *literature-based* implies a movement—particularly in literacy instruction—away from the exclusive use of the basal reader and toward teaching and learning through children's literature, both fictional and factual. The notion that it is possible and desirable to develop reading—and writing—ability by using genuine literary works is by no means new, but only recently has the movement toward literature-based instruction become widespread. Its growth represents efforts to combat both illiteracy and aliteracy by acknowledging that authentic literature—works by writers with something to say and the skill to say it well—has the potential to motivate children to read. The movement is also part of a general trend, particularly in literacy education, away from fragmented, largely teacher-directed approaches toward those which are holistic and child-centered, the latter more in keeping with new scientific knowledge about how language is acquired and developed.

Modern research in all aspects of language development leads us away from how it is approached in traditional classrooms. There reading, writing, and speaking typically are studied and practiced apart from each other in a fragmented manner; each is assigned a separate slot in the timetable, with its own separate activities and exercises. Reading is broken down into a skills sequence focusing first on words and parts of words. But taking this route toward language development runs counter to what we now know about how language develops. Language is not learned part to whole, but from whole to part; all language functions interrelate, developing together (K. S. Goodman, 1986; Smith, 1983). Language skill flourishes in situations where actual purpose and function are clear to learners, where children are active participants in every step of the process, receiving affirmation of their efforts from those around

them who are already speakers, readers, and writers (Halliday, 1975; Smith, 1983, 1986).

Literacy begins in hearts, not heads; children who have never thrilled to hearing or speaking words will remain indifferent to reading them. Realizing this, educators are looking critically at reading material used in schools. Is aliteracy a response to force-feeding students with the boring banalities found in basal readers? Surely the exploits of storybook characters like Frog and Toad, Curious George, and Pippi Longstocking can revive literary interest dulled by exercises on the eccentricities of long and short vowel sounds. Indeed, children flourish as readers when they are allowed to choose and study books that interest, excite, and challenge them (Eldredge & Butterfield, 1986; Holdaway, 1984; Tunnell & Jacobs, 1989).

Developing readers need genuine reading material with function and purpose for them as individuals: stories and poems if they give pleasure; biography and history if they satisfy curiosity; informational books if they contain answers to perplexing questions; poetry if its imagery and rhythm bring delight. Language flourishes in situations that make sense to learners: reading what they choose to read because it interests them; reading to answer their own questions; speaking to persuade others to read their favorite books; listening to discover others' ideas about a book; writing to an admired author.

Kits of exercises, workbooks, and other prestructured materials are unlikely to meet the needs of each child in a particular group. All holistic instruction begins with a study of each child in a class. Aware of each one's unique needs, teachers can begin to select materials and set up situations to facilitate learning for all. For greatest success, opportunities for learning must be grounded in actual experience, in the real lives of the children.

Since reading is an important source of experiences—both personal and shared—literature-based classrooms are rich in reading material: books, periodicals, newspapers, pamphlets, travel brochures, catalogs, recipes, advertisements, lists, instructions, captioned displays. The very experience of reading—fact or fiction—leads naturally to talk about what one reads, to research, and to writing. In a literature-based classroom, purposeful activities develop from what is actually happening there: preparation for an author's visit by reading his or her books, preparing through research for an apple-picking expedition or a visit to the zoo, reading biographies and subsequently writing one's own family history.

The literature-based classrooms I have visited are lively, busy places where teachers help children take responsibility for their own learning and use of time. Teachers and students plan together; children are active in self-evaluation, in stating their own goals, and in deciding how to carry out these goals. Each of these classrooms is different, for it was designed with the needs and abilities of a particular group of children in mind, yet there are important similarities among them. The classrooms are communities of learners where teachers, clearly learners themselves, serve as guides and facilitators, motivators and mentors. I found the teachers organized, flexible, involved, interested, accepting, and enthusiastic. These teachers know their students well, having listened to and observed the students in order to discover how they were becoming effective language users and to ascertain what was needed to help them grow. In my experience, effective literature-based teachers demonstrate, in their teaching, the fact that true education has very little to do with explanation but everything to do with engagement and involvement.

From an informal survey of seventy-two self-styled literature-based elementary teachers who work in Queens and on Long Island, New York, I found all to be in transition—if not in philosophy, then in practice (Sloan, 1991b). Many, because of administratively mandated curriculum, are still using basals along with a literature *component,* such as regularly scheduled periods for independent reading from classroom libraries or, in several cases, regular use of the *Junior Great Books Shared Inquiry Program.* Large numbers reported using especially designed transitional programs from commercial publishers, such as *Bridges: Moving from Basal into Literature* (Scholastic) or obviously transitional "literature-based" readers such as that described by Christine D'Amico (1991):

> The literature-based reader I am using in my third grade is called *Going Places,* published by Silver Burdette. It tries to stimulate literature reading by using colorful displays and giving students an opportunity to select a book of their choice to read along with the reader. There are phonics exercises for the children to master as well as story analysis skills.

In an attempt to incorporate literature in more holistic programs, some of the teachers whom I surveyed reported that they found it useful to organize instruction around thematic units (Moss, 1984; Sloan, 1991a) or *text sets,* a variation of this approach. In this procedure, three to five core works are read aloud to the whole group or read by each of the children, if multiple copies are available. Ideally, these are exemplary books offering ideas worth thinking, talking, and writing about. The discussion, a planned sequence of presentation, focuses on relationships among the books in both form and content. Discussion in large and small groups is the favored means of "studying" the core texts. Twenty-five to fifty books and other materials on the topic or related to it are made available for independent reading and further discussion in small groups or with partners. Extensions of the reading-listening-discussing phase may be further reading, research, writing, or art activities.

Literature-based instruction is broadly interpreted by teachers in the survey. Two additional procedures frequently cited were guided study of a novel that was read or listened to by the whole group, and literature response groups or "literature circles," involving small-group discussion of books read in common.

Literature or Literature-Based Programs

While it is natural to be in transition between traditional and holistic approaches to literacy teaching and learning, it is important to have a clear view of the holistic approach. In "Literature-Based or Literature: Where Do We Stand?" Yvonne Freeman (1989) makes a distinction between *literature* and *literature-based* and cautions against misinterpretation or misrepresentation of "the real thing," literature.

The California *English Language Arts Framework* (1987) states that the new literature-based English language arts curriculum should provide students with (1) "an in-depth study of core literary works," (2) "reading of literature that extends the study of the core work, captures students' individual interests, and challenges them to explore new avenues on their own," and (3) "recreational-motivational reading that is based on students' natural curiosity and that encourages them to read for pleasure (p. 7)." In suggesting that many literature-based programs, especially those for the newer "literature readers," deal *only* with "the in-depth study of core literary works," Freeman expresses a concern of many literature advocates. (Another valid concern is that "in-depth study of core literary works" may be interpreted as an invitation to submit literature to the scrutiny prescribed in older basal reader manuals for the "stories" of directed reading lessons). No matter how well this in-depth study may be handled, however, it cannot stand alone. Effective literacy programs require a component of independent reading.

In an effort to align their materials with holistic theory, many commercial publishers have included literature in new versions of their basal readers. In some cases, the literature is unabridged; in others it is "basalized," to use a term coined by Kenneth Goodman (1988) to describe the practice of simplifying, rewriting, censoring, leveling, and otherwise mutilating works of literature for inclusion in basal readers. Furthermore, to fulfill a perceived need of teachers who are teaching literature, countless publishers—amateur to professional—have developed teaching guides to accompany works of children's literature. Many of these guides are longer than the books themselves. They, and the teachers' manuals accompanying the new, "literature-based" readers, are frighteningly familiar.

Although these materials now may deal with literature, their way of treating it echoes the earliest and worst basal-reader manuals. There are fill-in-the-blanks exercises, with words supplied; cause and effect maps; flow charts; word games often unrelated to the literature; questions with suggested answers for the teacher; and procedures for teaching the selection according to such formulas as the Directed Reading Thinking Activity, a specific stop-start technique involving predicting, checking the prediction, and predicting again.

By their very nature, prestructured literature-based programs lead teachers and learners away from freedom of choice back to control and constraint. Literature is graded for use at specific grade levels, although we know that in a given group, interests and abilities differ markedly. Kits of preselected books limit readers' choices. Teachers are "guided" in what to teach and when. Children, through worksheets, are directed to answer others' questions, to follow instructions, to find another's meaning, to write according to a formula. In short, the old basal systems, with all their faults, are reincarnated to sabotage the new ways.

What is to be done? Warned away from the basalization of literature, how do we proceed to use, but not abuse, works of genuine literature in our classrooms? Many of the teachers in my survey, although in transition in their practices, were clear in their notions of how an authentic literature-based, whole language literacy program should look (see Figure 1.1).

Defining the terms we use requires continuing reflection and exploration. Indeed, *transition* implies growth and change. Teachers in transition are in the good company of many colleagues. Most heartening, these teachers report that their struggle to move toward more holistic literacy programs is rewarding and worth whatever effort is required (Scharer, 1992).

To conclude, descriptive statements about the meaning of the term *literature-based*, developed collaboratively with classroom teachers, are offered in Figure 1.2. What emerges from these statements is an emphasis where it belongs—on *literature*.

Figure 1.1.
Elements of a literature-based, whole language literacy program.

Materials
- genuine, unabridged literature without manuals or guides

Organization
- discussion in small groups, in whole group, or one-to-one (with teacher, parent, or partner)

Methods for small-group work
- cooperatively develop guidelines
- large-group brainstorming first to develop questions and topics
- preset time limits
- postsharing in whole group

Best questions
- children's own
- those that probe from free responses
- interpretive
- those beginning with *Why*
- open-ended
- those with no single correct answer
- general, not focused on trivia
- pertaining to the whole poem or entire story

Best activities
- are initiated by the children
- relate to the reading
- relate writing to reading
- integrate the language arts
- are real and purposeful
- allow for choice

Problems that arise
- insufficient knowledge of children's literature
- uncertainty about how to "teach" literature, especially questioning
- overwhelming organizational aspects: grouping, integrating curriculum, record keeping
- difficulty in grading creative projects
- lack of confidence in ability to plan curriculum
- parental or pupil resistance

Suggestions for alleviating the problems
- observe in literature-based, holistic classrooms
- form support groups
- set up workshops and study groups to learn about literature, clarify goals, discuss methodology
- hold information sessions for parents

Figure 1.2.
Descriptive statements
about the term
literature-based.

L	Literature, the best of written expression, creates interest in words.
I	Interest begins in delight with genuine, unique literary works.
T	Trade books are authentic, real-world reading material.
E	Emphasis is on reading, not on reading-related exercises.
R	Readers have a wide choice of reading materials.
A	Activities in writing and other arts flow from actual reading.
T	Teachers and students create their own study plans.
U	Units of study are built around real books, not textbooks.
R	Responsibility for learning is required.
E	Evaluation of progress is developmental.
B	Books are the basics.
A	Application of ideas found in books is varied and personal.
S	Searching books for pleasure and information is what literacy is about.
E	Emphasis is on purposeful reading, not word-perfect reading.
D	Deep study of a book, an author, a genre, is possible.

References

Altwerger, B., Edelsky, C., & Flores, B. M. (1990). *Whole language: What's the difference?* Portsmouth, NH: Heinemann.

Anderson, R. C., Heibert, E. H., Scott, J. A., & Wilkinson, I. A. G. (1984). *Becoming a nation of readers: The report of the Commission on Reading.* Washington, DC: National Institute of Education.

D'Amico, C. (1991). *Description of a literature-based program.* Unpublished report. New York: School of Education, Queens College, City University of New York.

Dolch, E. W. (1950). *Teaching primary reading.* Champaign, IL: Garrard.

Durrell, D. (1940). *Improving reading instruction.* Yonkers, NY: World.

Eldredge, J. L., & Butterfield, D. (1986). Alternatives to traditional reading instruction. *The Reading Teacher, 40,* 32–37.

Freeman, Y. S. (1989). Literature-based or literature: Where do we stand? *Teachers Networking,* Summer, 13–15.

Goodman, K. S., (1986). *What's whole in whole language?* Portsmouth, NH: Heinemann.

———. (1988). Look what they've done to Judy Blume! The "basalization" of children's literature. *The New Advocate, 1,* 29–41.

Goodman, K. S., Shannon, P., Freeman, Y. S., & Murphy, S. (1988). *Report card on basal readers.* Katonah, NY: Richard C. Owen.

Goodman, Y., Watson, D., & Burke, C. (1987). *Reading miscue inventory: Alternative procedures.* Katonah, NY: Richard C. Owen.

Halliday, M. A. K. (1975). *Learning how to mean: Explorations in the development of language.* London: Edward Arnold.

Harste, J., Woodward, V., & Burke, C. (1984). *Language stories and literacy lessons.* Portsmouth, NH: Heinemann.

Henke, L. (1988). Beyond basal reading: A district's commitment to change. *The New Advocate, 1,* 41–51.

Holdaway, D. (1984). *Stability and change in literacy learning.* Portsmouth, NH: Heinemann.

Koeller, S. (1981). 25 years advocating children's literature in the reading program. *The Reading Teacher, 34,* 552–56.

Meek, M. (1982). *Learning to read.* Portsmouth, NH: Heinemann.

Moss, J. F. (1984). *Focus units in literature: A handbook for elementary school teachers.* Urbana, IL: National Council of Teachers of English.

Routman, R. (1988). *Transitions: From literature to literacy.* Portsmouth, NH: Heinemann.

———. (1991). *Invitations: Changing as teachers and learners.* Portsmouth, NH: Heinemann.

Scharer, P. L. (1992). Teachers in transition: An exploration of changes in teachers and classrooms during implementation of literature-based reading instruction. *Research in the Teaching of English, 26,* 408–45.

Sloan, G. (1991a). *The child as critic: Teaching literature in elementary and middle school* (3rd ed.). New York: Teachers College Press, Columbia University.

———. (1991b). *Literature-based literacy development: Teachers' perceptions of the process.* Unpublished results of a survey. New York: Queens College, City University of New York.

Smith, F. (1983). *Essays into literacy: Selected papers and some afterthoughts.* Exeter, NH: Heinemann.

———. (1986). *Insult to intelligence: The bureaucratic invasion of our classrooms.* New York: Arbor House.

Tunnell, M. O., & Jacobs, J. S. (1989). Using "real" books: Research findings on literature based reading instruction. *The Reading Teacher, 42,* 470–77.

2 Perspectives on the Use of Children's Literature in Reading Instruction

Mary Jo Skillings
California State University, San Bernardino

I n order to understand the current movement for using children's literature in the reading program, it is helpful to review what our predecessors used as materials and methods of reading instruction and to examine the current driving influences for change from a basal to literature-based curriculum.

Historical Background

The following account briefly outlines the history of literature-based teachings, some major thrusts in textbook change, and the professionals who caused these changes.

During our country's colonial period (1600–1776), children were taught by stern schoolmasters whose primary concern was to ensure students' salvation. *The New England Primer*, described as being "bare of beauty . . . rough and stern" (N. B. Smith, 1963, p. 4) was published without controlled vocabulary or the systematic introduction of new words.

The period of building a new nation (1776–1840) and developing an informed citizenry brought about texts that were replete with patriotism and historically informative selections to help build a united nation from many diverse groups.

Instruction during the mid to late 1800s was geared toward a broader reading content of science, history, and art, as well as morals, and the use of the sight-word method (N. B. Smith, 1963). McGuffey's graded series of readers, published around 1836, consisted of stories about the rewards of good behavior and everyday life, but the books also contained some literature, such as poetry by William Wordsworth. These readers were used well into the 1900s and "literally comprised the elementary curriculum" (Huck, Hepler, & Hickman, 1993; Vacca, Vacca, & Gove, 1991).

Folktales and excerpts from the classics appeared in the basic readers of the first decade of the 1900s and were designed to develop literature appreciation. Supplemental texts were introduced, and children were given a separate class period for memorizing phonic families. By 1925, publishers of basal reading programs began adding new features—for example, preprimers and workbooks to accompany the textbook (Vacca, Vacca, & Gove, 1991). Reading selections contained informative and realistic texts.

Literary readers were developed for basic reading along with standardized tests, phonic charts and cards, and word lists. Following World War I, new methods of silent reading and an interest in accommodating individual differences by ability grouping as indicated through the use of standardized testing came about. Reading selections contained informative as well as realistic material. Silent reading seatwork and a variety of workbook-type activities were used (N. B. Smith, 1963).

By 1940, many components of what we now call literature-based reading instruction were used in many classrooms. Concepts about "reading readiness" were discussed, and as a result teachers often postponed beginning reading for some children. Teachers became interested in composing experience charts and other cooperatively composed texts. Reading teachers used both silent and oral reading, and teaching through units became popular.

The armed forces, during and following World War II, charged that American young people could not read or follow directions. As a result, remedial reading clinics were instituted with highly organized skill-development programs. Teachers still used basic readers and workbook pages, but outside personal interest reading was encouraged (N. B. Smith, 1963).

The idea that instruction must be taught in a set sequence or arrangement of skills to ensure "continuity of skill development" (N. B. Smith, 1963) sprang from the 1948 *Ginn Basic Reader* lists of objectives (Vacca, Vacca, & Gove, 1991). Reading programs were arranged according to grade levels and included teacher's editions and diagnostic tests. Ability grouping was popular, and teachers listened to children read in round-robin fashion. This management system was prevalent into the 1970s.

The predominately white middle-class "Dick and Jane" characters from the 1940s to the 1960s gave way to more ethnically diverse characters in the 1970s. Following the demands of social change, stronger roles for girls and women as problem solvers and leaders began to appear in reading texts by 1976 (Farr & Roser, 1979). Controlled vocabulary with stilted language and story excerpts still prevailed. However, textbook publishers added new components in the area of assessment measures, such as preskill and postskill tests, pupil placement tests, and end-of-the-book tests. Teachers were given inservice instruction to ascertain causes of reading failure and the influences of listening, semantics, and linguistics as related to reading. Individualized instruction in reading was discussed, as was teaching, particularly remedial instruction, with the use of machines.

Concerns over accountability and competency-based education have been the impetus over the past decade in reading instruction and assessment tools. The Education Commission of the States (1983) and the National Assessment of Educational Progress (NAEP, 1990) have used standardized tests as a measure of educational effectiveness. This alignment with standardized testing contributes to the fact that 80 to 90 percent of American elementary classrooms are reported to use published reading programs (Tunnell & Jacobs, 1989; Vacca, Vacca, & Gove, 1991).

Reading instruction in the 1980s and into the 1990s has been a reflection of major movements: to use basals or to use "real books," or to supplement basal programs with literature. Publishing companies have responded to the momentum and enthusiasm of whole language advocates who cite the large body of research in the areas of emergent literacy (Holdaway, 1979; Wells, 1986) and whole language and literature-based reading instruction (K. S. Goodman, 1986; Tunnell & Jacobs, 1989). These studies indicate the need for stories and meaningful language experiences for children in order to foster literacy and the lifelong love of reading. Many basal texts now include literature by award-winning writers and illustrators with the original language intact as well. Some use literature as supplemental trade reading.

Though this saga of reading instruction has focused on general methods and materials that have dominated American classrooms, historically there have been insightful, innovative teachers and researchers who challenged the traditional skill-based, text-driven, mechanical approaches. They took original, less traveled paths. It is their voices that provide the foundation or first glimmerings of literature-based reading instruction.

First Awakenings

The use of literature as rich sources for reading instruction found its bearings in the progressive education and nursery school movements. Early in the 1920s, Lucy Sprague Mitchell, principal of the Bank Street School, put into practice many of the ideas practiced in present-day literature-based classrooms, implementing a wide variety of meaningful experiences for young children in written and oral language. The classes Mitchell conducted on writing for children greatly influenced author Margaret Wise Brown, whose works for young children are still popular today.

In 1943, Doris Lee and Lillian Lamoreaux published *Learning to Read through Experience,* in which they emphasized real experiences and "experience charts" (really the beginnings of shared reading), a component of literature-based instruction. This book was later updated by Lee and Roach Van Allen in 1963.

Research conducted in the 1950s and 1960s, particularly as it related to meeting the individual needs of the reader and the use of the language-experience approach, pointed the way to literature-based reading instruction of today. The work of Jeanette Veatch (1958) emphasized children selecting and reading real books at their own pace, child-teacher conferences, individual diagnosis, and flexible grouping. This program focused on the power of motivating children by listening to entertaining stories, helping them to read these books, and devoting time to discussion with children about their reading (Farr & Roser, 1979).

The courses of study in most teacher education institutions have regularly contained courses on children's literature, oral interpretation, or storytelling. The emphasis in these courses has been on determining children's preferences for particular books and finding "the right book for the right child." In 1925, Emelyn Gardner and Eloise Ramsey wrote *A Handbook for Children's Literature,* which was used in many of these courses. It helped prospective teachers determine what were the best books to use with children.

Charlotte Huck and Doris Young prepared a text in 1961, *Children's Literature in the Elementary School,* with three chapters devoted to the development of a reading program based on literature. The emphasis in this text was on the use of literature throughout the curriculum in teaching reading, social studies, science, and other subjects. This text predated the development of the whole language movement.

Whole Language

"The secret of it all lies in the parents' reading to and with the child" (Huey, 1968, p. 332). Literature-based and whole language movements have their theoretical framework in the early writings of John Dewey (1933) and Edmond Huey (1968); similarly, these movements believe in a holistic explanation of how reading ability develops. Both movements are grounded in the belief that students must be engaged in meaningful contexts and functional experiences with print, together with heavy exposure to children's literature. Like Dewey (1933), they challenge as "mechanical" and "passive" those practices with exercises that are isolated and broken down into a discrete hierarchy of skills.

The developmental theories of cognitive psychologists Jean Piaget (1970) and Lev Vygotsky (1986) have greatly influenced this shift in focus. Their beliefs that children are active participants in their own learning and that they co-construct meaning as they interpret and give meaning to the language events they experience provide the bedrock for the whole language and literature-based instruction of today. Linguists Noam Chomsky and Michael Halliday, among others, contributed much to our views that children learn language in social contexts.

International Beginnings

Men make some things to serve a purpose, other things simply to please themselves. Literature is a construct of the latter kind, and the proper response to it is therefore (in D. W. Harding's words) to "share in the author's satisfaction that it was as it was and not otherwise." (Britton, 1978, p. 106)

In 1966 a group of British educators and their American counterparts held a conference at Dartmouth to investigate the perspective and practices of teaching English and to participate in an international exchange of new ideas. Recommendations that pertained specifically to the use of literature in the classroom are identified below.

- Teachers need to select books that exemplify diverse visions of life and provide opportunities for discussion and exploration with students.
- Teachers need to provide rich literary experiences and examine selections for grade level appropriateness.
- Teachers need to eliminate superficial examination patterns related to literature.
- Teachers need to be informed about research theory and practice and to guide their use of literature accordingly.
- Teachers at all levels need to have preservice in the uses of literature in the classroom. (Cianciolo, 1988, p. 13)

The philosophical stance of James Britton, a primary mover at the conference, can be identified in the position statements that came from the conference. Attendees acknowledged the importance of the affective responses to literature through a variety of means and noted that sharing personal responses "should lead back to the particular work rather than focus on and stop with the students and their subjective associations in response to the work" (Cianciolo, 1988, p. 14). The influence of the Dartmouth Conference was significant to teachers in the late 1960s in the following ways: (1) documents were published from the proceedings that affected teacher education courses in the teaching of language arts; (2) the International Federation for the Teaching of English (IFTE) was formed for the express purpose of facilitating collaboration and exchange of ideas with scholars from different countries and regions; and (3) the

Dartmouth Conference provided the direction which eventually led to research in the study of literature use in the elementary school (Cianciolo, 1988).

The significance of early engagement with books in facilitating literacy was richly documented (Harste, Woodward, & Burke, 1984; Holdaway, 1979; Wells, 1986). Increased interest in the development of oral and written language and the importance of personal experiences in shaping children's learning had a profound influence on the British primary schools and the move toward open education and informal education.

Implications of these movements can also be seen in the Bullock Report (1975), named after Sir Alan Bullock, who chaired the committee. This report was conducted by the English government, and many of the same English educators participated who had been involved in the Dartmouth Conference. Committee recommendations included suggestions for developing critical thinking skills when teaching reading with literature. Emphasis was placed on the early introduction of books in the preschool years to give young children pleasurable experiences with reading. Both the Dartmouth Conference and the Bullock Report advanced the beliefs that teachers needed to provide an active response-centered approach to the study and use of literature.

Research: Foundations for Curriculum Change

This large-scale network of international educators prepared the way for research endeavors pursuing many different avenues in the area of language and reading. The model for this progression toward a more natural literacy-learning environment in the classroom came from the way children master other developmental tasks, especially those involved in spoken language.

Much of the educational literature of the 1970s reflected a move toward the integration of the teaching of reading, writing, listening, and speaking. This movement was preceded by the work of a number of scholars in New Zealand who were particularly interested in the influx of Polynesian people into inner-city schools (Holdaway, 1982). The work and writing of Sylvia Ashton-Warner (1963) detailed the uses of highly charged personal key words as the stimulus for reading and writing in language-experience events for the Maori children. Donald Holdaway (1979) was instrumental in popularizing a teaching strategy called the "shared book experience" using "big books." This involved the teacher creating an environment similar to the bedtime story where children could actively participate in the enjoyment of reading a story repeatedly. Through these repetitive experiences, young children begin to develop pleasurable associations and reading-like behaviors.

Marie Clay (1979), also in New Zealand, examined knowledge about print that children possess prior to formal instruction and how their understanding about print changes. She also developed the "running record" and Reading Recovery, early intervention strategies for children who were at risk of reading failure. About the same time, Ken Goodman (1973) developed a method for analyzing miscues in the United States. Now teachers had ways to evaluate children's reading during the act of reading, ways of looking at how children approach unfamiliar texts. With these analysis systems, teachers had significant evidence about the cues that the reader used to analyze words and to gain meaning from print. The focus of these systems was directed toward the uniqueness and specific needs of the reader.

The issue of how children learn to read sparked much controversy during this time frame. Psycholinguist theorists, such as Ken Goodman (1973) and Frank Smith (1976, 1977, 1978, 1985) contributed to the literature-based instruction movement. As proponents of literature-based or holistic language explanations, they argued that reading cannot be separated into discrete skills such as those demonstrated in published reading programs. Rather, they "learn to read by reading" (Smith, 1976) real books, real stories.

The work of Carol Chomsky (1972) and Donald Graves (1983) supported the importance of connecting reading and writing with the development of beginning literacy. Similarly, later works by Lucy Calkins (1983) and by Rob Tierney and David Pearson (1983) assisted the movement by proposing that the processes of reading and writing are reciprocal—that is, learning about one process assists in the development and strengthening of the other.

National Commissions on Learning through Literature

The educational reform movement that emerged during the late 1950s was a response to Russia's launching of Sputnik. The American public began questioning the effectiveness of the educational system, and as a result, Congress provided federal funding for educational reform in science, math, and foreign languages. After spokespeople for the National Council of Teachers of English (NCTE) testified before Congress about the need for research in the field of English, Congress authorized limited funds for the improvement of English instruction and the development of Project English. In 1962, six Curriculum Study Centers were established to study and improve English instruction. While the focus was oriented toward English, the centers did suggest a distinct place for literature in the elementary curriculum (Cianciolo, 1988).

Two professional organizations, the National Council of Teachers of English and the International Reading Association (IRA), had a major impact on the dissemination of current research on language and learning to educators. This outreach came in the form of cooperatively organizing Impact Conferences (Cullinan, 1989), which provided opportunities for educators to hear internationally recognized researchers in the field of reading and language who supported teachers' efforts to implement literature-based instruction.

Another surge of educational reform of the late 1960s, which gained momentum by the 1980s, was the back-to-basics movement. This philosophy emphasized a content-filled curriculum and accountability of the schools to the public. Emanating from this movement, the National Assessment of Educational Progress (NAEP) was created with the express purpose of conducting national surveys of achievement and knowledge of American students in both elementary and secondary schools.

One document emerging from the NAEP commission, *Becoming a Nation of Readers* (Anderson, Hiebert, Scott, & Wilkinson, 1984), was supportive of literature-based reading instruction. This report of the Commission on Reading suggested major reforms in the teaching of reading, such as the importance of children hearing stories read aloud as the foundation for learning to read, reducing the amount of time spent on unnecessary worksheet and workbook activities, and increasing time spent on actual reading and writing in the classroom.

The movement for accountability, promoted by boards of education and lawmakers for the purpose of creating more effective schools, and the literature-based, whole language advocates are at opposite ends of the assessment spectrum. Teachers who are forced to give these tests have tended to spend more time on subskill-type activities found in workbooks and on worksheets, similar to those found on multiple-choice tests. Whole language teachers have maintained that a variety of informal assessments during the act of reading are more accurate measures of what a child really can do with language and print.

In an attempt to alter the course of illiteracy in America and "mediocrity" in public schooling, individual states incorporated educational reform in the area of language arts; for example, in 1983, the California legislature authorized the California State Department of Education to prepare a document outlining the components of a literature-based curriculum, which resulted in what was called the California Reading Initiative. Two major publications, one focusing on appropriate books to use and the other on planning for a literature program, came out of that literature committee: *Recommended Readings in Literature, Kindergarten through Grade Eight* (California State Department of Education, 1986a) and the *Handbook for Planning an Effective Literature Program, Kindergarten through Grade Twelve* (California State Department of Education, 1987).

As a result of the California Reading Initiative, the National Reading Initiative (NRI) was formed for the purpose of creating public consciousness of the need for literature in the reading curriculum (Cullinan, 1989). The first order of business for the NRI was to identify successful literature programs, and at the IRA meeting in Toronto in May 1988, *Celebrating the National Reading Initiative* (California State Department of Education, 1988) was presented. This publication described more than sixty literature programs being implemented, with plans for featuring more at the next conference.

Cullinan (1989) conducted a survey to determine the extent to which literature-based programs were in place nationwide. Her findings indicated that these programs are taking hold and that "There are statewide literature/literacy initiatives in seven states and, in 16 others, programs in school curriculums that hinge upon the use of literature" (p. 27). The trend appears to be that while local districts are reluctant to mandate a literature-based program, they are moving in the direction of an integrated language arts program "with a strong literature strand" (p. 27).

Looking Ahead: Problems and Promises

Literature-based programs in the 1990s have many designs, reflected in the many forms that instruction has taken. The movement for literature-based reading has had monumental impact on reading instruction, and on the expanding children's literature market. While the movement has enthusiastic advocates, it is not without critics and some hurdles (Cullinan, 1989). One of the most problematic, particularly for the teachers who must implement a new program and the administrators who promote and oversee it, is in the area of evaluation measures. There is research that supports the success of literature-based programs, such as the "landmark" study by Cohen (1968) and other studies by Holdaway (1982) and Larrick (1987), but more documentation is necessary to present to a public rightfully concerned by statistics showing a growing illiteracy rate in America.

Teachers are urged to use individual folders or portfolios that include a variety of formal and informal measures of student growth. However, if success is gauged primarily by performance on traditional reading achievement instruments (i.e., standardized multiple-choice tests), then students in literature-based programs may fall short of their peers in programs stressing phonics skills.

Another problem to be addressed is the scarcity of support for staff development and supplies for appropriate literature-based instruction. To instill more confidence in teachers' professional decision making apart from a teacher's manual and workbook pages, teachers need staff development opportunities. Administrators at the state and local levels must be convinced by corroborating evidence that children will read and write better with literature—sufficiently convinced to invest curriculum funds on trade books for classrooms and school libraries. Also, as part of their core curriculum, teacher education institutions will need to provide courses which introduce a variety of books and suggest creative ways to use literature in the classroom.

Certainly the word is out that reading to children is important in their early development of reading concepts. Political figures and other celebrities on television and in print advertise the need for books and stories in children's lives as a source of nourishment and strength for character development. Publishers of reading textbooks have also gotten the message that real stories and books are important for getting children "hooked" on reading, as evidenced by the overwhelming number of reading programs being called *literature-based* and *literary readers*. Books are making their way into children's lives, and they will work their own enchantment.

References

Anderson, R. C., Hiebert, E. H., Scott, J. A., & Wilkinson, I. A. G. (1984). *Becoming a nation of readers: The report of the Commission on Reading.* Washington, DC: National Institute of Education.

Arbuthnot, M. H. (1964). *Children and books* (3rd ed.). Chicago: Scott, Foresman.

Ashton-Warner, S. (1963). *Teacher.* New York: Simon & Schuster.

Britton, J. (1978). The nature of the reader's satisfaction. In M. Meek, A. Warlow, & G. Barton (Eds.), *The cool web: The pattern of children's reading* (pp. 106–11). New York: Atheneum.

Bullock, A. (1975). *Language for life: Report of the Secretary of State for Education and Science.* London: Her Majesty's Secretary's Office.

California State Department of Education. (1986a). *English-language arts framework.* Sacramento: Author.

———. (1986b). *Recommended readings in literature, kindergarten through grade eight.* Sacramento: Author.

———. (1987). *Handbook for planning an effective literature program, kindergarten through grade twelve.* Sacramento: Author.

———. (1988). *Celebrating the National Reading Initiative.* Sacramento: Author.

Calkins, L. M. (1983). *Lessons from a child.* Portsmouth, NH: Heinemann.

Chomsky, C. (1972). Write now, read later. In C. Cazden (ed.), *Language in early childhood education* (pp. 119–26). Washington, DC: National Education Association.

Cianciolo, P. J. (1988). *Critical thinking in the study of children's literature in the elementary grades* (No. 5). East Lansing: Michigan State University, Center for the Learning and Teaching of Elementary Subjects, Institute for Research on Teaching.

Clay, M. (1979). *Reading: The patterning of complex behavior* (2nd ed.). Portsmouth, NH: Heinemann.

Cohen, D. (1968). The effect of literature on vocabulary and reading achievement. *Elementary English, 45,* 209–17.

Cullinan, B. E. (1989, April). Latching on to literature: Reading initiatives take hold. *School Library Journal,* 27–31.

Dewey, J. (1933). *How we think.* Boston: D. C. Heath.

Farr, R., & Roser, N. (1979). *Teaching a child to read.* New York: Harcourt Brace Jovanovich.

Gardner, E. E., & Ramsey, E. (1925). *A handbook of children's literature.* Chicago: Scott, Foresman.

Goodman, K. (1973). *Miscue analysis: Applications to reading instruction.* Urbana, IL: National Council of Teachers of English.

———. (1986). *What's whole in whole language?* Portsmouth, NH: Heinemann.

Goodman, Y. M., & Burke, C. L. (1972). *Reading miscue inventory manual: Procedure for diagnosis and evaluation.* New York: Macmillan.

Graves, D. (1983). *Writing: Teachers and children at work.* Exeter, NH: Heinemann.

Hall, M. A. (1970). *Teaching reading as a language experience.* Columbus, OH: Charles E. Merrill.

Harste, J., Woodward, V. A., & Burke, C. L. (1984). *Language stories and literacy lessons.* Portsmouth, NH: Heinemann.

Hickman, J., & Cullinan, B. E. (Eds.). (1989). *Children's literature in the classroom: Weaving Charlotte's web.* Needham Heights, MA: Christopher-Gordon.

Holdaway, D. (1979). *The foundations of literacy.* Exeter, NH: Heinemann.

———. (1982). Shared book experience: Teaching reading using favorite books. *Theory into Practice, 21,* 293–300.

Huck, C. S. (1977). Literature as the content of reading. *Theory into Practice, 16,* 363–71.

Huck, C. S., Hepler, S., & Hickman, J. (1993). *Children's literature in the elementary school* (5th ed.). San Diego: Harcourt Brace Jovanovich.

Huck, C. S., & Young, D. A. (1961). *Children's literature in the elementary school.* New York: Holt, Rinehart & Winston.

Huey, E. B. (1968). *The psychology and pedagogy of reading.* Cambridge, MA: MIT Press. (Original work published 1908)

Larrick, N. (1987). Illiteracy starts too soon. *Phi Delta Kappan, 69,* 184–89.

Lee, D. M., & Van Allen, R. (1963). *Learning to read through experience* (rev. ed.). New York: Appleton-Century-Crofts.

Meek, M., Warlow, A., & Barton, G. (Eds.). (1978). *The cool web: The pattern of children's reading.* New York: Atheneum.

Olson, P. A. (Ed.). (1966). *The arts of language: Needed curricula and curriculum development for institutes in the English language arts.* Lincoln, NE: University of Nebraska, Nebraska Curriculum Development Center.

Piaget, J. (1970). *Science of education and the psychology of the child.* New York: Orion.

Rosenblatt, L. (1978). *The reader, the text, the poem.* Carbondale, IL: Southern Illinois University Press.

———. (1982). The literary transaction: Evocation and response. *Theory into Practice, 21,* 268–77.

———. (1983). *Literature as exploration* (4th ed.). New York: Modern Language Association. (Original work published 1938.)

Smith, F. (1976). Learning to read by reading. *Language Arts, 53,* 297–99.

———. (1977). The uses of language. *Language Arts, 54,* 635–44.

———. (1978). *Understanding reading* (2nd ed.). New York: Holt, Rinehart & Winston.

———. (1985). *Reading without nonsense.* New York: Teachers College Press, Columbia University.

Smith, N. B. (1963). *Reading instruction for today's children.* Englewood Cliffs, NJ: Prentice-Hall.

Tierney, R. J., & Pearson, P. D. (1983). Toward a composing model of reading. *Language Arts, 60,* 568–80.

Tunnell, M. O., & Jacobs, J. S. (1989). Using "real" books: Research findings on literature based reading instruction. *The Reading Teacher, 42,* 470–77.

Vacca, J. A., Vacca, R. T., & Gove, M. K. (1991). *Reading and learning to read* (2nd ed.). New York: HarperCollins.

Veatch, J. (1958). *Individualizing your reading program.* New York: G. P. Putnam's Sons.

———. (1986). Individualized reading: A personal memoir. *Language Arts, 63,* 586–93.

Veatch, J., Sawicki, F., Elliott, G., Barnette, E., and Blakey, J. (1973). *Key words to reading: The language experience approach begins.* Columbus, OH: Charles E. Merrill.

Vygotsky, L. (1986). *Thought and language.* Cambridge, MA: MIT Press.

Wells, G. (1986). *The meaning makers: Children learning language and using language to learn.* Portsmouth, NH: Heinemann.

Yolen, J. (1986). *Ring of earth.* San Diego: Harcourt Brace Jovanovich.

3 The Literature-Based Movement Today: Research into Practice

Barbara A. Lehman
The Ohio State University at Mansfield

In the late 1970s and early 1980s, I developed a literature-based language arts program for my fourth graders. During graduate school, I had read and studied children's literature extensively, and I believed it was the best medium *and* message for literacy learning. I rejoiced each year when I saw literature captivate those nine and ten year olds. Now, I show university students the pleasure of children's literature in the same way and encourage them to convey their enthusiasm to children. Inevitably, though, they return wanting more research support for their ideas when they encounter questions from fellow teachers, parents of students, and administrators. Here is what I tell them.

Koeller noted in 1981 that for at least the previous twenty-five years, leaders in the field of reading had been advocating the use of children's literature in elementary reading programs. For example, Huck had presented the case for literature's centrality in her 1977 benchmark article, "Literature as the Content of Reading." Thus, the idea of teaching with children's books is not new, but only now has it gained attention on a larger scale. What has been happening in the years since Koeller observed that 80 to 90 percent of teachers still used the basal to teach reading? One noteworthy event in 1986, the California Reading Initiative, integrated literature with language arts instruction. By 1989, Cullinan found that there were "statewide literature/literacy initiatives in seven states and, in 16 others, programs in school curriculums that hinge upon the use of literature" (p. 29). Currently, many states and the United States Department of Education (Sweet, 1993) officially endorse literature inclusion in reading and language arts programs.

Given this demonstrated interest in many locations across the nation in the increasing importance of literature in language arts programs, what is the state of research to support such practice? This chapter briefly explores selected studies to define what research exists and to strengthen a rationale for literature's importance in elementary and middle school literacy instruction.

First, there are investigations that focus on teachers' beliefs, concerns, and insights about teaching with literature. Other studies explore what teaching practices are being used with literature and what instructional or curricular patterns exist. Finally, there is research that probes the effectiveness of using literature to support children's literacy growth and learning. Each of these areas is examined in turn.

Teacher Perceptions and Literature-Based Practices

The path toward literature-based instruction should begin with teachers and their perceptions. Scharer's (1992) case study research documented five elementary teachers' transition into literature-based reading programs. She focused on the change process itself, both in teachers' thinking and practices and the issues that teachers face in making changes. Among the changes in classrooms and teachers, she found increased literature use accompanied by decreased basal program use, more opportunities for students to participate in and lead discussions and projects related to books, and greater use of informal assessment measures (such as conferences, projects, observation, book logs, and running records). Corresponding issues and concerns coupled these changes: about evaluation (meeting district mandates, assigning letter grades, and translating assessment into planning for individual needs); program organization (content, activities, and grouping); and materials (knowledge of current children's books, book selection, and availability of books).

Another study, one by Hoffman, Roser, Battle, Farest, and Isaacs (1990), also probed teachers' learning and change from incorporating children's literature in primary classroom learning experiences. Teachers gained insights about their own learning in the following areas: "(a) Program/Curricular Insights, (b) Familiarity with Children's Literature, (c) Strategies and Techniques for Sharing Books, (d) Awareness of Children's Learning, and (e) Personal Response to Literature" (p. 95). Their insights about children's learning included "(a) Response to Literature, (b) Literacy Acquisition, (c) Oral Language Development, and (d) Appreciation and Enjoyment of Books" (p. 95). Both studies suggest that teachers themselves learn and change in the process of giving children's literature a more central role in their instructional programs.

A second current line of research bridges the focus on teachers' perceptions and the focus on teaching practices by examining the relationship between the two. Zancanella (1991) explored the interaction between attitudes and beliefs about literature and approaches to teaching literature for five junior high teachers. He discovered that in their own reading these teachers experience literature imaginatively, but that "institutional constraints and the teachers' lack of a theoretical framework for literary studies" (p. 5) hindered them from approaching literature that way in their teaching. Instead, they focused on comprehension and learning literary terms and concepts in their teaching. In addition, they felt conflict between the roles of teaching "reading" and teaching "literature."

Similar research (Lehman, Freeman, & Allen, in press; Scharer, Freeman, Lehman, & Allen, 1993) examined the congruence between teachers' beliefs about teaching with literature and their actual practices. Results from a survey conducted with kindergarten through seventh-grade teachers led to three conclusions: (1) Certain beliefs and practices produced wide agreement (teachers developing their own literature programs, making literature the major component of elementary reading programs, teaching children to think critically about books, reading aloud to students daily, and allowing children to read self-selected books independently), while others reflected considerable disagreement (reading many books versus studying one book in depth, the importance of recommended grade-level reading lists, self-confidence about teaching literature, basals' role in reading programs, grouping children for instruction, and assessing children's learning). (2) Beliefs predicted practice in areas associated with teacher-centered versus child-centered instruction, teacher-developed versus commercially prepared materials used for planning and instruction, and assessment through individual conferences. (3) Other teacher variables also relate to their beliefs and practices (teaching location, years of teaching experience, and grade levels of teaching).

Walmsley and Walp (1989) took a slightly different approach by investigating teachers' instructional philosophies for their literature programs, their knowledge of children's literature, and their teaching practices with literature. These researchers interviewed classroom, reading, special education, and gifted and talented teachers, language arts coordinators, and principals in six elementary schools. Like the study by Lehman, Freeman, and Allen (in press), this research upheld teachers' "belief in the importance of literature in the elementary curriculum" (p. 34) and the prevalence of teachers who read aloud to their students and who had children read books independently. Similar to the findings of Zancanella (1991), this investigation showed the philosophical tension between reading skills instruction and literary study. In fact, Walmsley and Walp concluded that "the amount of time allocated to the teaching of literature is a very small fraction of that allocated to the teaching of reading skills, despite the importance our respondents attached to the role of literature in elementary school" (p. 35). They also noted teachers' lack of formal education in children's literature and how little they knew about their students' literary experiences "[i]n contrast to the detailed record-keeping and monitoring of reading skills instruction" (p. 36). Rather, they seemed to approach read-aloud and independent reading activities from a "romantic" philosophical stance. Thus, research has begun to explore the congruence (or lack of it) between teachers' thinking and their practices in the area of teaching with literature, and the results are indicating a need for more integration between "knowing" and "doing."

Patterns of Literature-Based Instruction

Studies of teacher perceptions and practices also suggest the issue of different curricular and instructional patterns for literature teaching. Hiebert and Colt (1989) identified three patterns of literature-based reading instruction based upon the two dimensions of instructional format and literature selection from teacher versus student locus of control. Each pattern blends these variables: (1) "teacher-selected literature in teacher-led groups" (p. 16), (2) "teacher- and student-selected literature in teacher- and student-led small groups" (p. 16), and (3) "student-selected literature read independently" (p. 17). The authors then describe two exemplary classrooms in which the three patterns combine variously to form comprehensive reading programs.

Zarrillo (1989) observed the programs of twenty-three elementary teachers to determine their interpretations of "literature-based" reading. He also found three basic patterns: the core book (most prevalent), the literature unit, and self-selection and self-pacing (also known as "individualized reading"). Despite their differences, successful programs in each of these patterns shared five common elements: (1) literature presentation (e.g., reading aloud, readers theatre), (2) children's response to literature (often stimulated by teachers' interpretive questions), (3) independent reading time with self-selected books, (4) teacher-led lessons with the whole class, small groups, or individuals, and (5) book-related group projects. Overall, successful programs prospered from environments "typified by administrators who allowed teachers to design their reading programs and teachers who worked together to develop curriculum and activities" (p. 28).

O'Brien (1991) examined one successful literature program for "practices that students responded to positively and that seemed to increase their interest in, understanding of, and responses to literature" (p. 114). She identified the following twelve strategies that "minimized the basalization of literature" (p. 114):

- no required prereading vocabulary work
- no comprehension worksheets

- reading whole books (not excerpts or chapter-by-chapter segments)
- student book choice and varied discussion group sizes
- broadly defined book "grade levels"
- encouragement for varied responses to and interpretations of books
- consideration of literary elements included in book discussions
- student-led discussions
- in-depth study of authors, genres, and themes
- emphasis on deeper meanings in books
- connections made between life and reading
- inclusion of literature from many cultures

She argued, "Strategies that may be effective with the basal are not effective with literature. In fact, they may be harmful to the transaction between reader and writer" (p. 114).

Walmsley and Walp (1990) developed an integrated language arts curriculum that incorporated literature and writing as major components. Over a period of several years, they implemented the program in grades 3–6 in one school district. The plan revolves around a thematic approach, with related literature (some as read-alouds, some as guided reading, and some as independent reading), writing (both self-selected and assigned) related to the literature, and skills taught through application at the point of need. These researchers did not conduct a comparison study to assess the program's effectiveness, but they did collect standardized reading achievement data that showed good progress by students in the program. They also suggested ways to adapt the model in combination with more traditional skills-based, basal programs.

Finally, May's (1987) case study described the development of a schoolwide elementary literature curriculum. Stott's (1987) spiraled design formed the basis for the curriculum structure. In this model, basic themes and genres of literature (such as folklore and fantasy) and literary devices (such as anthropomorphism) were selected for the entire program, with successive grades returning to and expanding upon ones explored in earlier years. Writing assignments were consciously modeled after literary works studied. The program's success after two years became evident through "improvement in the students' attitudes toward reading and writing" (p. 136). Such accomplishment, according to the author, depends upon careful, comprehensive planning, discussion, evaluation, revision, and involvement by the entire school staff.

Effectiveness of Literature-Based Teaching

As these investigations attest, various curricular configurations work well, but we need to know if children can learn what they must to become literate human beings. Over twenty-five years ago, concern about national surveys that found relatively few adults who read "widely and willingly" (Pfau, 1967, p. 34) prompted Pfau's experimental study of the impact of planned recreational reading programs on children's reading interest and achievement. Randomly selected first graders were provided with trade books and daily time for reading and for engaging in follow-up activities. At the end of two years, children in the experimental groups showed significantly greater interest in reading than the control groups, according to such criteria as number of books borrowed from the library, reported preferences for reading-related activities at home and at school, and a reading interest inventory. Furthermore, the experimental groups achieved significantly greater gains in vocabulary and written fluency. (There were no significant differences in comprehension, word analysis, spelling, and oral fluency.) The results indicate that recreational reading programs are better motivators of reading interest and at least as successful as basal-only approaches in promoting reading achievement.

Two decades later, Eldredge and Butterfield's (1986) experimental investigation examined the effectiveness of five alternative approaches to traditional reading instruction: (1) basals with traditional homogeneous grouping combined with a specially designed decoding program (developed by one of the researchers); (2) basals with heterogeneous grouping; (3) basals with heterogeneous grouping and the decoding program; (4) a literature program; and (5) a literature program combined with the decoding program. Pretest and posttest comparisons of second graders in the study showed fourteen of twenty significant differences among the five experimental approaches to favor the literature supplemented with decoding program (alternative 5). Children in that group and in the literature-only program (alternative 4) both made significant gains in achievement and attitudes toward reading compared to children in traditional reading programs.

Finally, data from the 1992 National Assessment of Educational Progress on reading achievement in the United States provides encouraging information about literature-based reading instruction. Fourth-grade students of teachers who reported "heavy emphasis" on such instruction showed higher average reading proficiency than those students whose teachers claimed little or no literature-based emphasis ("Analyzing the NAEP data," 1993–94).

In addition to research with whole literacy programs, studies also support the effectiveness of specific practices for enhancing children's literacy development with literature. For a historical perspective, Cohen's (1968) investigation with 285 second-grade children in New York City public schools is notable. Selected teachers read aloud daily to their students from a list of fifty books and chose an appropriate follow-up activity for the children to do after listening to the books. Standardized achievement tests and a specially developed vocabulary test were administered at the beginning and end of the school year. Children in these classes achieved significantly more than those in the control group in vocabulary, word knowledge, and reading comprehension.

An oft-quoted study by Carol Chomsky (1972) examined the language acquisition of thirty-six children between ages six and ten. Of particular interest is her exploration of the relationship between children's rate of linguistic development through five identified stages and their exposure to written materials. She found that both the amount and complexity of books read to or by children correlated positively with their linguistic developmental stage. In other words, same-age children exposed to more books at a more complex level tended to be at higher stages of language development. Chomsky states that these results imply that elementary reading programs should incorporate wider, unrestricted reading with richer, more varied materials, "rather than limiting the child with restrictive and carefully programmed materials" (p. 33).

Beyond these earlier investigations, more recent research continues to support literature-based teaching practices. Like Chomsky, Gambrell and Sokolski (1983) focused on children's language development. Using a formula developed by Anthony Manzo and Alice Legenza, Gambrell and Sokolski examined how effective Caldecott award-winning picture book illustrations would be for stimulating the oral language of primary grade children. The results indicated that nineteen of twenty Caldecott books received a high or medium "picture potency rating," and thus, they argue, these books would be excellent pictorial sources for promoting oral language development. In contrast, the authors note that a similar study by Alice Legenza and June Knafle revealed that basal reader illustrations are "poor facilitators of language" (p. 868). Finally, Hiebert's (1990) review of research on oral language found evidence that literature-based classes fostered more social interaction (e.g., oral language) among peers and with the teacher in literacy instruction than skills-oriented classes did.

Three other studies compared the effectiveness of predictable children's books versus basal readers in teaching early reading. Rhodes (1978) studied the reading behaviors of thirteen first-grade children and found a significant positive relationship between children's use of effective reading strategies (i.e., greater focus on meaning) and the predictability of the stories they read. Bridge, Winograd, and Haley (1983) found that first graders who used predictable materials learned significantly more sight words than a comparison basal preprimer group. The experimental group also used context clues more often in decoding unknown words, as compared to the control group, which "still relied solely on graphophonic information" (p. 890). Finally, the experimental group reported more positive feelings about oral reading than did the comparison group. Likewise, Chandler and Baghban (1986) examined the success of first, second, and third graders with predictable books. Children reading these books improved significantly over those using only basal readers, as demonstrated by pretest and posttest reading achievement scores.

Researchers have also explored the effects of reading materials on children's writing. Eckhoff (1983) compared the impact of two different basal series on the writing of second graders. Series A text "more closely matche[d] the style and complexity of literary prose" (p. 608)—that found in children's literature—while Series B contained the simplified text characteristic of many basal programs. Examination of children's writing samples revealed solid differences between the two groups. Children's writing in each group tended to reflect linguistic structures of their basal readers, which were more elaborated for Series A. In addition, children's writing mimicked the respective format and style of each series, such as the sentence-per-line format of Series B. Previously, DeFord's (1981) study had produced similar findings. Children's writing in three first-grade classrooms reflected the language of reading materials used: a phonics approach, a basal reading-skills approach, or a literature-based approach. The writing of children in the literature-based classroom was more sophisticated, meaningful, and natural.

In 1984, Mikkelsen specifically probed the influence of literature on children's writing. She systematically exposed children to selected folklore and fantasy and then elicited stories from them. Analysis of their stories revealed that most were literature-based and could be categorized as retellings, borrowings, re-creations, blendings, and transformations. She noted that children's story-making methods parallel those of professional writers in adapting and reshaping folk literature. Likewise, Dressel (1990) investigated effects of different qualities of children's literature on the writing of forty-eight fifth graders. She used mystery books from two different series, one of which ranked higher for literary quality and genre development (that is, matching classical detective story traits) than the other. She found that listening to and discussing books of higher quality in both literary merit and genre development led to significantly higher-quality children's writing, regardless of reading ability.

These studies, then, suggest that what children read does influence their writing and, specifically, that literary merit can enhance the quality of children's writing.

Beyond the investigations cited here, many firsthand accounts by or about teachers who have developed literature-based language arts programs supplement the body of research to support teaching with children's books. Nelms (1988), for example, includes several such descriptions at varied grade levels, as do Hancock and Hill (1988) from Australia and Hickman and Cullinan (1989). Johnson and Louis (1987), Routman (1988), and Robb (1994) offer concrete suggestions, based upon their own experiences, for creating literature-based programs. Many other teachers have published articles in professional journals about their personal odysseys. Fellow travelers can refer to Tunnell and Jacobs (1989) or Galda and Cullinan (1991) for other research summaries on this topic. On the basis of this body of research, a solid rationale does exist for the centrality and effectiveness of children's literature in elementary and middle school language arts instruction.

However, concerns are being raised as teaching with children's literature gains more widespread interest and acceptance. First, Holland (1990) questions what the theory is supporting teachers' use of literature in their classrooms. Without a solid theoretical base, literature-based teaching risks becoming merely another "program." Second, Freeman (1989) elaborates this danger by comparing the underlying assumptions of "literature-based" teaching with teaching "literature." She argues that beneath the surface, "literature-based programs are really not very different from the basal programs that we have been objecting to for some time" (p. 15). Finally, Purves (1990) bluntly asks whether literature can be "rescued from reading"; in so doing, he pinpoints the philosophical tension between teaching "reading" and teaching "literature" discovered by O'Brien (1991), Walmsley and Walp (1989), and Zancanella (1991). While these issues may not be resolved easily or finally, they must be considered carefully by both researchers and practitioners as the movement toward teaching with literature gains maturity.

References

Analyzing the NAEP data: Some key points. (1993–94, Dec.–Jan.). *Reading Today*, pp. 1, 12.

Bridge, C. A., Winograd, P. N., & Haley, D. (1983). Using predictable materials vs. preprimers to teach beginning sight words. *The Reading Teacher, 36*, 884–91.

Chandler, J., & Baghban, M. (1986). Predictable books guarantee success. *Reading Horizons, 21*, 167–73.

Chomsky, C. (1972). Stages in language development and reading exposure. *Harvard Educational Review, 42*(1), 1–33.

Cohen, D. H. (1968). The effect of literature on vocabulary and reading achievement. *Elementary English, 45,* 209–13, 217.

Cullinan, B. E. (1989). Latching on to literature: Reading initiatives take hold. *School Library Journal, 35*(8), 27–31.

DeFord, D. (1981). Literacy: Reading, writing and other essentials. *Language Arts, 58,* 652–58.

Dressel, J. H. (1990). The effects of listening to and discussing different qualities of children's literature on the narrative writing of fifth graders. *Research in the Teaching of English, 24,* 397–414.

Eckhoff, B. (1983). How reading affects children's writing. *Language Arts, 60,* 607–16.

Eldredge, J. L., & Butterfield, D. (1986). Alternatives to traditional reading instruction. *The Reading Teacher, 40,* 32–37.

Freeman, Y. S. (1989, Summer). Literature-based or literature: Where do we stand? *Teachers Networking*, 13–15.

Galda, L., & Cullinan, B. E. (1991). Literature for literacy: What research says about the benefits of using trade books in the classroom. In J. Flood, J. Jensen, D. Lapp, & J. R. Squire (Eds.), *Handbook of research on teaching the English language arts* (pp. 529–35). New York: Macmillan.

Gambrell, L. B., & Sokolski, C. (1983). Picture potency: Use Caldecott award books to develop children's language. *The Reading Teacher, 36,* 868–71.

Hancock, J., & Hill, S. (Eds.). (1988). *Literature-based reading programs at work.* Portsmouth, NH: Heinemann.

Hickman, J., & Cullinan, B. E. (Eds.). (1989). *Children's literature in the classroom: Weaving Charlotte's web.* Needham Heights, MA: Christopher-Gordon.

Hiebert, E. H. (1990). Research directions: Starting with oral language. *Language Arts, 67,* 502–6.

Hiebert, E. H., & Colt, J. (1989). Patterns of literature-based reading instruction. *The Reading Teacher, 43,* 14–20.

Hoffman, J. V. , Roser, N. L., Battle, J., Farest, C., & Isaacs, M. E. (1990). Teachers' developing insights about the use of children's literature for language and literacy growth. *Literacy theory and research: Analyses from multiple paradigms* (National Reading Conference 39th Yearbook, pp. 89–98). Chicago: National Reading Conference.

Holland, K. E. (1990). If we use children's literature in our classrooms, what's the theory? *The CLA Bulletin, 16*(2), 8–12.

Huck, C. S. (1977). Literature as the content of reading. *Theory into Practice, 16,* 363–71.

Johnson, T. D., & Louis, D. R. (1987). *Literacy through literature.* Portsmouth, NH: Heinemann.

Koeller, S. (1981). 25 years advocating children's literature in the reading program. *The Reading Teacher, 34,* 552–56.

Lehman, B. A., Freeman, E. B., & Allen, V. G. (1994). Children's literature and literacy instruction: "Literature-based" elementary teachers' beliefs and practices. *Reading Horizons, 35*(1), 3–29.

May, J. P. (1987). Creating a schoolwide literature program: A case study. *Children's Literature Association Quarterly, 12,* 135–37.

Mikkelsen, N. (1984). Literature and the storymaking powers of children. *Children's Literature Association Quarterly, 9,* 9–14.

Nelms, B. F. (Ed.). (1988). *Literature in the classroom: Readers, texts, and contexts.* Urbana, IL: National Council of Teachers of English.

O'Brien, K. L. (1991). A look at one successful literature program. *The New Advocate, 4,* 113–23.

Pfau, D. W. (1967). Effects of planned recreational reading programs. *The Reading Teacher, 21,* 34–39.

Purves, A. C. (1990). Can literature be rescued from reading? In E. J. Farrell and J. R. Squire (Eds.), *Transactions with literature: A fifty-year perspective* (pp. 79–93). Urbana, IL: National Council of Teachers of English.

Rhodes, L. K. (1978). *The interaction of beginning readers' strategies and texts reflecting alternate models of predictability.* Unpublished doctoral dissertation, Indiana University, Bloomington.

Robb, L. (1994). *Whole language, whole learners.* New York: William Morrow.

Routman, R. (1988). *Transitions from literature to literacy.* Portsmouth, NH: Heinemann.

Scharer, P. L. (1992). Teachers in transition: An exploration of changes in teachers and classrooms during implementation of literature-based reading instruction. *Research in the Teaching of English, 26,* 408–45.

Scharer, P. L., Freeman, E. B., Lehman, B. A., & Allen, V. G. (1993). Literacy and literature in elementary classrooms: Teachers' beliefs and practices. *Examining central issues in literacy research, theory, and practice* (National Reading Conference 42nd Yearbook, pp. 359–66). Chicago: National Reading Conference.

Stott, J. C. (1987). The spiralled sequence story curriculum: A structuralist approach to teaching fiction in the elementary grades. *Children's Literature in Education, 18*(3), 148–62.

Sweet, A. P. (1993). *State of the art: Transforming ideas for teaching and learning to read.* Washington, DC: U.S. Department of Education.

Tunnell, M. O., & Jacobs, J. S. (1989). Using "real" books: Research findings on literature based reading instruction. *The Reading Teacher, 42,* 470–77.

Walmsley, S. A., & Walp, T. P. (1989). *Teaching literature in elementary school: A report of a project on the elementary school antecedents of secondary school literature instruction* (Report Series 1.3). Albany: State University of New York at Albany, Center for the Learning and Teaching of Literature.

————. (1990). Integrating literature and composing into the language arts curriculum: Philosophy and practice. *Elementary School Journal, 90,* 251–74.

Zancanella, D. (1991). Teachers reading/readers teaching: Five teachers' personal approaches to literature and their teaching of literature. *Research in the Teaching of English, 25,* 5–32.

Zarrillo, J. (1989). Teachers' interpretations of literature-based reading. *The Reading Teacher, 43,* 22–28.

4

Journey from Hypocrisy: The Teacher as Reader Becomes a Teacher of Readers

Donna Peters
Elida Middle School, Elida, Ohio

I have been a sixth-grade teacher for seven years. Fortunately, I have not been a hypocrite in the classroom for that long, although that is how I began my teaching career. What I mean is that all my life I have been an avid reader. Yet when it came to teaching reading, I failed to treat my students in the way I would like to be treated—that is, I neglected to allow them to read books of their choice. Instead, I taught as I had been taught to read as a child and to teach reading in college. I began my career using a basal series, replete with worksheets, drills, lists of questions, overhead transparencies, unit tests, and subtests. I used it all, *ad nauseam*.

After the first month I was bored. Bored! Bored! Bored! But being a hypocrite, I was not about to let my students think I did not find the work we were doing every day incredibly stimulating. So, for the next few years I pasted a smile on my face each day when I would announce reading time. I pretended that I did not see or hear the yawns and small groans that would follow.

Even though I used the basal series and all the accompanying materials for at least three years, I felt very uncomfortable with how things were going. My good readers remained good readers, but I suspected that I had nothing to do with it. My poor readers remained poor readers, and I began to suspect that I did have something to do with that. I often felt as if I were putting just another "nail in their coffin" of reading failure. They hated to read, and I was doing nothing to change that attitude. My hypocrisy was revealing itself to me, but I had no idea what to do about it.

Then one April morning toward the end of my third year, the truth of my hypocritical ways hit me full force. I had borrowed several books from the local library, one of which was a suspenseful page-turner. I had risen early that morning in an attempt to finish the book before school, but I did not complete it. I tucked the book in my bag, planning to finish it over my lunch period.

Later that morning, as my students quietly completed reading worksheets, I began paperwork at my desk. I happened to glance at the materials I had brought with me that morning, and I noticed the novel. I suddenly had a wicked thought. Could I surreptitiously read while my students were working? The idea was almost sinful because I would be enjoying myself while they toiled on worksheets. The desire to know how the book ended got the better of me, and I furtively opened it to where I had stopped reading.

I quickly became absorbed in the story, but I felt a twinge of guilt as I raised my eyes from the pages to look around the room. The students were still working diligently on the worksheets, so I returned to the story. A few minutes later I felt a presence, and I found a student waiting patiently in front of my desk for me to answer her question. Guilt flooded through me as I closed the book, shoved it aside, and stammered something about its being incredibly interesting. She said that she often read by flashlight at night after her mother told her to turn off the light and go to sleep. I confessed that I had done the same thing as a child. She smiled, and we got into a discussion of the book she had been reading by flashlight the night before. I also had read the book and found talking it over with her a fascinating experience. Later I remember thinking that it would be great if I could have that kind of discussion with all my students.

I took that thought home with me and mulled it over. Reading a book for pleasure was permitted in my classroom only after completing all other work. But, I thought, wasn't the "work" of reading actually to read and discuss one's reading thoughtfully and reflectively with someone else? The hypocrite in me said that reading instruction was a set of sequential skills to be mastered. I believed that I was teaching skills children needed in order to become readers. The implicit message was, "Now you have the skills. Go home and read." However, as any teacher will tell you, only a handful of children actually read on their own time.

I had to rethink my goals. Did I want students who performed well on worksheets and drills, or did I want students who developed a lifelong love of reading? The answer was simple: I wanted students who loved to read. The hypocrisy of my teaching was now clear. I thought that I had been teaching children to read. I was wrong. I had been teaching them how to fill in the blanks on worksheets.

My change of attitude and beliefs about reading instruction was the easy part. The hard part was knowing where to start. At the time, I was not a member of any professional organizations, and I had not done any professional reading on current reading instruction. I did remember attending teacher inservice meetings where the importance of reading aloud was discussed.

I then began my fourth year of teaching committed to reading aloud every day and to providing time for students to read books of their choice every day. I read them novels, picture books, short stories, comics, magazine articles—anything I thought they might enjoy. And enjoy they did!

Silent reading was not such a hit with all students, however. Students who disliked reading spent the time staring at one page or bothering other students. Once again I found myself wondering what was wrong. Once again I found that *I* was part of what was wrong. I had required that reading material of their "choice" be a novel of at least one hundred pages. As before, it took a student to make me rethink my actions.

I had just finished reading aloud *The Great Kapok Tree* by Lynne Cherry (1990) when one student asked me why I could read short books to them, but they were not allowed to read these books during free reading time. I stared at the child blankly and then admitted that the one-hundred-page rule was dumb. From then on they were free to read materials of any length. This change helped alleviate the nonreading behavior of several students during silent reading since they now could read what they wished.

I almost became a hypocrite again because during silent reading I would grade papers at my desk. I did this for about a month before I realized that my message was, "Do as I say, not as I do." From then on I read silently with the class.

At this point I was having fun during reading class and was not as bored, but only for a relatively small portion of the instructional time. For the rest of the time, I was still basal-bound and worksheet-weary. Eventually I concluded that the basal series was the source of my boredom. I had the students put the books away and then borrowed classroom sets of novels from our school library. However, for quite a while I created worksheets strikingly similar to the old reading workbook pages. And why not? This was what I knew. I had really switched only materials, not process. I still previewed vocabulary with students, I had them list events in sequence, I had them select the main idea from several choices, and my comprehension questions all started with *who, what, when,* and *where.* The reading material had improved, but we were still doing the same old things with it. I had "basalized" the novels, and the hoped-for reflective class discussions were not happening.

Then in the spring of that fourth year, I attended the Ohio Council of Teachers of English Language Arts (OCTELA) conference in Columbus. What an eye-opener! I was thrilled by the ideas I saw, but more than that, I was elated to find many others who shared my views on reading instruction. When I returned to my classroom, I used and expanded upon ideas and approaches to instruction that I learned at the conference. My homemade worksheets looked less like a basal worksheet. My questions became evaluative, inferential, and interpretative. I added activities like readers theatre, book talks, letters to the author, and finding appropriate background music to set the mood for reading aloud.

My professional growth was just beginning. I purchased two books at the conference that have helped greatly: *In the Middle: Reading, Writing, and Learning with Adolescents* by Nancie Atwell (1987) and *What's Whole in Whole Language?* by Ken Goodman (1986). These books provided sound, research-based philosophies and practical ideas for both reading and writing instruction. Most strikingly, both emphasized letting students exercise choice in what they learn. I remember this when I develop reading units of study. Keeping current with literature and attending language arts–related conferences have helped motivate me when some ideas and activities that I try are not as successful as I had hoped.

I am currently halfway through my eighth year of teaching, the second year that I have not even bothered to distribute basal reading books. My reading program is totally literature-based. Yet, I do not believe that I have somehow "arrived." My journey to excellence in reading instruction is not over. I do not feel it ever will be finished because I will continue to make mistakes, but I am on a challenging journey and am pursuing a philosophy and method of instruction in which I can believe.

This journey's best part is that I now discuss books with my students. Our discussions take place formally through reading journals and conferences and informally on our way to the lunchroom or the drinking fountain. I am no longer a hypocrite in my own classroom. I can hold my head high as I bring a fantastic page-turner to devour during silent reading. A problem I now face is tearing myself and my class away from our books when the time for silent reading or reading aloud is over. Not a bad problem to have, is it?

References

Atwell, N. (1987). *In the middle: Reading, writing, and learning with adolescents.* Portsmouth, NH: Heinemann.

Goodman, K. (1986). *What's whole in whole language?* Portsmouth, NH: Heinemann.

Children's Books Cited

Cherry, Lynne. (1990). *The great kapok tree: A tale of the Amazon rain forest.* San Diego: Harcourt Brace Jovanovich.

II Considering

5 Children's Literature, Language Development, and Literacy

Virginia G. Allen
Columbus, Ohio

Children's literature is rapidly becoming the keystone to literacy development. Besides being a strong influence in reading and writing, literature contributes to the development of oral language, which is central to children's social and cognitive growth.

When Carol Chomsky (1972) measured the language acquisition of young children between the ages of five and ten, she discovered a strong correlation between language development and previous exposure to literature. Courtney Cazden (1965) was interested in what type of adult language input best supported children's linguistic development: adults expanding the child's brief utterances into complete sentences or the adults reading stories with the child and talking with the child about those stories. She found that children who were read to and who had opportunities to talk with an adult during the story had, by far, the greatest growth in language. Clearly, children who come from homes in which stories are an ongoing part of their experience developed oral language that was richer and more complex, and they developed that language at a faster pace.

When the children move from the home to the classroom, the language environment changes in dramatic ways. The child who at home was often the central focus of an adult caregiver now becomes one of many children in the care of one teacher. While at home the child most often was the initiator of conversations, in the classroom it is more frequently the teacher who sets the agenda for talking. In the home setting, there may be a familial context of shared experience that supports talk. In the classroom, children and teachers typically have widely differing backgrounds of experiences.

One researcher interested in this home/school language environment, Gordon Wells (1986), conducted an extensive study that followed a group of children from the age of fifteen months through their elementary school years. He found that children who were viewed by their teachers as having strong oral language ability were those who had been read to frequently. Children whose early years included experiences with stories not only had richer vocabularies but were able to use language to narrate events in their lives and to describe things that they had experienced. However, Wells believed that what was most significant in explaining the teachers' higher assessment of these children was the ease with which they were able to understand the teacher's language. As Wells pointed out, even when teachers are speaking, they tend to use more literate forms of language. Frequently, their talk focuses, not on what is happening here and now, but on ideas, abstractions, and topics beyond the classroom. Thus, in order to understand the teacher, children need to reconstruct the teacher's message to get at the meaning. Wells found that children who had frequent opportunities to hear stories read aloud developed strategies that helped them become effective listeners. These children arrived at school with a strong academic advantage.

While young children's acquisition of language is most intense in the early home years, it continues to grow during the school years—for example, they must learn the new vocabularies required by various disciplines, take on more complex linguistic structures, and learn to use language for a much wider array of purposes. It is during these years that students need to learn to communicate effectively with a wide range of audiences and to use language to learn in varied contexts. Just as literature supports early language development, it can also support older children as they increase their communicative competence. Well-selected books can play a significant role in continuing children's oral language development in the following ways, which are then discussed in depth:

1. providing linguistic input of both vocabulary and structure

2. developing a context of shared experiences

3. creating opportunities to use language for many authentic purposes

4. allowing children to examine language to make discoveries about language systems

Providing Linguistic Input

Young children who hear stories read aloud discover the language patterns that authors use, and then are able to call upon these same patterns in their own talk. Their retellings of folktales like

"Goldilocks and the Three Bears" include such phrasing as "Once upon a time" and "They lived happily ever after." Given wordless books and asked to tell the story, children will often "talk like a book." For example, one six-year-old boy "read" the wordless book *Creepy Castle* by John S. Goodall (1975), a story about a brave mouse knight who rescues a beautiful little damsel mouse. In recounting the story, cued by the illustrations, the child used such language as: "They crept up the steps," "They peered around the corner," and "They leapt for joy!" This ability to speak using both oral and written registers is one means to examine the child's emerging literacy (Purcell-Gates, 1988).

Literature is unique in the opportunities it gives children to experience powerful and well-crafted language. The rich descriptive language found in *Amos & Boris* by William Steig (1971) lets the child see the "phosphorescent sea" and the beached whale "breaded with sand" and admire with Boris, the whale, "the gemlike radiance and quivering delicacy" of Amos, the mouse. Well-written literature lets us slow down language in order to savor the way in which authors choose words that create visions in the reader's mind. Nothing else does so much for vocabulary as extensive and regular reading of fine literature (Nagy, Anderson, & Herman, 1987).

Literature also provides the context for acquiring new language pertaining to a specific topic. Gail Gibbons's colorful picture book *Weather Forecasting* (1987) helps children gain meanings for such terms as *cirrus, wind vane, low pressure system,* and *anemometer.* David Macaulay's exquisitely detailed illustrations in his book *Cathedral* (1973) clearly convey the meanings of such architectural terms as *nave, apse, flying buttress,* and *keystone* in ways that no glossary entries in a textbook could.

Creating a Context of Shared Experiences

Children arrive in the classroom setting bringing vastly different backgrounds of experience. Books, read together, can provide a strong web of shared experiences and can create a community of readers. While it may be difficult for children to talk about their own feelings, they find it easy to talk about how Alexander felt about his day in *Alexander and the Terrible, Horrible, No Good, Very Bad Day* by Judith Viorst (1972), or about the frustrations of young Tomie in *The Art Lesson* by Tomie dePaola (1989) when the art teacher required him to use the uninteresting box of eight school crayons instead of his own box of sixty-four crayons, containing such wonderful colors as turquoise, gold, and copper. Good writers, by letting children explore the details of the experiences of others, help them to think about their own experiences from fresh perspectives and provide frameworks for talking about the events in their lives.

Children in American schools come from a variety of cultures. More than 15 percent of schoolchildren in this country are African American, some 10 percent are Hispanic, and 3 percent are Asian. These figures are increasing rapidly. It is predicted that by 1995, minorities will make up one-third of the school population (Foster, Landes, & Binford, 1990). If teachers are to create a true learning community in the classroom, it will happen only when children understand and respect each other. Again, books provide a way for children to talk about differences and discover universals. Children who have read the book *Maniac McGee* by Jerry Spinelli (1990) can talk about the events in the lives of Maniac and Mars Bar and thus can explore racial conflict, not simply from their own background knowledge, but from the context of a new and shared experience. Bette Bao Lord's *In the Year of the Boar and Jackie Robinson* (1984) and Laurence Yep's *The Star Fisher* (1991) let children share the thinking of Shirley Temple Wong, a young Chinese immigrant, and of Joan Lee, a young Chinese-American, both of whom entered the new and strange American culture. Such books allow children to develop the understandings necessary to talk meaningfully across cultures.

Using Language for Authentic Purposes

Well-written books create both a context for talk and a desire for conversation. When one has become fully involved in a book, it is sheer delight to discuss that book with someone else who has enjoyed it, too. A trio of fifth-grade girls who had read *The Great Gilly Hopkins* by Katherine Paterson (1978) were overheard discussing, at length, the outcome of the book. Two girls were convinced that the ending should be changed. Gilly, they insisted, belongs with Maime Trotter. The third girl insisted that while the ending was not the happy one she wanted, it was inevitable: "the way things happen in real life." This discussion, unaided by adult supervision or input, was generated by the girls' strong interest in Gilly and was supported by the relevance of the plot in the lives of the readers. Because Gilly was such a well-drawn character, they were able to hypothesize about how she would act and feel in new situations and how she might continue to grow and change.

Dorothy Strickland collaborated with a group of teacher researchers (Strickland, Dillon, Funkhouse, Glick, & Rogers, 1989) to study the nature and the quality of talk that occurred when elementary schoolchildren were engaged in literature response groups. The content of the talk was wide-ranging. Not only did children discuss the events of the story, but they also focused on literary aspects. For example, they often talked about other works by the same author; literary elements such as characters, setting, and plot; and the craft of the writer. Beyond this, they linked books to their own life experiences. The researchers found that these literature response groups led to the children's growing competence in organizing their explanations of the story. The children learned to shape their speech to suit both their purpose and their audience. They developed greater awareness of differences in points of view. Finally, they became more able to analytically relate information to issues under discussion.

Books provide many opportunities to use oral language for various purposes. Role-playing, drama, puppetry, and choral speaking offer children a chance to interpret orally the author's words with expression, inflection, and pacing. The power of drama in the classroom lies not in the finished product but in the reflection and talk that occur when children are in the process of developing the drama. Folktales, such as Tolstoy's *The Great Big Enormous Turnip*, illustrated by Helen Oxenbury (1968), and *Stone Soup* by Marcia Brown (1947), encourage dramatic improvisation. Children who have read a group of survival stories, such as *Julie of the Wolves* by Jean Craighead George (1972), *Hatchet* by Gary Paulsen (1987), and *Island of the Blue Dolphins* by Scott O'Dell (1960), could role-play a conversation that might occur if Julie, Brian, and Karana were to meet after their ordeals.

Cooperative projects that grow from books, such as conducting reader preference surveys, charting book comparisons, painting murals, building models, creating board games, and setting up book displays, provide language use for a variety of purposes: planning, negotiating, and questioning. Children will have opportunities for many kinds of talk: with partners or in small groups in order to get a task organized and completed, and to explain, describe, and discuss when sharing their work with a larger audience.

Discovering the System of Language

Traditionally, children were taught rules of grammar with the belief that it would help them to speak using standard forms of English. Dialects were viewed as "faulty" and "inadequate," and the role of the teacher was to stamp them out. Current linguistic knowledge suggests that functional forms of language are acquired through use, not by learning grammar rules. It is also understood that dialect is both systematic and adequate.

Dorothy Strickland (1973) wished to discover whether the dialect of African American kindergarten children from lower socioeconomic backgrounds could be expanded so that it would include some aspects of standard English. An experimental group of children listened each day to carefully selected children's literature and took part in oral language activities, such as drama, choral speaking, and role-playing stemming from books. She found that these five year olds greatly expanded their repertoire of standard English forms without erasing their home language. Cullinan, Jaggar, and

Strickland (1974) extended this study to primary-grade children and found similar results.

While teaching children language rules is not effective, children can and should learn about how language works. Carol Chomsky (1980) proposed that teachers need "to heighten children's awareness of language" (p. 57). The written language provided by good books, she suggested, is one way to do this.

On the other hand, the beauty and the rhythms of dialect can be explored in a variety of delightful books, allowing children to compare it with standard English and to accept it as a function of many cultural groups. One example is in *Possum Come a-Knockin'* by Nancy Van Laan (1990), where the Appalachian dialect fairly sings:

> Sis was tossin' Baby
> while Pappy was a-whittlin'
> when a possum come a-knockin'
> at the door. (unnumbered, p. 6)

The charm and feistiness of Flossie in Patricia McKissack's *Flossie and the Fox* (1986) is enhanced by her African American dialect as she puts a treacherous impersonator in his place. "All due respect Miz Cat, but both y'all got sharp claws and yellow eyes. So . . . that don't prove nothing, 'cep'n both y'all be cats." Sharing books by writers such as Lucille Clifton, Eloise Greenfield, Walter Dean Myers, Virginia Hamilton, and Arnold Adoff will demonstrate the value placed on the language that many children bring to school.

Children also need to learn that English is not the only language, or the best language, but one language among many. *Abuela* by Arthur Dorros (1991) and *Tortillitas Para Mama* by Barbara Cooney (1981) let children enjoy the sounds and form of Spanish. In *Abuela*, the Spanish phrases of the grandmother are an integral part of the text and are made comprehensible by the context. *Tortillitas Para Mama* offers Mexican children's rhymes in a bilingual format. *I Hate English!* by Ellen Levine (1989) follows a Chinese child, Mei Mei, as she moves into the American culture. We discover how much she loves her own language and what taking on a second language means to her, as she compares English, the new language, with her own comfortable Chinese language:

> Such a lonely language.
> Each letter stands alone
> and makes its own noise.
>   Not like Chinese.
>
> Sometimes English letters fight each other.
> "We will go on a class TRIP,"
> the teacher said
>   in English.

T-R-I-P thought Mei Mei.
The letters "T" and "R" bang against
each other, and each keeps its own sound.
   Not like Chinese. (unnumbered, p. 4)

Books that invite children to play with language have a vital role in their developing linguistic awareness. Children, who giggle at the many puns in Jane Yolen's *Commander Toad in Space* (1980) and chuckle when the mixed-up maid in *Amelia Bedelia* by Peggy Parish (1963) puts out the lights by taking the light bulbs outside, are showing a growing understanding of how language works. As Lindfors (1987) says, "the child has expectations. These expectations are the child's developing knowledge of language structure" (p. 73). Books such as Ruth Heller's *Many Luscious Lollipops* (1989) and *A Cache of Jewels, and Other Collective Nouns* (1987) provide interesting ways for letting the child discover how words can be categorized. Other books, such as *Summer Is Icumen in* by Eloise Greenfield (1978) and *Poplollies and Bellibones: A Celebration of Lost Words* by Susan Sperling (1977), give children a historical perspective on how our language changes and grows.

Conclusion

If language arts programs are to provide optimal experiences for children to increase their vocabulary, broaden the ways in which they are able to use language, and extend their understandings about the systems of language, children's literature must be a significant part of the curriculum. Too often, as children progress in school, oral language is seen as being less important, and reading and writing become more important. There are significant differences between oral and written language. Wells (1986) notes that in conversation the speaker's task is to make "the *words fit the world*," while in writing, the task is to "use *words to create a world*" (p. 156). Literature can give children real reasons to make words work for them in order to share their thoughts. It can also help them gain the power to create worlds for others to discover.

References

Cazden, C. (1965). *Environmental assistance to the child's acquisition of grammar.* Unpublished doctoral dissertation, Harvard University, Cambridge, MA.

Chomsky, C. (1972). Stages in language development and reading exposure. *Harvard Educational Review, 42,* 1–33.

———. (1980). Developing facility with language structure. In G. S. Pinnell (Ed.), *Discovering language with children* (pp. 56–59). Urbana, IL: National Council of Teachers of English.

Cullinan, B., Jaggar, A., & Strickland, D. (1974). Language expansion for black children in the primary grades: A research report. *Young Children, 29,* 98–112.

Foster, C., Landes, A., & Binford, B. (Eds.). (1990). *Minorities: A changing role in America.* Wylie, TX: Information Plus.

Lindfors, J. W. (1987). *Children's language learning* (2nd ed.). Englewood Cliffs, NJ: Prentice-Hall.

Nagy, W., Anderson, R., & Herman, P. (1987). Learning word meanings from context during normal reading. *American Educational Research Journal, 24,* 237–70.

Purcell-Gates, V. (1988). Lexical and syntactic knowledge of written narrative held by well-read-to kindergartners and second graders. *Research in the Teaching of English, 22*(2), 128–60.

Strickland, D. (1973). A program for the linguistically different black children. *Research in the Teaching of English, 7,* 79–86.

Strickland, D., with Dillon, R., Funkhouser, L., Glick, M., & Rogers, C. (1989). Research currents: Classroom dialogue during literature response groups. *Language Arts, 66,* 192–200.

Wells, G. (1986). *The meaning makers: Children learning language and using language to learn.* Portsmouth, NH: Heinemann.

Children's Books Cited

Brown, Marcia. (1947). *Stone soup.* Illus. by Author. New York: Charles Scribner's Sons.

Cooney, Barbara. (1981). *Tortillitas para mama.* New York: Henry Holt.

dePaola, Tomie. (1989). *The art lesson.* Illus. by Author. New York: G. P. Putnam's Sons.

Dorros, Arthur. (1991). *Abuela.* Illus. by Elisa Kleven. New York: E. P. Dutton.

George, Jean Craighead. (1972). *Julie of the wolves.* Illus. by John Schoenherr. New York: Harper & Row.

Gibbons, Gail. (1987). *Weather forecasting.* Illus. by Author. New York: Macmillan.

Goodall, John S. (1975). *Creepy castle.* New York: Atheneum.

Greenfield, Eloise. (1978). *Summer is icumen in: Our ever-changing language.* New York: Crown.

Heller, Ruth. (1987). *A cache of jewels, and other collective nouns.* Illus. by Author. New York: Grosset & Dunlap.

———. (1989). *Many luscious lollipops.* New York: Grosset & Dunlap.

Levine, Ellen. (1989). *I hate English!* Illus. by Steve Björkman. New York: Scholastic.

Lord, Bette Bao. (1984). *In the year of the boar and Jackie Robinson.* Illus. by Marc Simont. New York: Harper & Row.

Macaulay, David. (1973). *Cathedral.* Illus. by Author. New York: Houghton Mifflin.

McKissack, Patricia C. (1986). *Flossie and the fox.* Illus. by Rachel Isadora. New York: Dial Books.

O'Dell, Scott. (1960). *Island of the blue dolphins.* Boston: Houghton Mifflin.

Parish, Peggy. (1963). *Amelia Bedelia.* Illus. by Fritz Siebel. New York: Harper & Row.

Paterson, Katherine. (1978). *The great Gilly Hopkins.* New York: Thomas Y. Crowell.

Paulsen, Gary. (1987). *Hatchet.* New York: Bradbury Press.

Sperling, Susan. (1977). *Poplollies and bellibones: A celebration of lost words.* New York: Crown.

Spinelli, Jerry. (1990). *Maniac McGee.* Boston: Little, Brown.

Steig, William. (1971). *Amos & Boris.* Illus. by Author. New York: Farrar, Straus & Giroux.

Tolstoy, Alexei. (1968). *The great big enormous turnip.* Illus. by Helen Oxenbury. New York: Franklin Watts.

Van Laan, Nancy. (1990). *Possum come a-knockin'.* Illus. by George Booth. New York: Alfred A. Knopf.

Viorst, Judith. (1972). *Alexander and the terrible, horrible, no good, very bad day.* Illus. by Ray Cruz. New York: Atheneum.

Yep, Laurence. (1991). *The star fisher.* New York: William Morrow.

Yolen, Jane. (1980). *Commander Toad in space.* Illus. by Bruce Degen. New York: Coward, McCann & Geoghegan.

6 Literary Characters Who Write: Models and Motivators for Middle School Writers

Sharon Kane
State University of New York College at Oswego

Today many of us teachers encourage our students to be aware of the stages through which they go as they write. We also try to convince them that published writers go through these stages, too. We quote from biographical sources describing the trials and joys of writing experienced by the authors whom our children read. At times we even invite authors to our classrooms, interviewing them about their processes and purposes.

As well intentioned as this may be, the fact remains that published authors are usually adults, and our children might not be convinced that the work of mature writers parallels what young people like to do—or have to do—in school. Often, our students can identify with the *characters* of books more than with the *authors* of those books.

Given this situation, one way to connect reading and writing is to determine how writing is reflected in the lives of literary characters. Middle-grade students can learn about writing processes by noticing how realistic characters compose. While writing may not be a story's focal point, it often serves a purpose or enriches the characters' lives. This chapter discusses literary characters who write several different genres and describes ways in which teachers can invite these characters into their writing classes.

Characters as Poets

Do your students write poetry? I find that in any given class, a few enjoy poetry and maybe write secret love poems and other quite private verses. Some find it extremely difficult to commit a poem to paper. There are a number of books that have young characters composing verse; students can enjoy these creations and perhaps use them as models for their own poetry writing.

For example, in *Yellow Bird and Me* by Joyce Hansen (1986), Doris misses her best friend Amir when he moves away, and the finest gift she can give him is a poem expressing her love. Her inspiration and her composing process over time are described in detail; the ending comes while sitting in math class:

> I took the poem out of my bag and placed it between the pages of my notebook. I needed something to rhyme with beautiful and rare. As I watched Russell slowly divide $2\,^3/_4$ by $1\,^1/_4$ the rest of the poem came to me. I wrote it quickly and read the whole poem.
>
>> A friend is like a crown of rubies,
>> beautiful and rare.
>> You're the most precious jewel of all
>> the one, the only Amir. (p. 12)

Students are likely to appreciate both Doris's composing efforts and the results, and they may be encouraged to tell how they create poetry.

In *The Bat-Poet*, by Randall Jarrell (1967), a young bat's response to nature and life takes a poetic form. His composing processes are described at every step, complete with an example of writer's block and advice from a "peer consultant":

> But it was no use: no matter how much the bat watched, he never got an idea. Finally he went to the chipmunk and said in a perplexed voice, "I can't make up a poem about the cardinal."
>
> The chipmunk said, "Why, just say what he's like, the way you did with the owl and me."
>
> "I would if I could," the bat said, "but I can't. I watch him and he's just beautiful, he'd make a beautiful poem; but I can't think of anything." (p. 25)

But the Muses have not abandoned the bat forever. Later, he is listening to and thinking about a mockingbird:

> And at that instant he had an idea for a poem. . . . He flapped slowly and thoughtfully back to his rafter and began to work on the poem.
>
> When he finally finished it—he'd worked on it off and on for two nights—he flew off to find the chipmunk. (p. 27)

Students can appreciate, after reading this account of the bat's struggles, that finishing a poem requires hard work, inspiration, careful observation, and time. They might be inspired to write some nature poems in response to their environment.

In *King Kong and Other Poets* by Robert Burch (1986), Marilyn wins a newspaper poetry contest and is voted class poet laureate by her admiring classmates. A quiet girl and new to the school, she only reveals things about herself to the class through her poems, one of which is about her father's depression and alcohol use after her mother's death. The teacher recognizes the therapeutic value of poetry writing for Marilyn and uses peer review regularly. Students involved in writing workshops should find this book relevant. They even may ask to hold a poetry contest similar to the one described in the novel.

Sometimes characters also analyze their own composing process, and teachers who are urging their students to do the same can use characters in stories as examples. In Madeleine L'Engle's *A Ring of Endless Light* (1980), the narrator writes a sonnet for a dead baby dolphin and concludes, "I had not, as it were, dictated the words, I had simply followed them where they wanted to lead. . . . I felt the good kind of emptiness that comes when I've finished writing something" (p. 166). When a friend asks her where she is when she is in the middle of a poem, she replies, "I'm not sure. I'm more in the poem than I am in me. I'm using my mind, really using it, and yet I'm not directing the poem or telling it where to go. It's telling me" (pp. 162–63). Students can use this passage as a springboard to discuss how they feel when writing: for example, troubled at the beginning, euphoric in the middle, frustrated at the revision stage, or satisfied at the end. They can identify with a literary character or contrast that character's writing process with their own.

In *Anastasia Krupnik* (1979), Lois Lowry describes the hard work and feeling of accomplishment as Anastasia creates an assigned poem:

> There were so many poems being born in Anastasia's head that she ran all the way home from school to find a private place to write them down. . . . But she discovered that it wasn't easy. (p. 8)

After hanging a "Do Not Disturb" sign on her bedroom door, getting a glass of orange juice with ice to sip while she worked, and putting on her Red Sox cap, Anastasia makes a discovery:

> But it still wasn't easy at all. Sometimes the words she wrote down were the wrong words, and didn't say what she wanted them to say, didn't make the sounds that she wanted them to make. Soon her Snoopy wastebasket was filled with crumpled pages, crumpled beginnings of poems. (p. 8)

It takes Anastasia eight evenings to write one poem, and she reads it aloud in her room with satisfaction when she finishes. But when she reads it to her class during Creativity Week, the class laughs, and her teacher gives her an F because she has no capitalization or punctuation and the words don't rhyme. Students will be outraged, but their insight may deepen as Anastasia acknowledges that a true poet is not always appreciated or understood by her readers.

Characters as Letter Writers

Do your students write either friendly or business letters that serve a real purpose in their lives? Letters play a part in many juvenile and adolescent books. For instance, Beverly Cleary's *Dear Mr. Henshaw* (1983) features Leigh Botts, who writes to an author because his teacher requires everyone to do so. He requests advice on his own developing stories and responds to the author's works, and gradually his letters take on a therapeutic role as he writes of personal matters: "I am sorry I was rude in my last letter when I finished answering your questions. Maybe I was mad about other things, like Dad forgetting to send this month's support payment" (p. 31).

Some characters write to their parents, as Minna does in *The Facts and Fictions of Minna Pratt* by Patricia MacLachlan (1988). Her fictitious signature does not fool her author-mother, who gets the message: "My mother doesn't really hear what I say. She doesn't listen. She asks me the wrong questions. She answers with wrong answers" (p. 67). Her mother understands Minna's complaint. By contrast, in *The Great Gilly Hopkins*, by Katherine Paterson (1978), Gilly sends a letter to her birth mother about the conditions in her latest foster home:

> Dear Courtney Rutherford Hopkins,
>
> At the present time, [the situation] is very desperate, or I would not bother you. The foster mother is a religious fanatic. Besides that she can hardly read and write and has a very dirty house and weird friends. . . .
>
> I have saved up $39 toward my ticket to California. Please send me the rest at your earliest convenience. . . .
>
> P.S. I am very smart and can take care of myself, so I will not be a burden to you in any way. (pp. 76–77)

This letter does not achieve the desired effect, but it does lead to Gilly's eventual removal from the foster home, which she has come to love. Later, the letters to her foster mother and to her former teacher show increased maturity and acceptance of her situation. Students can discuss the effects of letters on writer and receiver after reading this book.

Our students can learn about historical events as well as about writing when they read letters in historical novels. In Irene Hunt's *Across Five Aprils* (1964), letters are interspersed from soldiers describing the Civil War. When young Jethro Creighton faces a dilemma about hiding a deserter, he writes to the president, who responds with a letter that ends:

> May God bless you for the earnestness with which you have tried to seek out what is right; may He guide both of us in that search during the days ahead of us.
>
> Yours very sincerely and respectfully,
>
> Abraham Lincoln (p. 147)

Letters from Rifka by Karen Hesse (1992) is a series of letters composed by a twelve-year-old Jewish girl as she flees Russia for America in 1919. She uses the blank pages and margins of her poetry book, a gift from her cousin, to write letters telling of the trials that so many immigrants had to endure. Her last letter is written from Ellis Island, before sending her cousin the book, in hopes that its words will offer comfort: "At last I send you my love from America. Shalom" (p. 145).

Virtually every student has found pleasure in passing notes in class. That experience can be enlisted in convincing students that writing serves real purposes. Some teachers even organize a mail corner or a note-exchanging bulletin board to legitimize the genre. Barbara Park's *Maxie, Rosie and Earl: Partners in Grime* (1990) begins with a series of urgent notes, not to fellow students, but rather to the teacher, informing him of transgressions: "Michael P. was in the girls' bathroom," and "At lunch Mona Snyder chewed up her ham sandwich and opened her mouth and showed everybody" (pp. 19–20). Rosie gradually realizes that if she continues tattling, she will have to include herself on the list of rule breakers. She just cannot resist writing the notes, but she learns to deliver them to the dumpster rather than to Mr. Jolly's desk. This novel will help students see writing's effect on other people as well as on the writers themselves, something we want them to realize as they write letters to persuade, amuse, or inform.

Characters as Keepers of Journals

Do your students write in journals? Do they think no one would really keep a journal if teachers did not require them to? There are dozens of books that show this is not the case. In *My Side of the Mountain* by Jean Craighead George (1959), the narrator uses birch bark to record his adventures. Harriet, in Louise Fitzhugh's *Harriet the Spy* (1964), uses a journal to keep her spy business organized. Sam, in E. B. White's *The Trumpet of the Swan* (1970) keeps a personal journal in which he wonders about life; his entries always end with a question, such as, "Why does a fox bark?" (p. 6) or, "I wonder what I'm going to be when I grow up?" (p. 34). Michael, in *Mostly Michael* by Robert Kimmel Smith (1987), uses a journal to respond to books he reads over the summer. He would make a good model for students beginning literature response logs.

The narrator of *The Keeping Days* by Norma Johnston (1973) gets a diary for her fourteenth birthday as well as an unusual present from her mother, whom she has decided is too old to really understand her. It is another journal, already filled with writing, containing thoughts like, "What is there about me that makes me so different that nobody understands?" "How can I be my parents' child when we don't even speak each other's language?" "What happens to you when you get old? Does the part of you that feels crumple up and die, like losing sight or hearing? I'm never going to get too old to feel!" The narrator asks her mother who wrote this and receives the surprising reply, "I did, . . . the year I was fourteen" (p. 21). Students may appreciate the value of recording in a journal how they feel and think at certain ages; they may want to preserve memories for themselves and others.

In Avi's *The True Confessions of Charlotte Doyle* (1990), Charlotte records events in her journal, beginning with a note to the reader: "Not every thirteen-year-old girl is accused of murder, brought to trial, and found guilty. But I was just such a girl, and my story is worth relating even if it did happen years ago" (p. 1). She explains that before she began an ocean trip, her father gave her a volume of blank pages and instructed her to keep a daily journal, cautioning her that he would comment on her entries and check them for spelling so that keeping the journal would prove to be of educational value to her. "Keeping that journal then is what enables me to relate now in perfect detail everything that transpired during that fateful voyage across the Atlantic Ocean in the summer of 1832" (p. 3). Quite a motivator for our students! Charlotte had no idea that she would be writing a book one day, and neither do our young writers know what their futures hold in terms of publishing fame and fortune.

Journals play a part in several other historical novels. In Jean Fritz's *The Cabin Faced West* (1958), a young girl's journal is her most precious possession. In *A Gathering of Days: A New England Girl's Journal, 1830–32* by Joan Blos (1979), readers can appreciate a character's emotional reaction to her best friend's death, while getting the flavor of an earlier style of journal writing:

> The church bell filled the air with sound as we walked toward the cemetery. The day was so bright, and the sky so clear, it seemed to enjoin us to praise. Yet no one was there whose eyes were dry; even the men were weeping. . . . I shall remember Cassie for ever—and shall strive to be good and kind, as she was, for her sake. (p. 111)

Perhaps the most famous journal ever written is Anne Frank's *The Diary of a Young Girl* (1967). Besides being compelling reading, the book can also demonstrate how valuable a journal can be. Students might discuss the fact that Anne never thought her work would be published. She had a personal purpose for her journal; we can surmise that it was therapeutic during her years in hiding and that she may have written quite differently if she had envisioned a wider audience. Students can realize that although Anne's life was short, her journal lives on as a result of its publication. Students changed by the experience of reading this special girl's journal may desire to start their own journals.

Characters as Writers of Stories

Our students all have stories to tell, and we would like them to have the pleasure of putting those stories in writing. They might get encouragement from Anne Shirley and her friends, who form a story club in L. M. Montgomery's *Anne of Green Gables* (1976), and from *Libby on Wednesday* by Zilpha Keatley Snyder (1990), in which members of the writing workshop, self-called "The Incredible Five," give each other feedback and encouragement. Snoopy goes through all the stages of the writing process, from brainstorming to publication, in *Snoopy and "It Was a Dark and Stormy Night"* by Charles Schultz (1971).

Another humorous example of student story writing is found in Gordon Korman's *Radio Fifth Grade* (1989). Brad, the class bully, reads his story over the radio, opening with:

> Fuzzy and Puffy . . . were two kittens who were best friends in the whole world. Fuzzy was called Fuzzy because he was fuzzier than Puffy. Puffy was called Puffy because he was puffier than Fuzzy." (p. 77)

A teacher might use this story-within-a-story to have students practice peer evaluation. They will recognize Brad's work as a weak, though funny, piece of writing, and they might tell how they would respond to the writer and what suggestions they could give in a peer conference. More adventures of the kittens follow in later chapters, providing students with further opportunities to discuss how to give honest evaluation and support to fellow writers.

Characters as Journalists

Many students get their first taste of being published by writing for the school newspaper. In this area, too, literary characters can lead the way, serving as both positive and negative models. In *Twelve-Year-Old Vows Revenge!* by Stephen Roos (1990), children start a newspaper and report on each other's activities. Claire starts her own "yellow journalism" press, using cheap, twisted stories, to get even with Shirley. Everyone learns a lesson by the end, and our students can learn added lessons in discussion about the concept of freedom of the press and abuses of this freedom.

The True Story of the Three Little Pigs, by "A. Wolf, as told to Jon Scieszka" (1989), consists of an editorial in *The Daily Wolf,* explaining what *really* happened when those three famous pigs went off to build their homes. Besides being great fun to read, the book can provide an effective mini-lesson on point of view as well as objective versus subjective reporting.

In Lois Lowry's *Anastasia Has the Answers* (1986), Anastasia aspires to a journalism career. Every chapter ends with her hilarious attempts, including revisions, at writing articles based on the classic reporter's questions: who, what, when, where, and why. It's a terrific model for our own budding journalists.

Conclusion

This chapter describes a sampling of books in which characters are writers. Once students become aware that book characters write, they will find more examples to add to the list. A teacher may hear, "The whole story of *The Outsiders* [by S. E. Hinton, 1967] is Ponyboy's English composition!" or, "I just read *Anastasia, Ask Your Analyst* [by Lois Lowry, 1984]. Anastasia keeps a daily log on her gerbils as part of a science project!"

There are many ways to make use of literary characters who write. If we want to demonstrate how the stages of the writing process are recursive, we can point out characters who write recursively rather than linearly. If we have students who tend to ignore or bypass a certain stage that we think is crucial, such as revising or editing, a character struggling with that particular stage can serve as a guide.

The last paragraph from E. B. White's *Charlotte's Web* (1952), a book in which writing plays a crucial part in a life-or-death situation, exemplifies this chapter's main point:

> Wilbur never forgot Charlotte. . . . None of the new spiders ever quite took her place in his heart. She was in a class by herself. It is not often that someone comes along who is a true friend and a good writer. Charlotte was both. (p. 184)

Charlotte, and all the other "good writers" found in children's trade books, can be true friends *and* writing helpers for our students.

Children's Books Cited

Avi. (1990). *The true confessions of Charlotte Doyle.* Illus. by Ruth E. Murray. New York: Orchard Books.

Blos, Joan W. (1979). *A gathering of days: A New England girl's journal, 1830–32.* New York: Charles Scribner's Sons.

Burch, Robert. (1986). *King Kong and other poets.* New York: Viking.

Cleary, Beverly. (1983). *Dear Mr. Henshaw.* Illus. by Paul O. Zelinsky. New York: William Morrow.

Fitzhugh, Louise. (1964). *Harriet the spy.* Illus. by Author. New York: Dell.

Frank, Anne. (1967). *Anne Frank: The diary of a young girl.* New York: Doubleday.

Fritz, Jean (1958). *The cabin faced west.* New York: Coward-McCann.

George, Jean Craighead. (1959). *My side of the mountain.* New York: E. P. Dutton.

Hansen, Joyce. (1986). *Yellow bird and me.* New York: Clarion Books.

Hesse, Karen. (1992). *Letters from Rifka*. New York: Henry Holt.

Hinton, S. E. (1967). *The outsiders*. New York: Viking.

Hunt, Irene. (1964). *Across five Aprils*. New York: Berkley Publishing Group.

Jarrell, Randall. (1967). *The bat-poet*. Illus. by Maurice Sendak. New York: Macmillan.

Johnston, Norma. (1973). *The keeping days*. New York: Viking.

Korman, Gordon. (1989). *Radio fifth grade*. New York: Scholastic.

L'Engle, Madeleine. (1980). *A ring of endless light*. New York: Farrar, Straus & Giroux.

Lowry, Lois. (1979). *Anastasia Krupnik*. Boston: Houghton Mifflin.

———. (1984). *Anastasia, ask your analyst*. Santa Barbara, CA: Cornerstone Books.

———. (1986). *Anastasia has the answers*. Boston: Houghton Mifflin.

MacLachlan, P. (1988). *The facts and fictions of Minna Pratt*. New York: Harper & Row.

Montgomery, L. M. (1976). *Anne of Green Gables*. Illus. by Jody Lee. New York: Grosset & Dunlap.

Park, Barbara. (1990). *Maxie, Rosie and Earl: Partners in grime*. New York: David McKay.

Paterson, Katherine. (1978). *The great Gilly Hopkins*. New York: Harper & Row.

Roos, Stephen. (1990). *Twelve-year-old vows revenge: After being dumped by extraterrestrial on first date*. New York: Doubleday.

Schultz, Charles. (1971). *Snoopy and "It was a dark and stormy night."* New York: Holt, Rinehart & Winston.

Scieszka, Jon. (1989). *The true story of the three little pigs*. Illus. by Lane Smith. New York: Viking.

Smith, Robert Kimmel. (1987). *Mostly Michael*. New York: Delacorte Press.

Snyder, Zilpha Keatley. (1990). *Libby on Wednesday*. New York: Delacorte Press.

White, E. B. (1952). *Charlotte's web*. Illus. by Garth Williams. New York: Harper & Row.

———. (1970). *The trumpet of the swan*. Illus. by Edward Frascino. New York: Harper & Row.

7 The Power of Story and Storying: Children's Books as Models

Karla Hawkins Wendelin
University of Nebraska–Lincoln

The day begins, a new story. I awake in my home on this small island off the coast of Maine. I dress and go for a walk through the woods to the shore . . . stories from the earth, stories in trees, stories in clouds and sky. I sit by the shore. Waves roll in with their stories. Returning home, I meet a neighbor. We talk, I am caught up in her voice, her gestures, her story. Stories are everywhere, in everything, in everyone. There are so many ways in which stories abound. There are so many ways in which storytelling may be pursued.

Ashley Bryan, "Storytelling and Writing for the Storyteller," *The Five Owls*

Rosen (1992) acknowledges that every world culture has accumulated traditional tales that have been retold and transformed, yet people find themselves telling the oral stories every day, and it is these stories that help make up the "fabric" of life and form the basis of storytelling. Because we tell so many of these stories, we are less likely to think they are significant. Because we tell so many of them, however, these stories are vitally important.

Storytelling is a natural part of life. Oral traditions begin at home as part of families. When children ask parents to talk about when they themselves were young, family oral traditions are started. The children, then, add these stories to their own stories when they become adults and pass these stories on to their own children. Some stories are told and retold and remain in a family's oral tradition (Bryan, 1992).

Barton and Booth (1990) suggest that "stories shape our lives and our culture—we cannot live without them" (p. 12). In their discussion of why children need stories and need *to* story, they view stories as a source of comfort, a means of connecting all aspects of life, and an opportunity to *live* experiences rather than merely *know about* them. Stories allow children to experience language, including unknown words, variety in language patterns, familiar words in unusual contexts, and the "literary language" that can be found only in stories. Stories provide the context for making meaning. For the teller, this involves choosing the story to tell, selecting some details and omitting others, and shaping the narrative, the story meaning. Storytelling is a process of construction that makes organized sense out of experiential pieces. Meaning permeates stories, and storytelling communicates meaning by inviting listeners to agree with meanings of a teller's story or to search for their own meanings to the story through meanings that they already possess (Barton & Booth, 1990; Rosen, 1992).

Storytelling serves a social function. Rosen (1992) notes that personal storytelling usually sets in motion more personal stories, not as a random collection of anecdotes, but instead a collective understanding of a theme that is important to a group of tellers. "Stories live off stories . . . in storytelling we are comfortably at home" (Rosen, 1992, p. 6). Storytelling is enjoyable. Stories connect people to life and to each other; they connect families; they cross generations. Everyone is a storyteller.

The natural qualities of storytelling easily adapt to a classroom setting. Paley (1990) places stories at the center of her classroom, believing that they link the children with each other and with the events that happen. She trusts the children's ability to story: "children are born knowing how to put every thought and feeling into story form. . . . That which we have forgotten how to do, the children do best of all: They make up stories " (pp. 4–5). Paley includes herself in the storytelling community and acknowledges Rosen's premise about stories' social meaning: that "every story in the classroom influences all the others" (p. 12).

Calkins and Harwayne (1991) believe that sharing stories creates community, and they urge teachers to bring children's lives into the classroom. They report classroom storytelling sessions in which students seek stories within their families, in their private family treasures, and in powerful scenes and images from their lives etched in their minds. As in Paley's classroom, teachers participate in these storytelling sessions, sharing pieces of their own lives. Sometimes they model where they look for stories; often they use books as examples of how authors tell personal stories in their writing. That stories can lead to other stories is a prominent theme in these storytelling classrooms.

Telling stories may lead to writing stories. Calkins and Harwayne (1991) pose a pertinent question to their research in classrooms: "How can we expect children to write well when we don't know their stories?" (p. 13). When an oral story is written, it has the potential of being shared with a wider audience (Bryan, 1992). We have ample models in children's literature of authors' and illustrators' personal reflections of the past, of places to find stories, and of storytellers who pass their stories on to children. Perhaps these books will help children learn to *listen for* stories. Pulitzer Prize–winning author Eudora Welty (1983) wrote:

> Long before I wrote stories, I listened for stories. Listening *for* them is something more acute than listening *to* them. I suppose it's an early form of participation in what goes on. Listening children know stories are *there.* When their elders sit and begin, children are just waiting and hoping for one to come out, like a mouse from its hole. (p. 16)

The remainder of this chapter discusses books that model storying. Possibly, these books will help children realize that stories are everywhere, in their families and their daily lives.

Personal Recollections and Family Stories

Many authors and illustrators use recollections of people, events, and places from their own childhoods to create stories. Virginia Hamilton (1987), in describing the talk of her family, the stories that grew and changed into a kind of "fold history" that marked passage of time, defines this kind of writing as "rememory: an exquisitely textured recollection, real or imagined, which is otherwise indescribable" (p. 16). "Rememory" allows true memory to lapse and creativity to enter, as is often the case when personal stories are recalled and retold.

Patricia Polacco effectively combines text and illustrations in books that reflect the traditions of family and friends. In *The Keeping Quilt* (1988), she traces her family's heritage from her great-grandmother's arrival in America to her own daughter's birth. A handmade quilt, passed down through the years, unifies the family across generations. Polacco relates how her *babushka* eased her fear of thunderstorms in *Thunder Cake* (1990), and in *Uncle Vova's Tree* (1989), she recounts the loving family celebration of Christmas in the Russian tradition. The memories of childhood friends Stewart and Winston and their "gramma," Miss Eula, provide the background for *Chicken Sunday* (1992), a story about accepting cultural differences and helping others. The richness of Polacco's memories has become a trademark of her work.

Donald Crews tells of summer trips on the train to his grandmother's house in Florida in *Bigmama's* (1991) and in its sequel, *Shortcut* (1992). Soft watercolor illustrations depict the warmth of family gatherings in the old house and the pleasantness of the countryside that Crews and his brothers and sisters explore. Similarly, Thomas B. Allen nostalgically views childhood summers in Tennessee with his two cousins in *On Granddaddy's Farm* (1989). The chalk illustrations on textured paper reflect a "fuzziness" that often accompanies past memories.

The setting changes to a West Virginia steel mill town in Anna Egan Smucker's *No Star Nights* (1989). The gritty, smoky air and ever present smokestack glow permeate the illustrations and the author's warm childhood remembrance of her hometown. Cynthia Rylant's *When I Was Young in the Mountains* (1982), also set in West Virginia, describes her home life in the Appalachians. Rylant's grandfather was a coal miner, as was Judith Hendershot's father in *In Coal Country* (1987), set in a small Ohio coal-mining town. Students might compare the memories and common story threads contained in these three books. Locations, daily family routines, children's play, and celebrations of special events are possibilities for comparison and contrast.

In *Tar Beach* (1991), Faith Ringgold transforms her memories of growing up in Harlem to the fictional story of a child's wish to go wherever she wants for the rest of her life. The Caldecott Honor Book illustrations were taken from a story quilt, an art form often used by Ringgold as a vehicle for her stories.

James Stevenson relates his childhood memories differently. Instead of telling a complete story, he shares moments from his childhood in a series of illustrated vignettes. In three books, *When I Was Nine* (1986), *Higher on the Door* (1987), and *July* (1990), readers assemble the pieces of Stevenson's boyhood to form a story.

In *Long Ago in Oregon* (1987) and *Up in the Mountains, and Other Poems of Long Ago* (1991), Claudia Lewis draws upon her memories to create a picture of life in a small Oregon town in the early 1900s. Each poem is a story in itself, complemented by black-and-white pencil sketches reminiscent of old photographs.

Closer examination of an author's recollections might help students identify characteristics of personal stories memorable enough for telling and retelling through writing.

Occasionally, authors will borrow the memories of other family members and tell *their* stories. Byrd Baylor nostalgically portrays her father George's hometown in the Texas hill country in *The Best Town in the World* (1982). Delight in his stories about a place where everything was "best" is evident in Baylor's retelling.

In *Three Names* (1991), Patricia MacLachlan relates her great-grandfather's life growing up on the prairie with his dog. In addition to vivid descriptions of the prairie landscape, an important part of the story is the affection that both MacLachlan's great-grandfather and the dog Three Names had for going to school.

School dominated the life of Arizona Houston Hughes in Gloria Houston's touching memoir, *My Great-Aunt Arizona* (1992). A dedicated teacher, Arizona influenced children's lives in the Blue Ridge Mountains for fifty-seven years. Houston's characterization of her great-aunt is rich in detail. Similarly, Barbara Cooney describes her mother's affluent New York upbringing and her determination to become an artist in *Hattie and the Wild Waves* (1990). Although it is her mother's story, Cooney incorporates actual places from her own childhood into the illustrations.

According to Pellowski (1987), shared storytelling is possible among today's families. Although she acknowledges a decline in family storytelling in this century because of growing media influences, Pellowski contends that "young people of today still like to hear stories told to them directly by a live person" (p. 3), and she encourages families to rejuvenate this activity. Books like those discussed above might prompt students to interview parents, grandparents, other family members, or elderly friends in order to collect their stories of the past. These books show children that memories of family outings, celebrations, school, play, and special people and places make good stories for telling and writing.

Oral family traditions are preserved in stories often accompanied by photograph albums or scrapbooks. Children might start their own scrapbooks, or a whole class might keep a scrapbook for recording memorable events of the school year. Children's books are available to model the process. In Eleanor Schick's *My Album* (1984), a young girl describes herself and her life through journal entries and accompanying photographs (as the black-and-white sketches in the book are intended to represent). Michael Bragg assembles photographs and artifacts with handwritten captions in a scrapbook depicting a family wedding celebration in *Betty's Wedding* (1988). Jodan's father, no longer living with his daughter, makes a scrapbook to remind her of times they have shared in *A Book for Jodan* (1975) by Marcia Newfield. The text of this book also clarifies that Jodan enjoys telling stories about how she got her name.

Children's book characters use different vehicles for storytelling. In *Grandma's Bill* (1980) by Martin Waddell, a grandmother shows her photo album to her grandson Bill to tell him the story of his grandfather namesake. Stories related to a white oak basket unite four generations of women in George Ella Lyon's *Basket* (1990). In *The Rag Coat* (1991) by Lauren Mills, Minna's patchwork coat becomes "full of stories" when her classmates realize that the patches represent pieces of their own lives. In Aliki's *Christmas Tree Memories* (1991), a family partakes in their Christmas Eve tradition of telling stories associated with each tree ornament. A cross-country trip is told through a postcard series in *Stringbean's Trip to the Shining Sea* (1988) by Vera B. Williams and Jennifer Williams. A Jewish grandmother has a story for each treasured item in Eth Clifford's *The Remembering Box* (1985). In an excellent companion book, *The Hundred Penny Box* (1975) by Sharon Bell Mathis, Aunt Dew tells about the year inscribed on each of the pennies that represent her long life.

Books such as these help children realize that stories may be found in all sorts of places.

Characters Who Tell Stories

Grandparents and other elderly family members are important storytellers in children's books, as they are in life. A blind Native American boy begs his grandfather to tell him a story in *Knots on a Counting Rope* (1987) by Bill Martin Jr. and John Archambault. His grandfather obliges with the often repeated account of the boy's birth, his first horse, and his participation in a horse race, and marks the telling with another knot in the rope. In Camille Yarbrough's *Cornrows* (1979), Sister and MeToo have their hair cornrowed while Mama and Great-Grammaw tell them about the African hairstyle's significance. Thomas marvels at his grandfather's stories of science, history, and his own African heritage in two books by Mary Stolz, *Storm in the Night* (1988) and *Go Fish* (1991). A grandmother's story of her childhood love for whales prompts a young girl to run to the ocean to hear the song herself in Dyan Sheldon's *The Whales' Song* (1990). In Jean Thesman's *The Raincatchers* (1991), Grayling wonders if she will ever have a story to tell and be part of the group of women who circle her grandmother's tea table every day to tell the stories that tie them together. Elderly aunts in *The Ring and the Window Seat* (1990) by Amy Hest and in *Aunt Flossie's Hats (and Crab Cakes Later)* (1991) by Elizabeth Howard delight their nieces with childhood stories.

Parents also tell stories in books. "Tell me a story, Mama, about when you were little," begs a young girl in Angela Johnson's *Tell Me a Story, Mama* (1989). She knows the stories by heart and helps her mother tell them. Rose's mother tells about growing up in Jamaica and about dolls she loved in *The Chalk Doll* (1989) by Charlotte Pomerantz. These books show what Ashley Bryan (1992) suggested, that oral traditions begin in families.

Children themselves sometimes tell stories in books. Bidemmi illustrates her stories in *Cherries and Cherry Pits* (1986) by Vera B. Williams, and a new colored marker always prompts a new story. In Dale Gottlieb's *My Stories by Hildy Calpurnia Rose* (1991), Hildy, a people watcher, tells stories about her friends, family, and neighborhood. So that she can know people better, she writes her stories in a journal. Grace loves stories, all kinds of stories, and dramatizes them in *Amazing Grace* (1991) by Mary Hoffman. In *Stories from the Big Chair* (1989) by Ruth Wallace-Brodeur, Molly's mother encourages her to tell "Molly stories" to help deal with her frustrations with an ever present little sister. When the family gathers each evening in the big chair, Molly discovers that she has lots of stories that belong just to her. Stories told by children themselves as well as stories told by others have an important place in books, just as they do in life.

Teachers who tell stories, encourage storytelling, and share books that model where to look for stories, the need for stories, and the enjoyment that comes from telling and hearing stories can perpetuate storying inside and outside the classroom. Children need to realize that they have stories and that their stories are worth telling. Calkins and Harwayne (1991) suggest that encouraging children to "reread" their lives and find the story line there gives them direction and forward movement. Jo Carson traveled through the Appalachian regions, gathering stories through conversations and "eavesdropping," and published them in a poetry collection, *Stories I Ain't Told Nobody Yet* (1989). The importance of storying is dramatically presented in the title poem's closing lines:

> I'd rather you come back now and got my stories.
> I've got whole lives of stories that belong to you.
> I could fill you up with stories,
> stories I ain't told nobody yet,
> stories with your name, your blood in them.
> Ain't nobody gonna hear them if you don't
> and you ain't gonna hear them unless you get back home.
>
> When I am dead, it will not matter
> how hard you press you ear to the ground. (p. 81)

References

Barton, B., & Booth, D. (1990). *Stories in the classroom.* Portsmouth, NH: Heinemann.

Bryan, A. (1992). Storytelling and writing for the storyteller. *The Five Owls, 6,* 49–51.

Calkins, L. M., with Harwayne, S. (1991). *Living between the lines.* Portsmouth, NH: Heinemann.

Hamilton, V. (1987). Ah, sweet rememory! In B. Harrison and G. Maguire (Eds.), *Innocence and experience: Essays and conversations on children's literature* (pp. 6–12). New York: Lothrop, Lee & Shepard Books.

Paley, V. G. (1990). *The boy who would be a helicopter.* Cambridge, MA: Harvard University Press.

Pellowski, A. (1987). *The family storytelling handbook.* New York: Macmillan.

Rosen, H. (1991). The power of story. *Teachers Networking, 11,* 1, 3, 6.

Welty, E. (1983). *One writer's beginnings.* Cambridge, MA: Harvard University Press.

Children's Books Cited

Aliki. (1991). *Christmas tree memories.* Illus. by Author. New York: HarperCollins.

Allen, Thomas B. (1989). *On Granddaddy's farm.* Illus. by Author. New York: Alfred A. Knopf.

Baylor, Byrd. (1982). *The best town in the world.* Illus. by Ronald Himler. New York: Charles Scribner's Sons.

Bragg, Michael. (1988). *Betty's wedding: A photograph album of my big sister's wedding.* New York: Macmillan.

Carson, Jo. (1989). *Stories I ain't told nobody yet: Selections from the people pieces.* New York: Orchard Books.

Clifford, Eth. (1985). *The remembering box.* Illus. by Donna Diamond. Boston: Houghton Mifflin.

Cooney, Barbara. (1990). *Hattie and the wild waves: A story from Brooklyn.* Illus. by Author. New York: Viking.

Crews, Donald. (1991). *Bigmama's.* Illus. by Author. New York: Greenwillow Books.

———. (1992). *Shortcut.* Illus. by Author. New York: Greenwillow Books.

Gottlieb, Dale. (1991). *My stories by Hildy Calpurnia Rose.* New York: Alfred A. Knopf.

Hendershot, Judith. (1987). *In coal country.* Illus. by Thomas B. Allen. New York: Alfred A. Knopf.

Hest, Amy. (1990). *The ring and the window seat.* Illus. by Deborah Haeffele. New York: Scholastic.

Hoffman, Mary. (1991). *Amazing Grace.* Illus. by Caroline Binch. New York: Dial Books.

Houston, Gloria. (1992). *My Great-Aunt Arizona.* Illus. by Susan Condie Lamb. New York: HarperCollins.

Howard, Elizabeth. (1991). *Aunt Flossie's hats (and crab cakes later).* Illus. by James Ransome. New York: Clarion Books.

Johnson, Angela. (1989). *Tell me a story, Mama.* Illus. by David Soman. New York: Orchard Books.

Lewis, Claudia. (1987). *Long ago in Oregon.* Illus. by Joel Fontaine. New York: Harper & Row.

———. (1991). *Up in the mountains, and other poems of long ago.* Illus. by Joel Fontaine. New York: HarperCollins.

Lyon, George Ella. (1990). *Basket.* Illus. by Mary Szilagyi. New York: Orchard Books.

MacLachlan, Patricia. (1991). *Three names.* Illus. by Alexander Pertzoff. New York: HarperCollins.

Martin, Bill, Jr., & Archambault, John. (1987). *Knots on a counting rope.* Illus. by Ted Rand. New York: Henry Holt.

Mathis, Sharon Bell. (1975). *The hundred penny box.* Illus. by Leo & Diane Dillon. New York: Viking.

Mills, Lauren. (1991). *The rag coat.* Illus. by Author. Boston: Little, Brown.

Newfield, Marcia. (1975). *A book for Jodan.* New York: Atheneum.

Polacco, Patricia. (1988). *The keeping quilt.* Illus. by Author. New York: Simon & Schuster.

———. (1989). *Uncle Vova's tree.* Illus. by Author. New York: Philomel Books.

———. (1990). *Chicken Sunday.* Illus. by Author. New York: Philomel Books.

Pomerantz, Charlotte. (1989). *The chalk doll.* Illus. by Frané Lessac. New York: J. B. Lippincott.

Ringgold, Faith. (1991). *Tar Beach.* Illus. by Author. New York: Crown.

Rylant, Cynthia. (1982). *When I was young in the mountains.* Illus. by Diane Goode. New York: E. P. Dutton.

Schick, Eleanor. (1984). *My album.* Illus. by Author. New York: Greenwillow Books.

Sheldon, Dyan. (1990). *The whales' song.* Illus. by Gary Blythe. New York: Dial Books.

Smucker, Anna Egan. (1989). *No star nights.* Illus. by Steve Johnson. New York: Alfred A. Knopf.

Stevenson, James. (1986). *When I was nine.* Illus. by Author. New York: Greenwillow Books.

———. (1986). *Higher on the door.* Illus. by Author. New York: Greenwillow Books.

———. (1990). *July.* Illus. by Author. New York: Greenwillow Books.

Stolz, Mary. (1988). *Storm in the night.* Illus. by Pat Cummings. New York: Harper & Row.

———. (1991). *Go fish.* Illus. by Pat Cummings. New York: HarperCollins.

Thesman, Jean (1991). *The raincatchers.* Boston: Houghton Mifflin.

Waddell, Martin. (1980). *Grandma's Bill.* Illus. by Jane Johnson. New York: Orchard Books.

Wallace-Brodeur, Ruth. (1989) *Stories from the big chair.* Illus. by Diane de Groat. New York: Margaret K. McElderry Books.

Williams, Vera B. (1986). *Cherries and cherry pits.* Illus. by Author. New York: Greenwillow Books.

———. (1988). *Stringbean's trip to the shining sea.* Illus. by Author & Jennifer Williams. New York: Greenwillow Books.

Yarbrough, Camille. (1979). *Cornrows.* Illus. by Carole Byard. New York: Coward-McCann.

Additional Children's Books

The following books model the collection and telling of stories.

Ahlberg, Allan. (1989). *Ten in a bed.* Illus. by Andre Amstutz. London: Viking.

Bornstein, Ruth. (1990). *A beautiful seashell.* New York: Harper & Row.

Conrad, Pam. (1989). *My Daniel.* New York: Harper & Row.

Davis, Maggie S. (1991). *Something magic.* Illus. by Mary O'Keefe Young. New York: Simon & Schuster.

Edwards, Michelle. (1990). *Dora's book.* Minneapolis: Carolrhoda Books.

Fox, Mem. (1985). *Wilfrid Gordon McDonald Partridge.* Illus. by Julie Vivas. Brooklyn: Kane/Miller.

Grifalconi, Ann. (1986). *The village of round and square houses.* Illus. by Author. Boston: Little, Brown.

Haskins, Francine. (1991). *I remember "121."* Chicago: Children's Book Press.

Hennessey, B. G. (1991). *When you were just a little girl.* Illus. by Jeanne Arnold. New York: Viking Penguin.

Ketner, Mary G. (1990). *Ganzy remembers.* Illus. by Barbara Sparks. New York: Atheneum.

Tompert, Ann. (1990). *Grandfather Tang's story.* Illus. by Robert Andrew Parker. New York: Crown.

———. (1990). *Grandmother's chair.* New York: Clarion Books.

Turner, Ann. (1985). *Dakota dugout.* Illus. by Ronald Himler. New York: Macmillan.

Yolen, Jane. (1990). *Baby Bear's bedtime book.* Illus. by Jane Dyer. San Diego: Harcourt Brace Jovanovich.

Yolen, Jane. (1991). *All those secrets of the world.* Illus. by Leslie Baker. Boston: Little, Brown.

III Preparing

8 Decisions about Curriculum in a Literature-Based Program

Patricia R. Crook
University of Virginia

Some years ago while teaching in an inner-city school, I knew little about curricular decision making to support children's achievement as literary readers. But I knew something of reading diagnosis and had read many children's books. Also, I knew something about the thirty-four fourth graders who greeted me every morning. Most hated reading and were well below grade level in reading achievement. I knew, too, that I desperately needed to move them ahead—at least to a point where they would enjoy school and the class, and not spend their time picking fights with one another. As I observed their daily interactions, I sensed that most of them had been behind for so long that they had few positive feelings about themselves and felt very insecure in a group. Their stories, both oral and written, showed preoccupation with violent subjects.

Yet it was in this setting that I made two conscious decisions. First, I sought support for using materials other than the required basal series, such as high-interest, low-vocabulary series books and newspapers instead of or, in some cases, in addition to the basal reader. Still, I found that I would have to administer the basal series–level tests to the students so that their next teacher would know each child's placement in reading. This was the preferred way to track children's progress in the school district.

Second, I decided to increase the time that I read aloud, using a chapter book that would hold student interest and give them something to look forward to each day. I chose *Charlotte's Web* by E. B. White (1952) merely because it was one of my favorite novels and because I knew the class was not familiar with it. After each daily reading of a chapter, we discussed what the characters were doing at that point, using chart paper to record students' interpretation of events. I hung those charts around the classroom and found that students were reading them constantly, reviewing events, and talking about the story. They were beginning to behave like readers! They grew attached to Charlotte and cheered her resourcefulness; they admonished Templeton's self-serving ways. I saw dramatic changes in students' attitudes toward classroom tasks, and I believe that they became motivated as they communicated with each other about something meaningful and of interest to them.

Wilbur's life-and-death struggle had supplanted the curriculum. Students' engagement with literature prompted curiosities that had not previously emerged. They wanted to know more, first more about spiders and then insects. These were little lives they could explore, and so a study began, with students agreeing to respect and maintain the lives of collected species in order for us to learn something by observing their habits and habitats. That required lots of trade books—informational mostly, including "how to" ideas for building insect cages, which we constructed. Galls found on ragweed, cocoons, and various types of egg sacs were brought in to be housed through the cold winter.

We witnessed new life emerging in the spring, and I witnessed new vitality emerging in the children. As they gained interest and enthusiasm for these small living things, they studied the insects and wanted to read and learn more. I brought toad eggs from my pond; we observed all the stages of metamorphosis and ended up with one tiny, but perfect, toad. It took a great deal of care to determine when to put in the rock, how to provide the correct water level with algae, and, finally, what to feed a fully developed tiny toad. (With apologies to E. B. White, we used the egg sacs from spiders for food.) As the spiders hatched in "Toad's" newly constructed vivarium, he (or she) was hungry and waiting. Toad lived for twelve years. No fancy name—just Toad. Who would have guessed that it would live so long!

Why do I tell this story? I think for two important reasons: First, it illustrates how important literature is. In the words of Joy Moss (1990), "Authentic literary experiences serve as powerful motivational factors in encouraging children to become readers" (p. 21). Second, by building on children's enjoyment with literary experiences, teachers can shape a literary framework from which to focus on elements of story structure and common features of all stories as they integrate reading, writing, and oral language in their classrooms.

Relevant to the first point about the importance of literature, without question the children's attitudes toward reading grew more positive as our classroom became infused with literature. Further, meaningful literary experiences developed as a result of the students' own enthusiasm. Personal values inherent in the story stimulated emotional responses and consequently discussion; further interest led to more extensions, and so on. Nothing was forced. Every activity was conceived naturally in the pursuit of finding out something students wanted to know.

What about the second point? The experience taught me that we need to look ahead. Because participating in literary experiences makes reading enjoyable and meaningful, we can engage children in ways that deepen their enjoyment and understanding of literature. What happened serendipitously in my fourth-grade classroom with *Charlotte's Web,* exemplary though it was, should not be left simply to chance. I now see that these encounters with stories can, and should, be part of a larger, consciously planned framework enabling children to discover how literary experiences fit into a logical design. For the remainder of this chapter, I focus on that design or framework for a literature-based program and the relevant decisions teachers face: Should there be a preselected group of books? When and how do you teach children to articulate their discovery of "theme"? At what point should children understand the elements of fiction? Should these concepts be taught in a systematic manner at all during the process of beginning such a program? How can one cover regular curriculum and still have a literature program?

Figure 8.1 illustrates variables worthy of consideration when making decisions about a literature-based curriculum. The categories pictured are not limited to the language arts but include other elements to be considered as well. A good place to start in the web is with "Teacher: knowledge base." Teachers' knowledge and their beliefs about reading can be strong factors that affect the success or failure of curriculum change efforts. Peterson, Fennama, Carpenter, and Loef (1989) note:

> Teachers' beliefs, knowledge, judgments, thoughts and decisions have a profound effect on the way they teach, as well as on students' learning in their classrooms. In addition, teachers' beliefs, thoughts, judgments, knowledge, and decisions affect how teachers perceive and think about teaching a new curriculum that they receive and to what extent they implement the training or curriculum as intended by the developers. (p. 2)

Therefore, read lots of children's books—all kinds, fiction and nonfiction. Do not leave out picture books, even if you work with older children. There are many enjoyable picture books, some of which delve into deeper meanings of life, as in *Wilfrid Gordon McDonald Partridge* by Mem Fox (1985) and his quest for memories. As you build your own knowledge by reading a wide variety of books

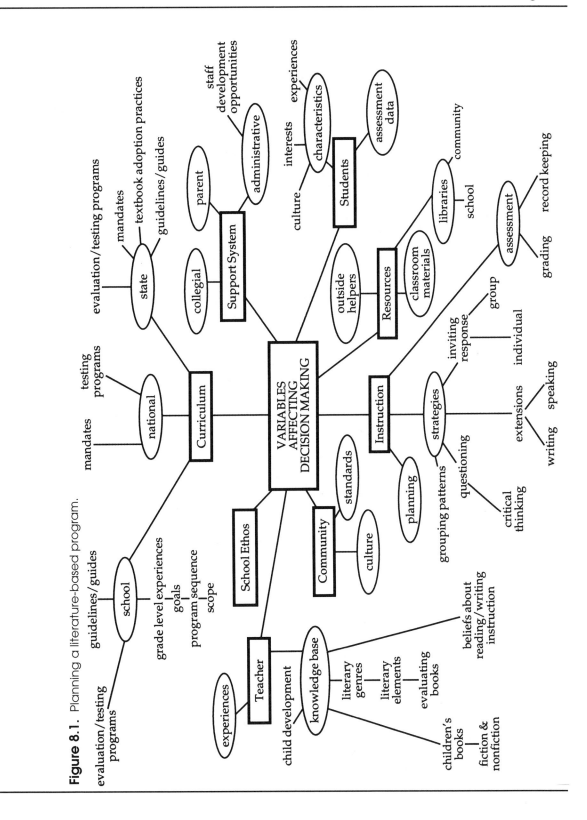

Figure 8.1. Planning a literature-based program.

exploring diverse genres, you will feel compelled to share the books you love with your students. Book talks by both students and teachers are an excellent component of a literature program. Through them, you will learn to recognize what types of books captivate your students and will become more discriminating in selecting appropriate books and in considering your students' interests, diverse backgrounds, and experiences when recommending books (as shown in the "Students" strand of the web). This will start you on your way to a literature-based curriculum.

The "Curriculum" strand of Figure 8.1 concerns the learning expectations addressed by national, state, and local guidelines since they are reflected in a school's formal curriculum. A school's explicit curriculum specifies the intended learning outcomes or, in other words, what concepts, skills, and attitudes a given child will have upon completing the school experience. The teacher translates these ideas into classroom activities in which children become involved from one day to the next.

Because the classroom is part of another context, the school, that organizational structure and the intended curriculum affect the teacher's decision-making flexibility. Curriculum guides and various textbooks, if included as curriculum, can be constraining for teachers in the types of choices they can make when planning for students. An example is the basal reading program that has provided the scope and sequence of the entire reading curriculum in most elementary classrooms for many years.

An alternative program, then, using literature for reading instruction instead of basal readers, requires considerable modification of the curriculum. Still, this modified curriculum should be conceived as a coherent framework that will guide teachers toward developing lifelong readers. What we know about curriculum development necessitates that a literature-based program be balanced so that experiences for children in later grades build on those that occur in the earlier school years. Teachers and curriculum specialists must work together to connect experiences and learning that result in a literature-based reading program that will accommodate children as they move from kindergarten through middle school and above. For classroom teachers, this means not only making instructional decisions about an individual classroom but being involved, if possible, in "collaboration among teachers in a school to insure that longer term continuity of student learning is sustained" (Comfort, 1990, p. 404).

Sloan (1991) states:

> The teaching of literature suffers in comparison with science and mathematics from not having more theory of this kind. It should be

as possible to educate the imagination systematically through literature as it is to train the reason through science and mathematics. It is as easy, if not easier, for children to grasp basic literary concepts like plot and rhyme as it is for them to understand sets and equivalent fractions. (p. 34)

All of this leads to my notion that the curriculum guides or guidelines in Figure 8.1 should be developed by a committee whose members are those teachers in the school, both knowledgeable about literature and interested in having a literature-based curriculum in their classrooms, and the library media specialist who will be able to share expertise about resources, particularly recently published books. The curriculum guides reflect common goals of the school and should contain a list of suggested books suitable for each grade so that there will be a balance of literary experiences throughout the grades reflecting the common goals.

There will be books representing various genres, chosen because they fit into a scheme appropriate for that school. Purves and Monson (1984) note that communities vary and that variety needs to be considered in curriculum development (as shown by "Community: standards, culture" in Figure 8.1). Some communities, according to Purves and Monson, might have a strong emphasis on preserving their heritage while others will emphasize individual creativity and imagination. Still a third group might stress skills and preparation for later education. Many, of course, would combine all three.

For example, I write this chapter from a community that lies within an hour of the site of famous Civil War conflicts. Children can take part in some of the historical experiences vicariously, following up their reading with actual site visits. Thus, a fifth-grade social studies unit in this community could offer a natural structure for organizing content using literature about these events that children can read and enjoy and that invites their participation and response through dynamic interaction. *Charley Skedaddle* by Patricia Beatty (1987) could provide an excellent starting point for making concepts about the Civil War personally relevant to children. This work of historical fiction is about a twelve-year-old drummer boy enlistee who "skedaddles" in the thick of his first battle, held in the wilderness just a short distance from where this class is meeting. The story gives children a vivid sense of what it was like to be there. Reading about the war, slavery, and the Underground Railroad can lead to a fascinating study of this era.

Not only is the above an example of how community can affect a teacher's decision about curriculum development; it also typifies using a thematic literature-based curriculum model. Teachers can decide to organize a literature study by topic or theme, by genre, by authors or illustrators, by literary elements (e.g., circular plots), by books too good to miss, or by indicated student interests (as shown by "Instruction: planning" in Figure 8.1). An organized study allows the teacher to be both a facilitator watching for resource needs and an observer of reading attitudes and interests. The teacher may be covering curricular subject matter (e.g., the Civil War) yet still be meeting long-term goals and short-term objectives in the language arts as well.

In the case of our fifth grade, the teacher (let's call her Ms. B) has made the decision to use *Charley Skedaddle,* an award-winning novel, as a read-aloud book for introducing the Civil War unit. It was included on the school curriculum committee's list because of both its literary quality and its relevant content for the grade level. The novel is a good choice for meeting a goal of familiarizing students with concepts about the Civil War and with literary concepts and forms as well. As responses to literature take shape, students become more aware of the author's craft, and stylistic elements and relation-ships between plot, setting, theme, and character development. They probe the very heart of literature, being no less moved because they are exploring what makes it work.

The school committee's recommended list contained a variety of books, including fantasy, poetry, and biography, representing many subjects as well as many choices having to do with the Civil War period. Ms. B has chosen some of the Civil War books for the children's independent reading. Such titles as Patricia Beatty's *Turn Homeward, Hannalee* (1984) and *Who Comes with Cannons?* (1992), Paul Fleischman's *Bull Run* (1993), Carolyn Reeder's *Shades of Gray* (1989), and G. Clifton Wisler's *Red Cap* (1991) all are of high literary quality. They evoke emotions from today's children that likely echo emotions of yesterday's children about whom they are reading, those from different times and settings. Also included on the unit library table are picture books for all ages, such as Patricia Lee Gauch's *Thunder at Gettysburg* (1975), and nonfiction such as biographies and reference books.

Again, in Figure 8.1, in the area of "Instruction," the strategies teachers use engage children both emotionally and intellectually with those stories selected for study. A major language arts goal emphasized by Ms. B's school curriculum committee was to enable children to develop a fuller understanding and appreciation of the literature they read. It was left to individual teachers to come up with short-term objectives and the strategies they would use to meet the goal. The committee agreed, however, that in all classrooms children should have opportunities to listen, speak, read, write, and think in real and meaningful situations. Ms. B's ideas for her inte-grated subject matter worked perfectly.

Ms. B believes that one important strategy is to read fine literature aloud to the class each day. She realizes that listening to and sharing stories help build the classroom as community. Part of her planning for the Civil War unit involved choosing passages to whet the children's appetite so that they would want to hear more about Charley's war adventures. She read the book herself, as she does all read-alouds, to achieve maximum aural effect. Students were highly motivated, ready to hear more, and open to deepening their understanding.

Strategies chosen by Ms. B for follow-up (extension) activities were based on her language arts process objectives, with Charley Skedaddle's adventure supplying the content. The first objective was for students to think actively and participate in discussions about books. The second was for children to synthesize ideas in writing that were generated from both reading and discussion. After children discovered, from their reading and discussion, something of the times and places of Charley's world and gained a deeper sense of the story's characters, it became natural for them to picture themselves in a similar setting. Ms. B formed smaller groups of three to five students for the writing tasks. Each group chose from a variety of carefully crafted suggestions, such as journal entries (e.g., Write an evening journal entry as though you were a Confederate or Union soldier and were preparing to stage an attack the next morning. What is going through your mind?). Newspaper articles, descriptions of battles, and letters from Charley to other important characters are other writing suggestions. Ms. B notes: "Even though we're satisfying a specific writing objective now, I never lose sight of the larger framework: that is, helping these kids see how individual works or stories are all part of the larger world of literature and, of course, human experience. It's really important to help them make these connections."

Small-group interaction is essential, containing teachable moments as Ms. B responds to ideas, asks questions, or helps children clarify their thinking. She carries her clipboard, noting who might need specific kinds of instruction when she calls together small instructional groups another time. It all happens naturally, this overlap of the "Assessment" and "Instruction" strands (see Figure 8.1). The teacher observes the processes children use rather than focusing only on the product—the final written piece.

While the above is an example of informal assessment, student learning can be assessed by using both formal and informal processes. Ms. B, in her interactions with children in the writing groups, provides them with constructive, ongoing (formative) feedback, and they find her direction and guidance useful. All of the various ways she uses to collect, record, and interpret information about her class members before, during, and after instruction are part of assessment. She is the professional decision maker who makes decisions about particular instruction as she watches or works with the children. For example, she noted to what degree children participated in the discussion and the quality of their responses. Also, when the writing groups were in session, she observed (and recorded) which children had difficulty synthesizing information from the story and developing those ideas on paper. When the final drafts come in after subsequent work sessions, she will analyze them carefully for how well children produce, organize, and express ideas, and she will check their mechanical skills. She will be interested, too, in their use of language, reference to the story's plot, and whether they show insights gained from reading in their writing. She will confer with each child about his or her progress, make decisions about instructional groupings to teach mechanical skills (e.g., use of quotations), and place the papers in the children's portfolios—the ongoing records of their literacy growth. Other items of students' work and teacher's records, such as evidence of books read, creative extensions of books, response journal samples, learning logs, and teacher and student checklists, are contained in each portfolio.

Because Ms. B's state still requires formal testing (standardized tests), she must have her fifth-grade students participate. She realizes, however, that information produced from the tests is limited to showing how students in her school and district compare to the population against which the tests were normed. Ms. B does not use the results of these tests for instructional decisions because they do not address the learning expectations she has for her students; anyway, by the time the scores are given to her, much learning opportunity has passed.

The portfolio containing teacher observations, records, and each student's work is the heart of the conference Ms. B has with each student's parents. She needs their support for this student-centered curriculum so, of course, she keeps parents well informed about their child's continuing literacy growth patterns (as shown by the "Support System" strand in Figure 8.1). The program was explained early in the year at the school open house. Each time a new unit is begun, a newsletter goes home with goals clearly articulated along with a list of available books. Often in the newsletter Ms. B requests specific kinds of at-home activities—another strategy to both involve parents and provide reinforcement for classroom learning.

There is ongoing communication with the school principal, who supports the move toward literature-based instruction for teachers who wish to design programs for student-centered classrooms. She has purchased sets of books requested by these innovative teachers since she no longer has to furnish them with basal texts and workbooks. In addition, she has encouraged parental support for activities in the classroom and in the larger community.

The support provided by the school and local libraries has been most rewarding. (See "Resources" strand in Figure 8.1.) Receiving the newsletter plus meeting regularly with teachers has enabled the librarians to know what units or projects are going to be part of the year's experiences so that appropriate books can be purchased. The school librarian always creates—with the help of students—special displays as incentives for reading. Both the librarian and Ms. B take great pride in seeing this school become an exciting community of learners.

Most of us believe that literature can enlighten and enrich the lives of children. Therefore, it deserves to be at the very center of the school reading program. These were beliefs I practiced with my fourth graders when we studied *Charlotte's Web* so many years ago. But I had not yet grasped the larger picture of how my instructional decisions could fit within a whole framework. In contrast, Ms. B illustrates a teacher who consciously makes decisions about her literature-based curriculum within the context of the total web of relevant variables.

New webs came with Charlotte's babies:

> Charlotte's children and grandchildren and great grandchildren, year after year, lived in the doorway. Each spring there were new little spiders hatching out to take the place of the old. But always two or three stayed and set up housekeeping in the doorway. (White, 1952, p. 183)

The story tells us well that endings imply beginnings—new beginnings. Our own web is indeed in place. We have to remind ourselves, however, that by consistently revisiting each of the strands, we know that the whole is secure. Tinkering with a few of the pieces has never been enough.

References

Comfort, R. (1990). On the idea of curriculum modification by teachers. *Academic Therapy, 25*(4), 397–407.

Moss, J. F. (1990). *Focus on literature: A context for literacy learning.* Katonah, NY: Richard C. Owen.

Peterson, P., Fennama, E., Carpenter, J. P., & Loef, M. (1989). Teachers' pedagogical content beliefs in mathematics. *Cognition and Instruction, 6*(1), 1–40.

Purves, A. (1990). Can literature be rescued from reading? In E. J. Farrell & J. R. Squire (Eds.), *Transactions with literature* (pp. 79–93). Urbana, IL: National Council of Teachers of English.

Purves, A., & Monson, D. (1984). *Experiencing children's literature.* Glenview, IL: Scott, Foresman.

Sloan, G. (1991). *The child as critic* (3rd ed.). New York: Teachers College Press, Columbia University.

Children's Books Cited

Beatty, Patricia. (1984). *Turn homeward, Hannalee.* New York: William Morrow.

———. (1987). *Charley Skedaddle.* New York: William Morrow.

———. (1992). *Who comes with cannons?* New York: William Morrow.

Fleischman, Paul. (1993). *Bull Run.* New York: HarperCollins.

Fox, Mem. (1985). *Wilfrid Gordon McDonald Partridge.* Illus. by Julie Vivas. Brooklyn: Kane/Miller.

Gauch, Patricia Lee. (1975). *Thunder at Gettysburg.* New York: Coward, McCann & Geoghegan.

Reeder, Carolyn. (1989). *Shades of gray.* New York: Macmillan.

White, E. B. (1952). *Charlotte's web.* Illus. by Garth Williams. New York: Harper & Row.

Wisler, G. Clifton. (1991). *Red cap.* New York: E. P. Dutton.

9 Teaching with Literature: Some Answers to Questions That Administrators Ask

Jean McCabe
Grand Haven Schools, Grand Haven, Michigan

A dministrators tend to be cautious people. Our days are spent solving and avoiding problems, and we are always in danger of becoming so absorbed with the problems that we forget about possibilities. If we are not careful, we begin to think of students as scores, rather than as readers, and of learning as the acquisition of skills, rather than as an individual adventure. We can miss out on the excitement of seeing a child's eyes light up over a good story and can lose the motivation to move into the use of literature.

This chapter responds to questions commonly asked by administrators. Some of the questions are great and some are small, but all have been voiced repeatedly by those who have administrative responsibilities. The answers, of course, are merely guidelines. Just as teachers must implement a literature-based program in their own fashion, so must administrators oversee a program that is appropriate for the needs and situations in their own building.

Question 1 | **What are the responsibilities of the principal in a literature-based program?**

The single most important thing that administrators can do to understand the contribution that literature can make to the curriculum is to *read.* The only way to understand the value of good literature is to experience it. Administrators who are readers themselves know the joy and pleasure of reading a good story and realize the impact such stories can have upon our lives and our understanding of the world.

Administrators also need at least a basic understanding of the philosophy behind literature-based instruction. Perhaps the key concept is a new definition of reading, the idea that reading is not a process of decoding symbols but one of creating meaning from the printed page. This simple distinction has enormous ramifications. When reading becomes a matter of constructing meaning, it implies, first of all, that the texts presented to students must be meaningful. Secondly, reading must be measured by comprehension and appreciation, for if it is simply an act of decoding, the meaning of a story has not been created.

Without an understanding of these two basic tenets—the value of literature and the definition of reading as constructing meaning—it will be impossible for any administrator to effectively advocate literature as the foundation of a language arts program. Administrators might be particularly interested in Smith's *Reading without Nonsense* (1985), Goodman's *What's Whole in Whole Language?* (1986), or Heald-Taylor's *The Administrator's Guide to Whole Language* (1989).

Administrators need to develop a plan for allocating sufficient resources to support a literature-based program. Although a high-quality program cannot be sustained without adequate funding, the cost of a literature-based program should be comparable to that of a textbook program.

Administrators need to provide support and education for their staff. Simply replacing basal texts with children's books will not create an effective literature program. Teachers who have been steeped in basal instruction may simply transfer basal strategies to literature if they do not have the time and understanding to develop new strategies. Teachers lacking sufficient skill in the use of children's books are also likely to succumb to the merchants of materials that are touted as literature-based but are actually just warmed-over skill sheets.

Finally, administrator guidance is needed as teachers develop a new repertoire of instructional techniques to use with both narrative and informational text. Strategies such as story mapping, Directed Reading and Thinking, SQ3R(Survey, Question, Read, Recite, Review), K-W-L (Know-Write-Learn), and Shared Inquiry are examples of well-researched, effective techniques.

Question 2

What can I expect to see when I go into a literature-based classroom?

Expect students to be involved in every aspect of reading, enjoying, sharing, and responding to literature. This is not limited to reading instruction but spills across all content areas, out of the classroom, and into the media center. Often the process will not be entirely quiet and orderly, but it will entail much discussion and activity.

One of the key features of good literature is that it evokes a powerful response from the reader. When we read a book that we enjoy, we are anxious to discuss it with a friend, read a portion aloud, or retell part of the story. Students also want to respond to their reading in many of the same ways. They should be encouraged to engage in a variety of responses, such as the following:

- Written response—response logs, patterned writing, story variations, poetry, wordplay, story maps
- Speaking and listening—discussions, book sharing, drama, choral readings
- Other media—art, music, movement
- Storytelling
- Readers theatre

Question 3

How can I explain this to parents?

Although parents will certainly have questions and concerns, they are often the first to see the benefits of using materials that interest and intrigue their children. Students' increased interest in and enjoyment of learning probably offer the most convincing evidence to support the use of literature.

Parents need to become involved as much as possible so that they can see firsthand the impact of literature upon their children's learning. The following are examples of effective strategies for helping parents understand the possibilities of using children's books:

- Encourage parents to visit the classroom.
- Use parents as volunteers to work with students on literature-related assignments.
- Publish (i.e., make public) student work arising from literature.
- Explain the importance of literature activities in parent newsletters.
- Have students write letters to parents about their work with literature.
- Provide parent inservices or workshops about literature.
- Celebrate literature with students and parents (readings, author birthdays, book weeks).
- Show student-made videos of literature activities.

Question 4

What are the costs of a literature-based instructional program?

One of the primary responsibilities for building administrators is the equitable allocation of resources. Administrators accustomed to routinely purchasing basal materials have begun to ask whether such funds might be more effectively used. Upkeep of basal programs, with their various consumable components, constitute a major portion of school budgets. It would not be unusual for the cost of basal reading materials to average over $50 per student a year. In the long run, basal materials are probably more expensive than buying children's books. Initially, costs inherent in implementing any new program may require expenditure of additional funds. For example, each classroom must be equipped with a basic stock of books sufficient to provide a range of levels and topics for students. Each year additional books may then be added as the budget allows.

Overall, it is crucial that literature-based programs fall within accustomed cost guidelines, as programs that are expensive to sustain seldom survive for long. Additional funding for purchase of trade books can also be provided through various means, including book clubs, book fairs, discount houses, parent-teacher organization donations, and individual donations of books.

Question 5

How can I be sure that skills are covered?

Among the illusions carefully perpetuated by publishers of basal texts are the existence of (1) a single set of basic skills and (2) a means of assuring that all students acquire these skills. Incredibly, the fact that no two textbook series have the same list of skills and the fact that many students are not acquiring skills covered in basals do not seem to dissuade us from these two beliefs.

Currently, most researchers agree that many phonetic rules that we have been teaching are simply not consistent enough to be useful. For example, the Commission on Reading (Anderson, Hiebert, Scott, & Wilkinson, 1984) suggests that it is probably unnecessary to teach many of the commonly taught rules. In an analysis of the utility of forty-five phonetic rules, Clymer (1963) found that many phonetic rules apply less than half of the time while others occur so seldom that they are not worth learning.

In the content areas as well, the body of factual knowledge once thought necessary has proved to be in a state of constant flux. What is a fact today may not be a fact tomorrow. Students need to learn not so much the facts and rules of history, science, and mathematics, but how history's lessons about our past shape both the present and the future and how science and mathematics have transformed our way of seeing and coping with the natural world.

It can be argued that if indeed there are such things as "basic skills," the need for them would surface in almost any sort of endeavor one might pursue. Therefore, students and teachers engaged in any learning task might be expected to repeatedly encounter opportunities to acquire these skills. For example, students who want to protect a woodland area against development would need to discover what governmental agencies had control over the area, investigate local, state, and federal laws governing such issues, study the impact upon various plants and animals in the area, analyze the costs and benefits of various alternatives, and communicate with the people involved. Such a project would activate speaking, listening, reading, and writing skills and would require research (including the use of nonfiction children's books) in the areas of civics, science, and mathematics.

Those who wish to substantiate the acquisition of skills can readily accomplish this by observing students at work and by documenting the skills they demonstrate in the course of their endeavors. Learners engaged in meaningful tasks will show repeatedly that they can identify initial consonants or word endings, for example. Furthermore, it is the demonstration of skills in real-life contexts that is a far more accurate and less intrusive measurement of learning than the imposition of artificial testing situations.

Question 6

How do we know what books to use?

Selection of literature is an important and significant task that should not be undertaken casually. There is such an abundance of good literature available that there is no reason for not using high-quality material. There are a number of lists, such as the California list of Recommended Readings in Literature (1986), that suggest books in various genres, subjects, and grade levels.

Librarians or media specialists are also an important professional resource and should play a key role in making trade book selections. Anyone responsible for selecting and using literature needs to become familiar with the authors whose work has been recognized for its high quality. Kits or packages that have been produced to fit a topic are frequently not of comparable quality.

Question 7

What teachers should be involved?

It is difficult to think of a subject area or grade level that could not benefit from literature study. Even the publishers of basals recognize this and typically recommend literature to be used with their program. Similarly, content-area texts also cite various trade books to supplement their basic program. The real question is not whether literature should be used but how extensively. Rather than creating a dichotomy between literature-based and nonliterature-based classrooms, it is more realistic to think of literature use in terms of a continuum ranging from a completely basal program on one end to a completely literature-based program on the other.

Teachers in any given district might align on the continuum. For example, the following patterns might be found:

- Basals are used for basic reading instruction and are supplemented with a free reading time from children's books of choice.
- Basals are used for basic reading instruction and supplemented with whole-class literature study.
- Children's books are used to accompany a unit or theme study in a content area such as science or social studies.
- Basals are used three to four days a week; literature is used on the remaining day or days.
- Basals and children's books are rotated among groups of students.

Rather than attempting to implement the use of children's books by fiat, administrators might adopt the more reasonable goal of moving teachers gradually, but steadily, toward the literature end of the continuum.

Question 8

Will students who have not been using basals be a problem for next year's teacher?

This question arises when some teachers in a building use only literature while others use basals. Indeed, students who have become accustomed to reading good literature may be unhappy if they are expected to confine themselves to textbook materials. We need to ask ourselves whether the solution to this problem is to deprive all students of quality literature, or to provide it for more and ultimately all of them.

Teachers who are concerned about the range of experiences and skills demonstrated by students who have been using literature need to ask themselves the following questions: Is it possible, or even desirable, to create uniformity in our students? Do basal textbooks produce uniformity of skill acquisition? Isn't one year of literature study better than none at all?

Question 9

What students can benefit from the use of children's books in their instructional program?

Accelerated students will benefit from the use of literature, which provides the opportunities to go well beyond the boundaries imposed by textbooks. They, in turn, can share the information and insights they have acquired with other students in the class.

Struggling students typically spend most of their time reading vocabulary-controlled stories and doing skill sheets. Is it any wonder that they are not interested in reading? Studies also show that these students spend less time actually reading than do other students.

Increased opportunities to read good stories and well-written informational books certainly would do much to revive their interest in reading and writing.

Average students also need to have access to materials that can enliven and expand their learning. Using trade books for reading and in the content areas can enrich learning enormously for these students.

Question 10

How can we assess the effectiveness of a literature-based program?

Assessment has been and surely will continue to be one of the thorniest of problems for educators. Nowhere is this more true than in the assessment of nontraditional programs. The crux of the problem is that traditional measures are simply inappropriate and inadequate for measuring nontraditional programs. They are based upon a model that assumes that a task such as reading can be measured by reducing it to individual parts, measuring the parts, and then summing the scores.

One of the reasons for advocating a literature-based approach is recognition of the personal and idiosyncratic nature of the act of reading. Implicit in this vision of reading is that it is a holistic act that cannot be divided meaningfully into discrete parts. While various reading skills can be described, the act of reading is certainly not the sum of these parts, but the interaction among these parts. In fact, suggesting that the magic of reading a fine story can or would be reduced to a set of scores does violence to our whole idea of what reading is really all about.

Another problem with assessment is the enormous variety of reading experiences that certainly will ensue as a result of introducing choice into a reading program. The impossibility of assuming the acquisition of standardized vocabulary or a set of skills becomes apparent when one considers the range of reading materials that might be used in a literature-based classroom.

This is not to say that it is impossible to measure or document the progress of students using a wide range of learning materials. Indeed, there are various methods and instruments that can be used to gather data on students' growth. Anecdotal records, student self-evaluations, portfolios, reading response logs, teacher-student conference notes, personal reading lists, rubrics, inventories, work samples, checklists, and video tapes are all examples of effective means of documenting various aspects of students' growth in literacy. It would be obvious that such measures yield richness and depth of information vastly superior to the sparse and artificial numbers we call test scores.

Administrators who want more specific information on alternative assessment measures are encouraged to consult the following sources: Anthony, Johnson, Mickelson, and Preece (1991); Goodman, Goodman, and Hood (1989); Harp (1991); and Tierney, Carter, and Desai (1991). These sources document the problem more explicitly and contain samples of a wide range of alternative measures.

In spite of their limitations, standardized measures have been used to evaluate the growth of students in literature-based programs. As early as 1965, Stauffer found that students in a language-experience program outperformed students in a basal program on a variety of measures. Eldredge and Butterfield (1986) used the Gates-MacGinitie Reading Test and other measures to compare a traditional basal approach to five other experimental methods, two of which were literature-based, and found that the literature-based programs had a positive effect upon both achievement and attitude. White, Vaughan, and Rorie (1986) found that 80 percent of economically disadvantaged first graders who did not use a basal but were immersed in print scored above grade level on standardized tests administered toward the end of the school year. Other studies by Larrick (1987) and Cohen (1968) confirm these findings. Although the performance of students on these measures is somewhat satisfying, they are a poor substitute for the richer, "thicker" collections of data described earlier that more accurately reflect the complexity of the reading task.

Like reading itself, using literature as part of instruction is a process of discovery. No two teachers, no two administrators, will deal with it in the same way. What is certain is that use of trade books in all parts of the curriculum will add a necessary depth and richness to learning.

References

Anderson, R. C., Hiebert, E. H., Scott, J.A., & Wilkinson, I. A. G. (1984). *Becoming a nation of readers: The report of the Commission on Reading.* Washington, DC: National Institute of Education.

Anthony, R., Johnson, T., Mickelson, N., & Preece, A. (1991). *Evaluating literacy: A perspective for change.* Portsmouth, NH: Heinemann.

California State Department of Education, Language Arts and Foreign Language Unit. (1986). *Recommended readings in literature, kindergarten through grade eight.* Sacramento: Author.

Clymer, T. (1963). The utility of phonic generalizations in the primary grades. *The Reading Teacher, 16,* 252–58.

Cohen, D. (1968). The effect of literature on vocabulary and reading achievement. *Elementary English, 45,* 209–13.

Eldredge, J. L., & Butterfield, D. (1986). Alternatives to traditional reading instruction. *The Reading Teacher, 40,* 32–37.

Goodman, K. (1986). *What's whole in whole language?* Portsmouth, NH: Heinemann.

Goodman, K., Goodman, Y., & Hood, W. (1989). *The whole language evaluation book.* Portsmouth, NH: Heinemann.

Harp, B. (1991). *Assessment and evaluation in whole language programs.* Norwood, MA: Christopher-Gordon.

Heald-Taylor, G. (1989). *The administrator's guide to whole language.* Katonah, NY: Richard C. Owen.

Larrick, N. (1987). Illiteracy starts too soon. *Phi Delta Kappan, 69,* 184–89.

Smith, F. (1985). *Reading without nonsense.* New York: Teachers College Press, Columbia University.

Stauffer, R. G. (1970). *The language-experience approach to the teaching of reading.* New York: Harper & Row.

Tierney, R., Carter, M., & Desai, L. (1991). *Portfolio assessment in the reading-writing classroom.* Norwood, MA: Christopher-Gordon.

White, J. H., Vaughan, J. L., & Rorie, L. (1986). Picture of a classroom where reading is for real. *The Reading Teacher, 40,* 84–86.

10 Developing a Teaching Guide for Literary Teaching

Marilou R. Sorensen
University of Utah

Amy and Bruce were both new teachers, hired only days after completing student teaching. Neither had time to prepare materials before they took the reins of their new assignments. Amy found a room devoid of materials. It had been stripped of everything except the basal series for reading and a set of ancient social studies texts. The teachers on her team advised her to "follow along" with them; they had plenty of ditto sheets, and the monthly units were all prepared. When she asked about children's books, a classroom library, or "extra reading materials," she was told that the children were not ready to handle things like that.

"I felt defeated from the first! Where were all the good books that I wanted my students to read? Would I really be shackled to that basal?" But then Amy remembered that the decision was hers. She visited the media center and the public library, collecting several copies of the same novel. It was a slow start, but she ventured into "making literature lovers" from the beginning. "Some of my team have started to use literature pieces a little bit, too," she commented. She was shy at first, but lately she has shown them how she plans teaching guides for the novels she is using.

Bruce, on the other hand, had numerous book sets in his room *and* the published guides to go with them. "I couldn't believe what I saw in those guides! Imagine having to count the syllables as part of the literature lesson!"

Bruce and Amy have found ways to develop personal guides for their own classrooms based on professional objectives and considering the needs, interests, and abilities of their students. Both Bruce and Amy made a decision based on their successful experiences with literature and on the research attesting to the authentic learning involved in literature-based teaching. Some teachers hesitate to go the way of these two young teachers. Perhaps you are one who still needs a nudge to try, an assurance about ways to plan lessons and make realistic assessment of the learning.

This chapter is written for you. It is the outcome of years of trying diverse strategies and evaluating the results. Because my students are a major part of the development of this approach, we wish you well and hope that you enjoy the journey on the path to literature-based teaching as much as we have.

Deciding on Literature-Based Teaching

When you first make a decision to use literature-based instruction, you are likely to have some questions about planning: How and where do I begin? Are there lists of stories I should use with questions that will assure learning? Isn't it easier just to use a published guide to find the strategies to teach a novel rather than trying to develop my own?

All three concerns are justified, but any change in teaching requires taking risks. At first it may be like walking a tightrope without a net. The "safety" of prescriptive basal programs may have been an assurance assumed from the publisher's written goals and sequences. The network of interschool and cross-country testing scores and of evaluation materials provided by these programs has perhaps satisfied your statistical-minded peers and administration.

To answer the first question, how and where to begin, moving away from the constriction of a prescribed set of materials is necessary. Beginning to teach with literature means taking one step at a time. Each step—albeit a small one—will reflect a measure of success resulting in safer footing for later accomplishments.

To respond to the second concern, no canon of literature pieces or "just right" questions are appropriate for all groups, all teachers, at all times. This is a myth perpetuated by publishers proclaiming the "universality" of their core works. What they do not, and cannot, provide are stories suited to your unique classroom. Only *you* can provide the appropriate choices of titles for your students. Also, you realize when a teachable moment occurs: perhaps a political issue becomes paramount in the minds of the readers and can best be studied with trade books.

This leads to the third question regarding the development of teaching guides. It *may* be easier to use a published guide for a book you want to study, but ease and enjoyment are not synonymous; nor are ease and understanding.

Guidelines for Literature-Based Lessons

The adage "out of nothing comes nothing" can be applied here. Guidelines may be necessary and even recommended to attain the goals of a literature-based lesson, but uncertainty about *what* guidelines to use has perpetuated a plethora of published guides for literature. As the basal readers include more literature, they also provide outlines for teaching that often reflect the same prescriptive format as the traditional reading methods, which has been called "basalization of literature" (K. S. Goodman, 1988). In addition, paperback distributors sell guides that are meant to be used as reading methods. Some companies have as their focus the mass production of teaching guides to accompany picture books, fiction, and poetry.

The assumption cannot be made that all these guides are helpful or advisable for your class. Before even considering the prepackaged lessons, ask yourself the following questions:

1. Does the guide meet *my* objectives of encouraging responses to relevant ideas, themes, and styles? (Don't let it dictate your objectives; they are for you to determine.)

2. Are the strategies active (open-ended questions) versus passive (fill-in-the-blank responses)? Do they promote higher-level thinking skills?

3. Does the guide provide for various methods of teaching and learning? In particular, does it encourage ways that are unique to me?

4. Does the guide teach the story with meaningful learning and deep involvement of literary understanding? (Watch for busywork and peripheral activities.)

5. Does the guide suggest *more* than I want or think is necessary for using this book? (One example is a published guide that has forty-five pages of ditto sheets for one picture book!)

6. Is the cost of the guide worth it? Could I purchase other pieces of literature for my collection in place of this guide?

7. If I choose not to use a guide, what basic questions can *I* begin with? What decisions about the sequence of teaching can I glean from the students' interests, needs, and questions?

There are numerous ways to plan and guide literature-based lessons. Ideas gleaned from some of these sources may suggest a strategy for you to consider. Susan Hepler (1988), with a group of students, developed a five-step paradigm to fit their needs in planning lessons for literature: summary, initiating activities, questions for creative thinking, activities, and related readings.

Wood, Lapp, and Flood (1992) have collected seventeen different models of study guides, which include interaction, mapping, and conceptual outlines. While these offer many ideas, you may find them more related to teaching skills than literary response.

Sloan (1992) suggests that terms of form and structure be discussed that will assist students in designing patterns common to different kinds of stories. She provides some generic questions as guidelines, such as, "Did the story end as you expected it to? Did the author prepare you to expect the ending? How?" and "In what ways is this story and its characters like others you have read, heard or seen?" (p. 78).

Huck, Hepler, and Hickman (1993) and Norton (1995) suggest ways to prepare lessons for teaching. Corwin, Hein, and Levin (1976) advise a webbing process to provide a visual outline of teaching ideas related to materials and diverse activities. Flender (1985) charts the book discussion to represent a graph of story elements. At a more analytical level, Temple (1991) suggests two literary devices, the dramatic role of Etienne Souriau and the contrastive model of Levi-Strauss, which will lead to a greater appreciation of story.

I have seen teachers use a prescriptive question taxonomy based on Sander's (1966) model of knowledge, analysis, comprehension, synthesis, application, and evaluation. Saul (1989) shares the concern about reverting to such a presupposed format and provides a scenario of teachers who develop "literary questions."

Moss (1990) and Raines and Canady (1991) have designed guides to help teachers develop topical units by combining many children's book titles. Somers and Worthington (1979) have developed examples of activities for specific book titles, with the suggestion that teachers use discretion and their own personal ideas in selecting the strategies.

Teaching Guides: Choosing the Middle Ground

Most educators will agree that a teacher often needs more than the story and the students' spontaneous response to make a literature-based lesson successful and meaningful. Two misconceptions surface about what that entails. One theory advocates the necessity of guided, structured lessons to dictate individual skills that *must* be taught to assure comprehension. It is assumed that correct answers and directives provided in such a guide will alleviate the possibility of "misreading" a literary piece. The other misconception is the "hands-off approach," which warns that there is no inherent meaning in a story, just the meaning that readers can construct for themselves. Table 10.1 presents these misconceptions about teaching guides.

In reality, to make literature-based lessons successful, there must be a middle ground. Teachers need to set objectives but need to do so with the input of students and in consideration of their interests, skills, needs, and background knowledge. Teachers should experiment with literature of different genres, address the ideas of literary elements, and examine the way in which stories work. With this knowledge base, they can nudge young readers' responses in critical ways, to elicit questions that enhance parts of the text that may have been overlooked and to guide discussion with issues that have no single answer, thereby encouraging diversity in the responses.

Teachers may need to keep a deductive framework in mind even though they teach inductively. It is at this point where a teacher "holds a gentle rein" on literature teaching. The objective may be to (1) develop skills, (2) set a framework for later learning, (3) attain a level of comprehension, or (4) merely enjoy a literary piece and the consideration it gives to the kinds of activities that encompass a structure (the text) while encouraging a response-based approach (the reader).

With these thoughts in mind, an outline called a Cycle was developed as a middle ground between "hands-off" and structured lessons. (See Figure 10.1.) The Cycle is a four-step plan: *Exploration* is a study of text and structure. Activities to encourage responding to the text and reaching beyond are *Enrichment*. The Cycle schema gives ideas for *Extension* into other curricula. Finally, a reaction to the experience, or *Reexamination*, returns the reader to the text. The recursive nature of the Cycle, or *Recycle*, leads this experience to the next literature event.

The Cycle model encourages selecting from any or all of the parts as a teaching guide. This could merely be to read a picture book while encouraging spontaneous comments (Enrichment). Or it

Table 10.1.
Misconceptions about
teaching guides.

Structured Lesson	"Hands-Off" Lesson
Lesson Objective: Predisposed by publisher	Lesson Objective: Comes from student

1. A dictated order of lesson:
  • labeling (no need to justify answer)
  • prescriptive assignments
  • learn words that "may give problems" before reading text
  • directives of prompts (a routine of these will make it easy to follow)
  • questions always result in answers
2. One interpretation of the lesson.
3. Usually one correct answer.
4. Right answer results in comprehension.
5. Teacher will provide the right answer if you wait long enough.
	1. Meaning only comes from the reader, who constructs it.
	2. Interpretation need never be replaced with the "intent of the author."
	3. Ideas of students are only source of information and insight.
	4. No framework such as knowledge or contrasts is needed to "understand" literature.
	5. Shared responses will automatically result in understanding and enjoyment.
	6. There are no right or wrong answers.
	7. "Right" answers will be discovered, if there are any; no prompts are necessary.

Assessment: Product only (test scores, length of written piece, no errors found on work sheets, etc.). *Assumption:* Knowledge is inherent in text.	*Assessment:* Process only (staying on task, appearance of enjoyment, "appreciation"). *Assumption:* Knowledge is never inherent in text.

Figure 10.1.
Cycle: A
literature-based
lesson.

Lesson Objective: Student and teacher at all levels.
Conceptual framework for the objective is "Thinking about thinking."

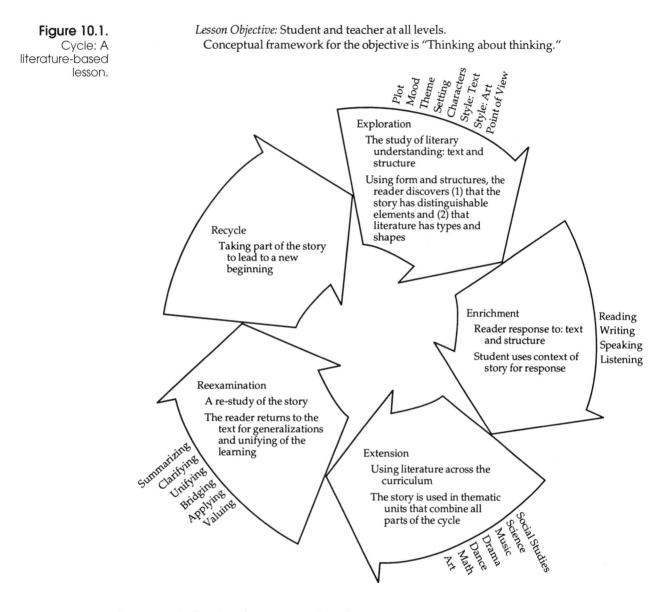

Assessment: Authentic tasks, process and product
Assumptions: There is more than one way to read a text

could be an ongoing unit directed to the study of text (Exploration), responding to the story in holistic language activities (Enrichment), or deciding to link the book to other curriculum (Extension). The Cycle process is simple and predictable, while the direction it may take never is, particularly when students' interests, questions, and input are considered at each level of the planning.

A teacher reading *Anno's Counting Book* by Mitsumasa Anno (1977) asks a kindergarten class about the page labeled "5," thinking that they will see the relationship of the number to the illustrated objects and the stack of blocks on the left-hand page. David, sitting in the back of the group, says, "I know! That's population explosion!" By accepting this divergent (and explosive) answer into the discussion, the teacher is able to extend the meaning of the counting book far beyond Anno's original intent. It becomes more than a shared counting book; it becomes a way to look at neighborhoods, transportation, and the extended world in changing seasons.

Considering children's answers and their questions is an integral and ongoing part of the Cycle process. For example, the teacher who has only one objective may initiate the discussion by asking, "What is on this page?" When the student answers, "It is a 5," there is an immediate evaluation, "That's right!" Or if the answer is not "correct," the teacher turns to other students until someone responds in the presupposed manner. In this kind of classroom interaction, there are no "creative enterprises," no extensions that reach into the lives of the learner.

A group of children in a fifth-grade class see a stack of empty barrels behind a commercial building close to their school and question the contents. By discussing the consequences to them and their community if the material is hazardous, and through nonfiction exploration of the repercussions, the children determine what should be done and end up becoming community activists regarding waste disposal. (For a complete report on this award-winning classroom, see Lewis, 1991.)

While there *may* be "right" answers in the discussion of a literary work (which is necessarily justified by redirecting the issue to an examination of the text), most of the teaching is open-ended, certainly individual, and always valued.

The questions and teaching strategies presented in Figure 10.2 are only examples. They are generic in nature, making them appropriate for almost any story. They are "launching off" ideas that may begin a lesson but that are not intended to be inclusive. Readers' responses are what give "flight" to the story.

Figure 10.2.
Literary questions and
strategies.

Exploration: The Study of Text and Structure

Genre

- What kind of story is it?
- What details define what kind of story it is?
- What other stories do you know with similar patterns? characters? settings? themes?

Plot

- What is the story about?
- How would it look if we diagrammed the structure?
- What are the major conflicts?

Characters

- What were the "literary fingerprints" of the characters?
- What do the actions, dialogue, description, and monologue tell about the characters?

Theme

- In what ways or words does the author tell about the "big idea"?

Setting

- How do time and place add to the story?
- Explain how the time or place is a friend or foe.

Style

- What style of art is used?
- What sensory or formal properties did you find?
- What voice (point of view) does the teller take?
- Select words or phrases that are "just right" for you.
- What feelings (mood) did you experience?

Extension: Using Literature across the Curriculum

Social Studies

- What are the political and religious issues in the book?
- How do fiction and nonfiction expand the understanding of a time in history?

Science

- What inventions and discoveries have made an impact on the twentieth century?
- How does the study of biography help us understand recent discoveries?

Math

- How has the author or illustrator

developed details to assist in understanding mathematical concepts?
- Develop a time line of the story plot.

The Arts

- *Visual arts*: What media are used by picture book illustrators today? Design an advertisement for a book.
- *Dance*: During one of the tense times in the book, how would you show that tension in body movement?
- *Music*: Set the picture book to music. What pieces of music would you choose? Why?
- *Drama*: Decide which part of a book would make an after-school television special.

Enrichment: Reader Response to Text and Structure

- Discuss two stories of the same genre. Develop a chart of comparison for the two.
- Write a journal entry in answer to some of the problems faced by one of the characters.
- Debate one of the conflicts found in the theme.
- In your own words, describe how you feel about the setting.
- Write a prequel or sequel to the story.
- Develop a readers theatre from the monologue and dialogue.
- Locate examples of simile, metaphor, irony, and hyperbole.
- Discuss the literature meanings and how the author used them figuratively.
- Develop new chapter titles. How is the book organized into sections?

Reexamination: Returning to the Book to Unify the Learning

The following questions are used to unify or bring together the students' thinking about the book. In all cases, it is a *return to the book* for clarification, bridging information, and summarizing what was felt, learned, and acted upon.

- What do you know (or believe, question, wonder about) that you did not know before?
- What conclusions can be drawn from the story?
- What might have precipitated the conflict which resulted in the ending of the story?
- Can you explain how the idea (plot line) evolved?
- Tell me more about how the conflict was resolved.
- Can you explain your answer in other

words? from another point of view?
- This book will be in the learning center with others by the same author or illustrator. Find some generalizations among the books.
- In what way do you have the same feelings as when we first read the book? What feelings are different?
- How do you rate the story? (Think about your overall impression and your feelings about the various elements of the story.)

State your reasons for your rating.
- List three elements of the story that were factual. List three elements that were fiction.
- What is your interpretation of the final conflict?

Recycle: Leading to a New Beginning

- What do we still wonder about the story?
- How can we find out more?

To Understand More Is to Enjoy More

The Cycle was first developed to assist my students and practicing teachers in adapting basal series instruction. I believed that if the basal stories were modified by removing the stultifying effect of the prescriptive questions and teaching strategies provided in the teachers' manuals, they would be more palatable to teachers and readers. Not only did that prove to be true, but strategies selected from the Cycle framework that were applied to supplemental literature in social studies lessons were equally successful.

This resulted in "real" reading in all curriculum areas. We soon found ourselves selecting from the Cycle framework to discuss and interpret books which were read aloud, and surprisingly enough, we applied the principles to nonbook reading, labels, charts, and graphs.

The important finding was the recursive nature of the Cycle schema. Using any or all parts of the Cycle led naturally into another. Each Cycle made connection to the next, with the end (Recycle) becoming the beginning of something else.

A Word about Questions and Teaching Strategies

There are some cautions about questions or strategies selected from the Cycle pattern:

1. Try the Cycle, but do not let it control your direction, format, or teaching style.

2. Listen, watch, and wait for the children's questions and interests to develop. Their relevant concerns produce a quality literature experience and a love of reading.

3. Redirect the discussion if it gets completely off the target.

4. Select questions pertaining to things that also make *you* wonder. You will not have all the answers, either.

5. Evaluate and listen to yourself. You are controlling the discussion if you provide information or realizations that readers can discover for themselves.

6. The Cycle works with a variety of class models:
   - Whole-class work (e.g., the whole class reads or listens to the same book)
   - Groups that are assigned a book, directive, theme, or issue
   - Groups where they choose their own directive or strategies, such as individualized reading
   - Thematic or topical units of literature study

Evaluating and Assessing the Cycle

The Cycle planning scheme allows "kidwatching" (Y. Goodman, 1985) for observing and assessing students' actual experiences with literature pieces. These authentic and functional measures are both product- and process-based: how children respond to a story by retelling it, how they apply what they understand in various registers—group discussions, charts, story maps, and related writing or further reading.

The Cycle evaluation is based on the notion that literature learning is a developmental process, a simple foundation leading to a perceptive and analytical understanding. The developmental levels of literary understandings are the following:

1. *Enjoyment of story:* primary level at which students talk about the story, predicting and choosing the pleasurable parts.

2. *Guided study:* intermediate level at which students determine meaning of the plot, compare tales, and examine ways that words and illustrations interface with moods or setting. This is an active process involving social interaction, reasoning, and silent appreciations. Questions and strategies depend on the readers' understanding and perceptions.

3. *Critical reflection:* advanced level that becomes an emotional experience (sense, feelings), response to values (judgments, explanations, disassociations), and intellectual change (thoughts, actions).

Figure 10.3 provides some general observational guidelines for each level of literary understanding.

Figure 10.3.
Observing and assessing the literature lesson.

Exploration: The Study of Text and Structure

This assessment is determined by how students understand, define, formulate, or explain stories and the literary elements, story type, and patterns.

- recognizes different genres and provides patterns or elements that give the structure
- identifies such elements as sequence of ideas, direct statement of the characters, main idea and theme, point of view, language elements (imagery, sound patterns, figurative language), and setting (time and place)
- demonstrates understanding of relationship of elements through writing and storytelling
- can retell the story
- finds similarities between stories or themes and can chart them
- can discuss cause and effect in plot
- asks questions that lead to understanding of form or structure
- can make predictions about the characters
- can locate sections or phrases that substantiate his or her beliefs
- understands and discusses the figurative language used
- compares the media version of a book with the text
- can write a critical essay about the theme

Enrichment: Reader Response to Text and Structure

Students are observed as they participate in activities that are holistic in nature. They write and read (both assigned and spontaneous activities) and think ahead to verify from the text. They ask questions. They continue to make connections from what was read (text) and their own responses (reader) through patterns, quotations, and discussions.

- can match the print to his or her speech
- can sustain attention to literary pieces
- makes literature a choice
- anticipates a sequence of events and ideas
- interested in a variety of genres
- dictates stories before trying to "invent" personal narrative
- uses "sketch to stretch" to augment writing
- responds to elements and features of a story in light of personal experiences

- participates in book talks or writing groups and in reading and writing "buddy" groups
- choices of leisure reading reflect increased variety, quality, and personal interest
- uses strategies to assist in decoding, grammar, spelling, and composition
- understands the relationship of reading/writing and writing/reading
- reports of reading reflect creativity; sometimes incorporates author's or illustrator's style
- continues to write in imaginative ways
- self-correction strategies are used
- expansion of "book message" is evident
- uses background knowledge to investigate a story
- accepts, questions, or rejects stories and can give reasons for these choices
- sees different levels of meanings in a work
- makes choices for leisure reading that reflect a growth in understanding
- develops a reading portfolio (a collection of reading and writing related to literature) that sustains interest and that is a measure of accomplishment

Extension: Using Literature across the Curriculum

Generally, students are able to see that books and other media are concerned with people, places, ideas, and things that integrate all curriculum areas in the classroom.

- can use books to help solve problems
- understands the terms in propaganda or in stereotypical plots
- combines genres (e.g., fiction/nonfiction) to discover and explore
- uses various media (arts, dance, music) for expression as demonstrated in trade books
- uses trade books to find answers to personal and community issues
- uses schematic methods (maps, organizers, graphs) as demonstrated in trade books as meaningful context for his or her own writing
- develops understandings across a range of works (art, music, dance, drama)
- shows a sensitivity to other points of view
- understands literature as a method of stating and exploring values
- continues to ask questions

Two Sample Cycles

Recurring plots, types of characters, themes, and symbols are all fundamental patterns that appear in literature. "It is the teacher's business to know it and to structure the student's experiences with literature in such a way that the child will discover for himself the significant patterns in literature at the same time as he enjoys each literary experience for its own sake" (Sloan, 1992, p. 44).

In adventure stories, the idealized person is the hero traveling in a world to test his or her abilities and to seek a quest. The sample Cycle below demonstrates this archetype for animal heroes.

I. *The Tale of Peter Rabbit* by Beatrix Potter (1902)

   A. Exploration and Enrichment

     1. Why did Peter go to the garden? What other possible reasons can you think of? What was he looking for?

     2. How is Peter different than his sisters? (Discuss both text and art.) If the girls had gone into the garden, what might have happened?

     3. Did Peter get what he was looking for?

     4. What were his feelings when he returned home? Will he go again? Why or why not?

     5. Write about what happens the next time Mrs. Rabbit gives a warning. (Dictate the story, if necessary.)

     6. Make a chart showing what the sisters did all day while Peter was in the garden.

   B. Extension

     1. Using simple props (apron, hat, pot, jacket), act out the story.

     2. Have a tasting party of what Peter might have sampled (lettuce, radishes, cabbages, blueberries, chamomile tea).

   C. Reexamine

     1. Reread the story. Put it in a learning center with other stories by the same author.

II. *The Three Little Pigs* by L. Leslie Books (n.d.)

   A. Exploration and Enrichment

     1. Why didn't the pigs just stay home? Use the artwork to determine if there may have been different feelings for each of the pigs.

     2. What does "seek your fortune" mean?

     3. Does this story remind you of any others that we have read? Which ones and in what ways?

     4. Why did each of the pigs choose something different with which to build his house?

B. Extension

1. Locate as many different versions of *The Three Little Pigs* as you can (different authors, illustrators, and media). Compare and contrast them.

2. Act out (mime) what you would do if you went to "seek your fortune."

C. Reexamine

1. [Present students with a Venn Chart.] Compare Peter Rabbit and the third little pig.

D. Recycle—The teacher introduces other stories in which the characters have gone on a quest, such as the following books:

1. Two heroes who sailed on their quest: *Where the Wild Things Are* by Maurice Sendak (1963) and *The Fool of the World and the Flying Ship* by Arthur Ransome (1968)

2. Two heroes who were Native Americans: *Arrow to the Sun: A Pueblo Indian Tale* by Gerald McDermott (1974) and *The Legend of Scarface* by Robert San Souci (1978)

3. Three heroines who went on a quest: *East of the Sun, West of the Moon*, retold by Ingri and Edgar d'Aulaire (1969), *The Wizard of Oz* by L. Frank Baum (1900), and *The Wild Swans* by Marcia Brown (1963)

4. Three heroes from different nations: "The Golden Fleece" by Margaret Evans Price (1924), *Jack and the Beanstalk* by Virginia Haviland (1959), and *The Flower of Happiness on Sunnymount Crest,* selected by Elsa Olenius (1973)

A second sample Cycle, shown below, focuses on a single book, *Lyddie* by Katherine Paterson (1991). In this novel, a young farm girl from Vermont, struggling to keep her family together, is contracted out to work at an inn to pay her father's debts. Later, Lyddie finds better-paying work in the factories of Lowell, Massachusetts, but she misses her younger brother and sister and finds the work tedious and hard. What keeps her going is her dream of further schooling and regaining the family farm. This book of self-discovery also gives insight into the lives of factory workers in the 1880s.

Exploration and Enrichment

A. Characterizations

1. Describe Lyddie, her mother, Charlie, and Rachel. Find a place in the first three chapters that gives details about them. Write a character sketch for each or draw what you think they look like.

     2. Discuss Lyddie's adjustment to the working conditions at the inn and the factory.

     3. How does Lyddie describe herself to Mr. Marsden? How does Ezekiel describe her?

     4. Lyddie stares down the bear early in the story. Later, she decides to stare down another "bear." What is that?

  B. Setting

     1. Compare the Worthens' and Stevens' farms.

     2. If you had only the descriptions from this book, how would you sketch Lowell for a land survey?

  C. Theme

     1. What meanings or messages did you find in the story?

     2. Describe Lyddie's journey.

     3. "Slavery" is used in two ways in this book. Discuss both meanings and give examples from the story about who is a slave. Who is free?

  D. Style

     1. Who tells this story? How would it be different if it were told by the innkeeper? Mr. Stevens? Lyddie's voice?

     2. What does "the kiss of death" mean?

     3. Write a petition for changing working conditions from the viewpoint of Lyddie.

II. Extensions

     1. Research the factories in Lowell; compare the information that Paterson provides and that presented in history books.

     2. Debate the benefits of industrialization.

     3. Discuss the different economic, political, and religious classes in the story.

     4. Interview someone who can tell about the beginning of the women's movement during the early 1900s. Read about the conflicts of the 1800s.

     5. What can we learn about the author that would give insight into the story?

III.   Reexamine

     1. Did Lyddie feel differently at the end of the book than at the beginning? In what ways? Does she really know who she is? What will happen next?

     2. How is this book different from or similar to anything in your life?

     3. In what way does *Lyddie* remind you of any other story you have read?

Summary and Assumptions

Literature-based teaching—with or without a teacher's guide—has no single model. However, the following basic assumptions can be applied:

1. Teachers using trade books see literature learning as developmental. Therefore, teaching strategies and assessment measures should first reflect enjoyment, then guided study, and finally conscious and critical examination of the story.

2. There are many options for using a work of literature, many of which are dictated by active and natural responses. Student input is necessary to determine which options are effective.

3. Teachers should prepare for literature learning. More is needed than producing a text and awaiting students' spontaneous reactions. A deductive framework may be kept in mind although the actual teaching may be thoroughly inductive. This does not mean having a predetermined goal or product and being inflexible toward change.

4. Teachers need to be learners, to be able to think in "literary ways."

5. It may be necessary or advisable to include both reader interpretation and author intent as part of a literature study.

6. There are many ways and reasons to read a story: for information, to question, for enjoyment, as a model for writing and viewing the writing act, and making connections to "the story," to "other stories," and to "my own story."

References

Corwin, R., Hein, G. E., & Levin, D. (1976). Weaving curriculum webs: The structure of nonlinear curriculum. *Childhood Education, 52(5)*, 248–51.

Flender, M. G. (1985). Charting book discussions: A method of presenting literature in the elementary grades. *Children's Literature in Education, 16*(2), 90–92.

Goodman, K. S. (1988). Look what they've done to Judy Blume! The "basalization" of children's literature. *The New Advocate, 1*(1), 29–41.

Goodman, Y. (1985). Kidwatching: Observing children in the classroom. In A. Jaggar and M. Smith-Burke (Eds.), *Observing the language learner*. Newark, DE: International Reading Association.

Hepler, S. (1988). A guide for the teacher guides: Doing it yourself. *The New Advocate, 1*(3), 186–95.

Huck, C. S., Hepler, S., & Hickman, J. (1993). *Children's literature in the elementary school* (5th ed.). San Diego: Harcourt Brace Jovanovich.

Lewis, B. A. (1991). *The kid's guide to social action*. Minneapolis: Free Spirit.

Moss, J. F. (1990). *Focus on literature: A context for literary learning*. Katonah, NY: Richard C. Owen.

Norton, D. (1995). *Through the eyes of a child* (4th ed.). Englewood Cliffs, NJ: Prentice-Hall.

Raines, S. C., & Canady, R. J. (1991). *More story s-t-r-e-t-c-h-e-r-s: More activities to expand children's favorite books.* Mt. Rainier, MD: Gryphon House.

Sanders, N. M. (1966). *Classroom questions: What kinds?* New York: Harper & Row.

Saul, E. W. (1989). What did Leo feed the turtle? and other nonliterary questions. *Language Arts, 66*(3), 296–303.

Sloan, G. D. (1992). *The child as critic* (3rd ed.). New York: Teachers College Press, Columbia University.

Somers, A. B., & Worthington, J. E. (1979). *Response guides for teaching children's books.* Urbana, IL: National Council of Teachers of English.

Temple, C. (1991). Seven readings of a folk talk: Literary theory in the classroom. *The New Advocate, 4*(1), 25–35.

Wood, K. D., Lapp, D., & Flood, J. (1992). *Guiding readers through text: A review of study guides.* Newark, DE: International Reading Association.

Children's Books Cited

Anno, Mitsumasa. (1977). *Anno's counting book.* Illus. by Author. New York: Thomas Y. Crowell.

Baum, L. Frank. (1900). *The wizard of Oz.* New York: William Morrow.

Books, L. Leslie. (n.d.). *The three little pigs.* New York: Frederick Warne.

Brown, Marcia. (1963). *The wild swans.* Illus. by Author. New York: Charles Scribner's Sons.

d´Aulaire, Ingri, & Edgar Parin d´Aulaire (Retellers). (1969). *East of the sun, west of the moon.* Illus. by Retellers. New York: Viking.

Haviland, Virginia. (1959). *Jack and the beanstalk.* Boston: Little, Brown.

McDermott, Gerald. (1974). *Arrow to the sun: A Pueblo Indian tale.* Illus. by Author. New York: Viking.

Olenius, Elsa (Comp.). (1973). "The flower of happiness on Sunnymount Crest," in *Great Swedish fairy tales.* Illus. by John Bauer. New York: Delacorte.

Potter, Beatrix. (1902). *The tale of Peter Rabbit.* Illus. by Author. New York: Frederick Warne.

Price, Margaret Evans. (1924). "The golden fleece," in *Myths and enchantment tales.* Chicago: Rand McNally.

Ransome, Arthur. (1968). *The fool of the world and the flying ship.* Illus. by Uri Shulevitz. New York: Farrar, Straus & Giroux.

San Souci, Robert. (1978). *The legend of Scarface.* New York: Doubleday.

Sendak, Maurice. (1963). *Where the wild things are.* Illus. by Author. New York: Harper & Row.

IV Modeling

The Different Faces of Literature-Based Instruction

11

Barbara A. Lehman
The Ohio State University at Mansfield

A teacher's transition from relying on basal language arts textbooks to developing a literature-based program is a critical time period. The change involves more than a different *approach* to teaching reading and writing; it also requires an altered *philosophy* about the power and potential of literature in children's lives to help them become fully literate human beings. In other words, through *literary* experiences, *literacy* is accomplished.

Previous and subsequent chapters describe how the path to literature-based teaching can begin with small steps and may progress gradually. Among many other decisions a teacher must make are those regarding what curricular model to follow in designing a new program. This chapter describes different "faces" of literature-based instruction and notes strengths and weaknesses of each.

First, however, we need to consider three sets of variables that affect instructional decision making, for whatever model a teacher chooses to follow is further shaped by these variables as well. The variables can be arranged along intersecting continua as shown in Figure 11.1.

The first continuum relates to whether a classroom is teacher-focused or student-centered. For example, who selects what books to read? Who plans and leads discussions about those books? Who determines what meanings from those books are important? Who decides what activities will be used with those books? Who groups children for reading, discussion, and activities? Who plans when literacy events and experiences will occur? Who chooses what skills will be introduced and when? Who decides how readers' and writers' growth will be evaluated?

The second variable concerns whether content will be integrated or segmented, both within the language arts and among other curricular areas. Will reading and writing be interrelated or separated? How and when will skills be addressed—within the context

Figure 11.1.
Instructional variables.

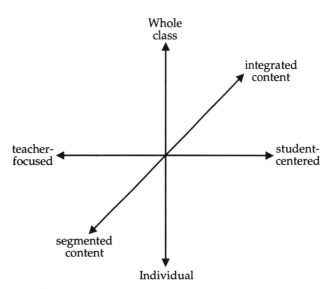

of reading and writing or apart? How will language arts be related to math, science, social studies, health, art, music, and physical education? How can trade books be an integrative force across the curriculum?

Finally, grouping children for instruction ranges along a continuum from whole class to small groups to individuals. When is it appropriate to work with a large group, engage smaller gatherings, or assist individuals? What activities work best with which configurations? Which children need particular support and instruction? Who works well with whom? (For more on the art and complexity of instructional and curricular decision making, see chapter 8 by Patricia Crook, "Decisions about Curriculum in a Literature-Based Program.")

Thus when we examine literature-based "faces," we need to remember that there are many facets to each one. Yet even as each "face" and its angles differ in subtle ways, they also share some essential components. Huck, Hepler, and Hickman (1993) have detailed certain necessary features of a literature program: (1) an enthusiastic teacher who conveys a love for literature by reading aloud and by sharing books in other ways with children; (2) a wide selection of children's books available in the classroom; (3) a classroom reading center containing these books; and (4) displays of books and children's literature-related work in the classroom. Additional elements identified by Kulleseid and Strickland (1989) include time for reading, discussing, and responding to books; opportunities and materials for writing; art, music, creative dramatics, and other activities developed in response to books; and a library media center well integrated with the literacy program.

The Spiral Curriculum Model

The first model of literature-based instruction is based upon a spiral curriculum design, as exemplified by Stott (1987). Basic themes or genres (e.g., folklore or fantasy) are selected for an entire, schoolwide program. These are introduced at the earliest grade levels, and successive grades return to and build upon themes or genres previously explored, working at more advanced levels. Writing is modeled after literature selections studied. In light of the variables discussed earlier, teachers may need to consider such issues as how much input students will have in choosing and sequencing the themes or genres, who will decide what books are used to accompany particular themes and genres, how much flexibility there will be in writing assignments based upon books read, and how much literature study will be integrated across the curriculum.

The strengths of this model include its strong literary focus and integrated reading and writing. On the other hand, it also requires that teachers have a strong literary background themselves and understand how to approach literature study systematically and in depth. The fact that the spiral model depends upon careful, comprehensive planning and involvement of the whole school staff might make it difficult to implement in situations where commitment to literature is less unified. Still, the excitement and challenge of implementing this model could revitalize teachers' interest in literature and their desire to further their own literary education. Chapter 12 by Jill May, "A Literary Studies Model Curriculum for Elementary Language Arts Programs," would be compatible with the spiral design. Patricia Cianciolo, in chapter 16, "Teaching and Learning Critical Aesthetic Responses to Literature," and Renea Leonard, in chapter 17, "Guiding Children's Critical Aesthetic Responses to Literature in a Fifth-Grade Classroom," provide two other companion pieces that emphasize a strong literary stance.

The Individualized Reading Model

The individualized reading model has been described succinctly by Veatch (1968). Key ingredients to this approach include a large collection of children's books (at least one hundred); a classroom library to house those books; children's self-selection of books to read by themselves; ample time for reading, for writing about reading, and for projects; and individual conferences between teacher and child. Additional segments involve small-group work on similar needs and interests and whole-class time for planning and sharing. Decision-making variables may relate to who picks books for the classroom collection, how teachers can assist self-selection, how closely skills are linked to children's reading and writing, how groups are incorporated into literacy activities and discussions, who decides the group's composition, and how reading and writing are related to other content studies.

Strengths of this model include its accommodation of individual diversity in terms of needs and interests. Because of the appeal of self-selection and the responsibility and experience of making their own choices, children may tend to read more and to make better selections for reading. On the negative side, some teachers express frustrations with the management chores of this model: having enough books for children to read, finding enough time to confer with individual children and with small groups when needed, and tracking children's reading and their progress in mastering skills. However, these problems are not insurmountable; teachers can find creative ways to organize the class efficiently—by using book buddies, for example, to reduce the number of individual conferences with children. Chapter 13 by Mary Jo Fresch, "Self-Selected Books of Beginning Readers: Standing before the Smorgasbord," describes a classroom that employs many of the aspects of individualized reading.

The Core Book Model

The core book model is one of the most prevalent configurations, according to Zarrillo (1989). As implied by its name, a whole class will read one book together, which is supplemented by independent reading of other books, writing, and activity choices related to the core book. Potential variables may include who selects the core book, activities related to it and books for independent reading, the relationship of skills instruction to the core book, how the core book may be linked to other curricular areas, how to meet the needs of individuals for whom the core book is not the best match in terms of ability or interest, and how and when to use small groups within a core book format.

This model can be a good bridge between basal and literature-based instruction, and some teachers find it an easier way to begin teaching with trade books or even to combine literature with basals. The teacher still controls most of the whole-class instruction (i.e., assignments, discussion, and assessment); thus the structure seems somewhat more manageable than other configurations may be. However, there are also trade-offs. Using a single book with the whole class rarely meets every child's abilities, needs, and interests. Having the whole class read a core book may take longer and may become more tedious than reading individually or in small groups, and mass assignments may kill children's interest in the book entirely. Finally, there is a danger for teachers in "basalizing" a core book, particularly if the basal model of instruction is simply applied to a trade book. Core books (or perhaps short stories) could be alternated with other patterns, though, and still provide enough worthwhile whole-class experiences.

The Thematic Unit Model

Thematic literature units are often developed through a process known as *webbing* (Norton, 1982). This model integrates subject areas and incorporates many children's books on the same topic. Typically, the teacher will read aloud one or more of the books to the whole class; small groups will choose or be assigned to read other books; and children will select still other books to read individually. Group and/or individual projects will accompany book reading. A unit may last from one to six weeks, depending on the topic. In using this model, a teacher may need to consider the following variables: who picks the unit theme, who chooses books to be included in the unit (for reading aloud, small-group reading, and individual reading), who plans projects that attend book reading, what place skills will have in the unit, what content areas will be integrated in the unit, how groups will be composed and for what purposes, and what work is appropriate for individual endeavors.

One of this model's strongest features is that a whole class can study the same topic while also exploring options for individualizing content within the unit. Furthermore, use of themes is an excellent way to integrate other curricular areas with reading and language arts. Finally, the model provides a good opportunity for teachers and children to collaborate in planning educational experiences. (See chapter 24 by Linda Lamme, "Collaborating with Children on Theme Studies.") Potential drawbacks include the time needed to develop thematic units, especially if teachers try to plan by themselves rather than working together and with their students. Thus units may also take longer to implement and may involve more long-range planning and an overview of the year's curriculum. If they do not incorporate necessary curricular areas, danger exists that thematic units simply will be add-ons and, therefore, frustrating, if not impossible. Sylvia Vardell, in chapter 14, "Thematic Units: Integrating the Curriculum," and Peggy Oxley, in chapter 23, "Literary Tapestry: An Integrated Primary Curriculum," paint a more detailed portrait of this "face." Gail Tompkins also describes experiences with thematic units in chapter 19, "Hear Ye, Hear Ye, and Learn the Lesson Well: Fifth Graders Read and Write about the American Revolution."

Combination Models

Finally, various permutations of models can be devised. A core book may provide a thematic unit focus, for instance. Individualized reading usually accompanies both core books and thematic units. Thematic units, core books, and individualized reading could easily fit within a spiral curriculum design.

Combinations of literature with a basal reading program are also possible (and sometimes necessary or even desirable). Several teachers in this book recount ways in which they have combined basals with literature, particularly as an intermediate step in their journeys toward literature-based instruction. For example, in a traditional three-group reading class, such groups can rotate, with two reading in the basal and the third studying a thematic literature unit. Alternatively, one group could read in the basal, a second group could read individual selections, and the third group could read a children's book together. Some teachers prefer to alternate the whole class between reading in the basal and reading literature (core books, individualized reading, or thematic units).

Such combinations of basal programs and children's books allow teachers to experiment with literature-based instruction without entirely relinquishing the basal's security. Combinations also enable some teachers to reconcile conflicting expectations, as in the case where the teacher prefers literature-based instruction, but the school system requires a basal program. Inherent dangers to such combinations include extension of basalized instruction to reading literature, philosophical incongruence and fragmentation between basal and literature-based instruction, inconsistent assessment priorities between the two approaches, and stagnation if teachers stop growing beyond this point. In any case, a teacher need not rely heavily on a basal reading program and should feel free to adapt it to children's needs, rather than allowing the basal to dictate instruction.

Teachers' choices about the design of literature-based programs are constrained by many factors (some of which Patricia Crook discusses in chapter 8). Teaching style influences this decision, since some styles match better with certain models than others. The children one teaches, availability of resources, building and district mandates, support of colleagues, parents, and supervisors, and physical layout of the school building itself, while not *excuses*, are possible considerations among others. The point is that no one way is right or best; we all must experiment and construct or adapt models that work well for us. In that spirit, these "faces" of literature-based instruction are offered.

References

Huck, C. S., Hepler, S., & Hickman, J. (1993). *Children's literature in the elementary school* (5th ed.). San Diego: Harcourt Brace Jovanovich.

Kulleseid, E. R., & Strickland, D. S. (1989). *Literature, literacy learning: Classroom teachers, library media specialists, and the literature-based curriculum.* Chicago: American Library Association.

Norton, D. E. (1982). Using a webbing process to develop children's literature units. *Language Arts, 59,* 348–55.

Stott, J. C. (1987). The spiralled sequence story curriculum: A structuralist approach to teaching fiction in the elementary grades. *Children's Literature in Education, 18*(3), 148–62.

Veatch, J. (1968). *How to teach reading with children's books.* Katonah, NY: Richard C. Owen.

Zarrillo, J. (1989). Teachers' interpretations of literature-based reading. *The Reading Teacher, 43,* 22–28.

12 A Literary Studies Model Curriculum for Elementary Language Arts Programs

Jill P. May
Purdue University

Harvard educator Jerome S. Bruner (1966) has argued that instruction should have four major elements: learning experiences that encourage a desire to learn; a structured program that moves from simple to complex concepts; variety in teaching methods and a sequencing of knowledge; and a gradual shift in learning from dependency on teacher reinforcement to independent problem solving and solutions to questions. Bruner, acknowledging that each child will approach learning in different ways, concludes: "If a curriculum is to be effective in the classroom it must contain different ways of activating children, different ways of presenting sequences, different opportunities for some children to 'skip' parts while others work their way through, different ways of putting things. A curriculum, in short, must contain many tracks leading to the same general goal" (pp. 39–72).

If a model for literary criticism within language arts instruction were to be developed, teachers would use theory similar to that advocated by Bruner in order to build a prototype yearlong program of learning for each of the school's elementary grades, including kindergarten. The program would be unique to that school and would develop children's understanding of literature in its place in society.

Instruction for literary studies should be planned and instituted by the teacher, beginning with a statement of the basic principles and concepts which all of the staff agree are the heart of the program. Teaching units included in the program should be based on a theory of literature that focuses on helping children understand literary texts and the pleasures to be gained from enlightened reading. This theory of literary instruction should be the core of any program, not the specific lessons that have been developed or books that are included within the plans. The introduction should empha-size that literary study will be defeated if other schools simply take someone else's model and try to institute it.

Since each school's professional staff will vary in its under-standing of literature and knowledge of children's books, one pro-posed study of literature would not fit the needs of all school sys-tems. Each school's model must address the needs of a particular audience; it cannot assume that the same audience would be found within all American school districts. The schoolwide program could suggest how the teachers might test the program's effectiveness and demonstrate how individual classrooms are related to each other.

Within each class, teachers would strive to outline a structure for optimum learning. The designed activities for literary study would consider what each child might be expected to bring to the program from his or her real-world experiences, how that knowl-edge might generate new learning, what earlier classroom experi-ences might be reinforced, and what materials could be shared to instill each of the children with an eagerness to learn. The teacher would need to plan effective sequencing in teaching literary concepts and to collaborate with similar teaching in other classes in the school.

I joined forces with a group of teachers and their principal to create a model curriculum that would replace language arts text-books used in the classroom. The teachers determined what literary principles they wished to emphasize, wrote a guide that placed certain books and experiences within certain grades, and established which literary terms would be used throughout the school. The guide was published and given to all teachers in the school; the program was instituted in the fall of 1984.

The first books to be shared within the classrooms were se-lected through teacher recommendations to extend curriculum areas beyond reading. For instance, the kindergarten guide stated that books would be shared in a unit that discussed children's fears. The unit introduced personified animals as characters, the importance of setting in a story, and the differences between fantasy and realistic fiction. Books chosen to be shared included *Will I Have a Friend?* by Miriam Cohen (1977), *You're the Scaredy-Cat* by Mercer Mayer (1974), *Bedtime for Frances* by Russell Hoban (1960), and *Stevie* by John Steptoe (1971).

In the third grade, the teaching guide concentrated on the literary merits of books. It named several types of literature that would be introduced, including animal fables, American tall tales and legends, fantasy, and realistic modern fiction. The teacher developed the children's understanding of point of view in writing, foreshadowing in plot, and symbolism in stories. Books included

E. B. White's *Charlotte's Web* (1952); a version of *Aesop's Fables* illustrated by Heidi Holder (1981); Chaucer's *Chanticleer and the Fox*, retold and illustrated by Barbara Cooney (1958); and *The Incredible Journey* by Sheila Burnford (1961).

Although the guide suggested ways of approaching the books, flexibility in planning and teacher modifications of the program were stressed. Once a month, the faculty talked about what had worked and what had failed to work. They suggested ways to alter instruction and recommended abandoning certain books at particular grade levels. Thus, the third-grade teacher returned her set of Kenneth Grahame's *The Wind in the Willows* (1961) to the textbook library once she realized that her students did not enjoy the book and were not following the plot development. The fourth-grade teacher discovered that her students could not read the Yorkshire dialect in Frances Hodgson Burnett's *The Secret Garden* (1938). However, because they enjoyed the story, she read it aloud to them while they followed along in their copies.

A program like this allows children to systematically explore works of literature for their specific meanings and attitudes. Children learn to express their individual interpretations in different ways; they also learn to listen to others when they discuss shared readings and to respond to the critical theories of others.

Besides the books used in each grade, a literary studies program should stress the conventions found in most literature within a particular genre, including story structure, stereotypical characterizations found in the stories, and predictable endings. Genres are based upon archetypal patterns established within classical pieces of literature; often similar motifs can be found in contemporary works. Teachers can stress that "stealing patterns in literature" is an important part of writing and developing an appreciation for both the writer and the text.

Another strategy for literature study is to examine various versions of a tale. Readers who have shared the original archetypal story will enjoy the new tale more than an uninformed reader will. For instance, changes in tone, theme, and perspective can be seen when traditional patterns are first explored and then reinforced with a study of contemporary titles holding similar patterns. Versions of the Brothers Grimm tales show how authors have used the traditional characters and plots to rewrite popular stories. One story that has been told in many versions is *Little Red Riding Hood*. A classroom study that explores the original French version by Charles Perrault (1969) and the original German version by the Brothers Grimm (1963) and then turns to contemporary picture book retellings by Trina Schart Hyman (1983), John S. Goodall (1988), and Michael Emberley (1990) would show how stories change, how cultures reshape the original plot to fit their needs, and how authors manipulate archetypal patterns to create new interpretations of plot, characterization, or even theme.

Students should also be challenged to consider the idea that literature need not be relevant to their lives to be enjoyable. For example, children have long enjoyed the inane capers that confront Alice in Lewis Carroll's *Alice's Adventures in Wonderland* (1907). While adult critics have found a good deal of British social and political commentary in the book, children view the book differently. Usually they love the story for its absurd plot and for Alice's saucy way of handling the unknown. Few children hope to live in Wonderland, and fewer still hope to emulate Alice's physical and emotional changes, but lots of children continue to enjoy Alice's adventures.

The Bicycle Man by Allen Say (1982) is historical realism based upon Say's childhood experiences while living in Japan. Adults reading the story can infer the significance of World War II on Japanese culture to which Say alludes and can admire Say's training in Japanese graphic design demonstrated in the illustrations. However, children are more apt to see this story as an adventure in a faraway land. The "heroes" in this story are two American adults. Because they are adults, children will probably view them from the perspective of the narrator—a child participating in his Japanese school's sports day.

If teachers share both classical and modern literature that allows children to escape from their everyday world, they will help students see that much of literature is designed around a circular journey—home/away/home—and that most adventure stories end "happily ever after."

Likewise, when children share the original classical tales found in a modern adaptation, such as those produced by the Disney Studio, they should learn to form opinions about the tale's rewriting based on story form, characterization, and language. Sometimes their opinions will be based upon the values held within the stories. Teachers must allow children to openly express their own attitudes about adaptations and encourage them to listen to the opinions of others. Classroom discussions of contemporary media can help youngsters evaluate for themselves future television, movie, book, and even interactive video reproductions of traditional tales. Teachers should show students that they cannot determine the worth of a new production without looking for the archetypal patterns found in the original version and for the changes made in each new rewriting. Children should learn that much of literature depends upon the traditional journeys of heroines or heroes, and they should be encouraged to consider how they might adapt stories if they were creating an artistic adaptation.

The goal in literary studies (and the teaching of reading) in the elementary school is to offer children a variety of story approaches from which to choose, approaches that will make reading a meaningful activity in their lives. Literary theories can inform all readers' textual understandings and can enhance their appreciation for children's literature.

The professional readings listed in References can help teachers and administrators understand how children's literature can be brought into language arts instruction. These books provide a starting point in a study of literary patterns. They contain references to other writings in the field and suggest ways to approach literature and classroom teaching. They are not prescriptive; they do not comprise a "canon of critical theory." Instead, these readings are representative of the recent scholarship acknowledged by experts within the field of children's literature who hope to see critical literary theory find a place in the elementary schools.

References

Bettelheim, B., & Zelan, K. (1982). *Learning to read: The child's fascination with meaning.* New York: Alfred A. Knopf.

Bruner, J. S. (1966). *Toward a theory of instruction.* Cambridge, MA: Belknap Press of Harvard University Press.

Campbell, J. (1972). *Myths to live by.* New York: Viking.

Farrell, E. J., & Squire, J. R. (Eds.). (1990). *Transactions with literature: A fifty-year perspective.* Urbana, IL: National Council of Teachers of English.

Frye, N. (1970). *The stubborn structure: Essays on criticism and society.* Ithaca, NY: Cornell University Press.

Lehr, S. (1991). *The child's developing sense of theme.* New York: Teachers College Press, Columbia University.

Lukens, R. (1990). *A critical handbook of children's literature* (4th ed.). Glenview, IL: Scott, Foresman.

May, J. P. (Ed.). (1983). *Children and their literature: A readings book.* West Lafayette, IN: Children's Literature Association.

Nodelman, P. (1988). *Words about pictures: The narrative art of children's picture books.* Athens: University of Georgia Press.

———. (1992). *The pleasures of children's literature.* New York: Longman.

Nodelman, P. (Ed.). (1985–87). *Touchstones: Reflections on the best in children's literature* (Vols. 1–3). West Lafayette, IN: Children's Literature Association.

Probst, R. E. (1988). *Response and analysis: Teaching literature in junior and senior high school.* Portsmouth, NH: Boynton/Cook.

Rosenblatt, L. M. (1983). *Literature as exploration* (4th ed.). New York: Modern Language Association. (Original work published 1938)

Sloan, G. D. (1991). *The child as critic* (3rd ed.). New York: Teachers College Press, Columbia University.

Tchudi, S. N., Boomer, G., Maguire, M., Creber, J. W. P., D'Arcy, P., & Johnson, F. (Eds.). (1986). *English teachers at work: Ideas and strategies from five countries.* Portsmouth, NH: Boynton/Cook.

Temple, C., & Collins, P. (Eds.). (1992). *Stories and readers: New perspectives on literature in the elementary classroom.* Norwood, MA: Christopher-Gordon.

Vandergrift, K. E. (1980). *Child and story: The literary connection.* New York: Neal-Schuman.

Children's Books Cited

Aesop. *Aesop's fables.* (1981). Adapted and illus. by Heidi Holder. New York: Viking.

Burnford, Sheila. (1961). *The incredible journey.* Illus. by Carl Burger. Boston: Little, Brown.

Burnett, Frances Hodgson. (1938). *The secret garden.* Illus. by Tasha Tudor. New York: J. B. Lippincott.

Carroll, Lewis. (1907). *Alice's adventures in wonderland.* London: Heinemann.

Chaucer, Geoffrey. (1958). *Chanticleer and the fox.* Adapted and illus. by Barbara Cooney. New York: Thomas Y. Crowell.

Cohen, Miriam. (1977). *Will I have a friend?* Illus. by Lillian Hoban. New York: Greenwillow Books.

Emberley, Michael. (1990). *Ruby.* Boston: Little, Brown.

Goodall, John S. (1988). *Little Red Riding Hood.* New York: Margaret K. McElderry Books.

Grahame, Kenneth. (1961). *The wind in the willows.* Illus. by Ernest H. Shepard. New York: Charles Scribner's Sons.

Grimm, Johann, & Grimm, Wilhelm. (1963). *Household stories.* Retold by Lucy Crane. Illus. by Walter Crane. New York: Dover.

Hoban, Russell. (1960). *Bedtime for Frances.* Illus. by Garth Williams. New York: Harper & Row.

Hyman, Trina Schart. (1983). *Little Red Riding Hood.* New York: Holiday House.

Mayer, Mercer. (1974). *You're the scaredy-cat.* Illus. by Author. New York: Parents Magazine Press.

Perrault, Charles. *Perrault's fairy tales.* (1969). Illus. by Gustave Dore. New York: Dover.

Say, Allen. (1982). *The bicycle man.* Boston: Houghton Mifflin.

Steptoe, John. (1971). *Stevie.* Illus. by Author. New York: Harper & Row.

White, E. B. (1952). *Charlotte's web.* Illus. by Garth Williams. New York: Harper & Row.

Self-Selected Books of Beginning Readers: Standing before the Smorgasbord

13

Mary Jo Fresch
Royal Melbourne Institute of Technology, Coburg, Victoria, Australia

Step into Mrs. A's first-grade classroom. The room is a profusion of print—every bit of wall space displays something for children to read. Children have created most of the "readable walls." Group efforts contributed to word-family posters, science predictions and observations, and language-experience charts. A large open area accommodates activities such as big book reading, show and tell, and "author share" during writing workshop. Throughout the day children use this area to spread out for individual reading and writing.

Next to the open area is the reading corner, housing approximately 100–150 books. Some books are from Mrs. A's own collection. Others are borrowed from the public library for four weeks, with popular ones renewed for another four. Big books with accompanying small copies are also available. Finally, school library books or small books from the *Literacy 2000* series (published in New Zealand in 1988–89) are in the corner. Nearby is the Young Author's Shelf containing stories written, illustrated, and compiled in the school's publishing shop by class members. Two notebooks complete the reading choices—a collection of poetry to which the children add throughout the year and a compilation of the weekly class newsletters.

Mrs. A announces group one's B.E.A.R. time (Being Excited About Reading). Half the students go to the reading corner to make their selections. The other half write on topics of personal interest in their journals. A flutter of activity ensues in the reading corner as the self-selection process begins. Tracy and Sara decide to buddy-read (or read together) and discuss which books to choose. David and Nick negotiate over the same book—who will read it first and pass it on—since they both want to read the same book alone. Mitch makes several quick choices and returns most of them to the shelf. Nick hunts for another book and asks where it is. Quietly, Christopher pulls it from his desk, puts it on the bookshelf, and points out to Nick that it was on the shelf after all. Some children return to their desks; others choose nooks and crannies in the room where they will begin reading.

Mrs. A checks what the selections have been. Once again, Jim chose a book much too hard to read by himself and walks toward her, finger on the first page, to request help. Jill picked all new, unfamiliar books. Nick has selected the same book for the third day in a row. Mrs. A wonders whether she should place some parameters on what books the children *can* choose. Is B.E.A.R. time a chance for self-selection of reading materials, an activity that encourages growth of these beginning readers' skills?

Literature-based classrooms such as Mrs. A's are organized to make learning meaningful and to encourage growth in young readers. Children have opportunities throughout the day to self-select various books with which to practice their new skills. They stand before a smorgasbord of reading materials, encouraged to select whatever might appeal to them. We may notice a child safely returning to the same book over and over. Research suggests repeated readings are a way to gain confidence. Eventually, the child may scan the smorgasbord for something new. Meek (1988) states that "the move from 'more of the same' to 'I might try something different' is a clear step" (p. 99), indicating growth in reading development. Teachers encourage self-selection to aid in the development of independent readers. While they may choose familiar selections, it is also hoped they will try one that challenges their developing skills.

The Study

My six-month study illustrated that first-grade children can make literature selections that advance their developing literacy skills. The study also indicated ways to assess beginning readers in literature-based instruction. Mrs. A's students self-selected books to read and worked cooperatively throughout the day. Reading abilities ranged from those still learning the alphabet to several children comfortably reading beginning books. All children could select from any of the texts in the library corner described in the scene above. As children's self-selections were tracked and recorded for six months, interesting patterns emerged supporting this important component of a literature-based classroom. (For an in-depth description of this study see Fresch, 1991).

Patterns in Self-Selection

At the beginning of the school year, many children selected a variety of books, not necessarily at their reading level. They experimented with exploring illustrations, leafing through pages, or simply handling numerous books. Many children needed to establish important understandings about print and stories—and thus needed to "dig in" to different types of books.

Within a month or two, the first self-selection pattern was observed: children began to reread. They sometimes reread a big book shared by the teacher, or they simply chose repeatedly a particular book from the classroom collection. Often, self-selected reading would not begin until a specific book was secured.

Ownership of a "special" text became obvious in children's self-selection during these first two months. Children sometimes made great efforts to obtain a particular book, such as hiding books in their desks or in an odd spot in the room, following other children around—watching and waiting for the opportunity to request the book, offering trades, or negotiating in other ways to gain possession. Jim became excited when he saw that *One Hungry Monster* by Susan Heyboer O'Keefe (1989) had been renewed from the library again. "Oh good, she got my book!" he remarked and immediately claimed it that afternoon. Rereading chosen books was an important activity. Both Smith (1985) and Meek (1988) claim that children reread books to gain control of reading strategies. Repetition helps children gain confidence by drawing on what they already know and provides positive reinforcement and immediate feedback.

A second self-selection pattern emerged: a delayed revisiting of big books presented during shared reading. This strategy was consistently evident with one particular child. From the first big book introduced in September to those presented as late as December, Katie waited two weeks between the whole-group introduction and her self-selecting the book for B.E.A.R. reading. During that time, the teacher read the book each morning, related activities were completed, and Katie observed other children reading the book. Finally, after two weeks, she self-selected the book to read and reread for several days. For example, *There's a Dragon in My Wagon* by Nelson (1982) was first read by Mrs. A on August 30. Katie watched and listened for two weeks. On September 12, she self-selected the book and then reread it several times over the next four days. This pattern was obviously dependent on prolonged availability of small copies of shared big books.

The third pattern of self-selection was that many of the children had an "anchor" book, or one particular book they returned to time and again—a pattern reliant on the library corner's stock. Many days of experimenting with new books might pass, and then, as if to say, "Here's something I know and know I can do well," the child would return to a favorite book. For example, Nick reread many different books, but returned to an alphabet book by Eve Merriam called *Where Is Everybody?* (1985) once or twice a week throughout

September and October. He then replaced this "anchor book" with a story he wrote that was typed, bound, and illustrated. Many children continued throughout the six months to integrate some risk taking (or moving way from the familiar) while maintaining a "safe" approach to reading with an anchor book. Having access to certain books, even after several weeks, was a key factor in children's ability to select something with which they felt secure.

A fourth clear selection pattern was movement between "easy" and "difficult" books. Children typically selected books within a comfortable reading range for several days and then attempted a book well above their reading level. The next selection might return to an easy level, but gradually movement to more difficult books was observed. For example, in October Sara selected *Elephant in Trouble* by Thomas Crawford (1970), a text well above her instructional level at the time, followed by *Mary Wore Her Red Dress, and Henry Wore His Green Sneakers* by Merle Peek (1985), a text below her instructional level, followed by *There's a Nightmare in My Closet* by Mercer Mayer (1968), again above her instructional level. As with Sara, other children needing the most support for learning to read sometimes selected texts far too difficult for them to practice their new reading strategies. Yet, these children did not abandon the difficult books since interest motivated their selections. By October, the majority of children integrated attempts to read new, more difficult books, particularly with support from a buddy or the teacher.

Many factors influenced book selection: the child's personal need at the time (e.g., rereading to build confidence or trying something new to test new strategies), buddy recommendations, cover or title attractiveness, or curiosity in a newly introduced book. Whatever the reason, children decided if the book seemed like a good choice for that moment. Availability of all book types—new and familiar, easy and difficult—enhanced children's selections.

Evaluating Readers' Strategies

Observations of children reading their self-selected books were useful in evaluating their growing repertoire of strategies. Mrs. A used the time to informally observe and make notations on the children's literacy learning.

First, by watching children reread familiar texts, information was gathered concerning their use of reading strategies. Text familiarity enabled them to use all strategies—contextual, structural, and analytical—to read the words. For example, Lee and Jim read the big book version of *Hattie and the Fox* by Mem Fox (1986). In this story, Hattie warns the other farm animals that a fox is emerging from the bushes. Each page, highly supported by the illustration, adds a new part of the fox that Hattie can see. When Lee and Jim came to "I can see two ears, a nose and two eyes in the bushes" (unnumbered, p. 12), they got stuck on the word *ears*. They mutually decided to "skip that one" and tried to read on. They faltered again on the word *eyes*. Unsure of two words on the page, Lee pointed to *ears* and suggested they "go back to where we first saw that one." The two boys flipped back to the beginning and, using both text and illustration, discovered that the word was *ears*. When they returned to their original page, Lee pointed to the words and said, "See that one's *ears* and this one's *eyes*." They continued, successfully reading aloud the entire story. The boys showcased the reading strategies they knew. They used familiarity with the text along with contextual and analytical clues to "unlock" a word independently.

Second, the children developed understandings of print and books that could be evaluated through their actions. For example, Jill explained that she never picked books that looked "easy" because "in shorter books the part that's exciting happens too fast. The books that are longer are usually better." Then, pointing to a simple concept book, she said, "That one's not really that exciting." Jill's self-selections indicated her definition of literacy learning—choose a good story to read.

Another day, Tom read the supplemental reader *I Like* (1971), a simple concept book featuring photos with the caption "I like," with his eyes closed. Lee was appalled. "This is a preschool book!" he said. "Hey . . . this is not a story. I can't believe a guy got that published!" Jill's and Lee's reactions suggest that we should remember that learning to read requires "a good story"—to practice "reading the words" is just not enough.

Third, selected texts signaled a child's current stage of learning to read. Rereading generally indicated a confidence-building time. The familiar was sought to reaffirm what skills and strategies were well in hand. New book selection suggested risk taking. Strategies were stretched, tested, and explored in new texts. After trying new texts, children were observed for using new strategies. After two or three months of self-selecting, children picked books that better fit their reading needs—rereading to build confidence or trying something new to stretch themselves.

Finally, children often used familiar books to find words for other purposes. When in need of a word's spelling, they were observed saying, "I know where I heard that word," locating a particular book, and searching the familiar text for the needed word. This indicated their understanding of the interactive process of reading and writing. Self-selected books provided children with a source for expanding their writing vocabulary.

Jim and Lee found another purposeful use of familiar text. They compared the big book copy of *Yes Ma'am* by Mesler and Cowley (1982) to the small copy in their attempt to read the word *will.* They decided to skip the word. Then, when they stopped at the word *what,* Jim stated, "There's that word again." Lee used the big and small copies to show Jim that *what* begins with "wh," not the same as *will.* Comparing familiar texts allowed for valuable learning to take place. The children were permitted (and encouraged) to use books to help in the reading and writing process. These moments of displayed understanding were recorded to further document their literacy growth.

Using Self-Selection with Beginning Readers

Self-selection is one important aspect of a literature-based classroom. It provides a powerful source for beginning readers to practice their developing skills. The following components are important for self-selection:

1. *Provide a large, varied book collection that remains constant over a prolonged period of time.* Books from all genres and all levels of difficulty should be included. Each child can select the type of book that seems most useful at the time. Having books available for at least eight weeks allows for the rereading of familiar texts over extended time periods, confidence building through repeated exposure before attempting a new book, and balancing the selection of a more difficult book with returning to a known text. At the same time, new books added weekly spark interests and provide new possibilities for becoming someone's favorite.

2. *Organize books by genre or source (e.g., borrowed library books versus teacher-owned books), but avoid labeling such as "difficult," "beginner," or similar descriptors that might discourage selection.* Children often are motivated to read a book that looks attractive or is recommended by a friend, regardless of the difficulty level. By not classifying books by difficulty, children are not limited in their selections.

3. *Include children's own publications as additional available texts to select.* This provides the "author" with another familiar text for reading. It also creates an in-class authority on the story's words, so other children can go to the author for needed help.

4. *Allow opportunities for children to read alone or with a buddy.* Reading alone is a time to experiment with texts and strategies. The choice to read a new book alone may indicate growth. At the same time, buddy support can help both

readers strengthen their reading skills. Conversations about words, illustrations, and decoding strategies can be instructive to both children. These conversations also inform the teacher about the children's understanding of various reading strategies.

5. *Be available to provide support by "jogging" a child's memory of previous strategies learned during one-on-one or small-group instruction.* Help children see connections between what they learn during instruction and what they encounter when they read independently. This is also a good time to circulate and note children's progress.

6. *Do not require a list of books read.* This may interfere with the desire to reread texts and is tedious for beginning readers. Also, books that are started and then judged too difficult by the reader can be replaced easily, without making notations on a reading list.

7. *Provide time each day for children to self-select.* Plan at least twenty minutes of reading time. There should be enough time to select books, find a comfortable spot, and read several complete stories. Self-selected reading can coincide with journal writing. Half the class might spend time writing in their journals, while the other half reads self-selected books. Reverse the groups, and two important curricular areas have been touched. This plan also allows more books to be available to students since only half the class at a time is making selections. Children can insert bookmarks labeled with their names if they must stop reading before finishing their books. In this way, books return to the shelf for the next group to use while still respecting each reader's need to complete the story at another time.

The Smorgasbord of Texts

After observation of the children for two months, the importance of a classroom library corner that remained constant over a prolonged period of time became obvious. While new books were consistently added, most books remained for an eight-week minimum. Small copies of shared big books remained permanently on the shelf months after they first were introduced. Library books being reread were renewed, returned to the library for a while, borrowed again, and then renewed once more to provide sixteen weeks of availability. Books were grouped on the shelves by source (i.e., teacher-owned books versus library books) to ease organization. They were not identified by difficulty level in any way. Adult perceptions about what is too difficult for a child to read may be different from the child's. Grouping or classifying books by difficulty limits children's choices. The smorgasbord must remain open in order for children to select old favorites or risk picking something new.

Summary

Children approach learning to read along an individual path. What appears to be a stalled reader rereading the same book again and again may be a child gathering confidence in his or her own skills. The child choosing a book that seems much too difficult for his or her skill level may be a motivated reader trying something new at the "smorgasbord." Risk taking comes when the challenge of selecting a more difficult text balances with the option to revisit an old favorite at any time. Each reader in this study made significant strides in learning to read. Children's developing skills were nurtured and challenged through book self-selection. Their choices continued to nudge them to new literacy learning.

References

Fresch, M. J. (1991). *Becoming an independent reader: Self-selected texts and literacy events in a whole language classroom.* Unpublished doctoral dissertation, The Ohio State University, Columbus.

Meek, M. (1988). *How texts teach what readers learn.* England: Thimble Press.

Smith, F. (1985). *Reading without nonsense* (2nd ed.). New York: Teachers College Press, Columbia University.

Children's Books Cited

Crawford, Thomas. (1970). *Elephant in trouble.* Mahwah, NJ: Troll Associates.

Fox, Mem. (1986). *Hattie and the fox.* Illus. by Patricia Mullins. New York: Bradbury Press.

I Like. (1971). (Supplemental Reader). Glenview, IL: Scott, Foresman.

Literacy 2000 Series. (1988–89). Auckland, New Zealand: Shortland Publications; Crystal Lake, IL: Rigby Education.

Mayer, Mercer. (1968). *There's a nightmare in my closet.* Illus. by Author. New York: Dial Books.

Merriam, Eve. (1985). *Where is everybody?* New York: Greenwillow Books.

Mesler, J., & Cowley, J. (1982). *Yes ma'am.* Auckland, New Zealand: Shortland Publications; Crystal Lake, IL: Rigby Education.

Nelson, J. (1989). *There's a dragon in my wagon.* Cleveland, OH: Modern Curriculum Press.

O'Keefe, Susan H. (1989). *One hungry monster: A counting book in rhyme.* Illus. by Lynn Munsinger. Boston: Little, Brown.

Peek, Merle. (1985). *Mary wore her red dress, and Henry wore his green sneakers.* New York: Clarion Books.

14 Thematic Units: Integrating the Curriculum

Sylvia M. Vardell
University of Texas at Arlington

A s the students enter Ms. Long's room in the morning, she is quickly taking attendance and lunch count, eager to start teaching. The first item on the agenda is literature, which is read aloud by the teacher. Today she is reading Doris Lund's *Attic of the Wind* (1966), a poetic musing on where things go when they are lost in the wind. Next, she reviews the day's routine: date, schedule, special classes (library, computer, etc.). This is followed by one of Ms. Long's favorite activities, a sing-along—with songs chosen by the students from an assortment of song cards featuring the lyrics. After a brief session with students sharing recent personal experiences in cooperative groups, they continue working on previous individual or small-group projects and activities related to the current theme, "Wind and Air." Among other options, they may do additional reading, plan a puppet show, write, paint, conduct science experiments, or listen to special music or a story on tape. Then it is time to gather again as a whole class for a science lesson using sheets of plain paper (wadded up, flat, folded into paper airplanes) to demonstrate principles of lift, thrust, and gravity. In a class collaboration, students produce rebus writing combining pictures or icons with words to describe their findings. Sometime before lunch, individual journals are updated, too.

In the afternoon, the math lesson includes using balloons to look at rate, time, and distance. Later, the class collaborates again by writing their reflections on the day's events. To end the day, Ms. Long reads aloud *Flash, Crash, Rumble, and Roll* by Franklyn Branley (1985), a nonfiction book about thunderstorms. Then, by student request, she also shares *The Storm Book* by Charlotte Zolotow (1952), which vividly describes a fictional summer storm.

Throughout the day, students have read, written, listened, spoken, calculated, speculated, investigated, and thus experienced various aspects of the natural phenomena of wind and air. The integration of subject areas around this common theme has enabled them to make important connections. It has enabled them to see that things they are learning *are* connected. Many more such days will follow in which the teacher guides their learning with additional literature and other resource materials, including guest speakers. Students will actively participate in all these learning activities by asking questions, working together, and suggesting additional possibilities for involvement. They are learning by doing, by using language to learn, and they may well be developing an ongoing interest in wind and weather, airplanes, or kite flying. Through thematic teaching, Ms. Long is introducing her students to the world of "Wind and Air."

Ms. Long teaches kindergarten.

Thematic teaching, like the whole language movement, is grounded in the notion that we learn best when things make sense. As teacher Diana Hansen put it: "Thematic teaching, I feel, is a more natural way to teach. In real life we don't usually break our day into little discrete units and only do something for 15 minutes, then drop that and arbitrarily do something completely unrelated for 25 minutes, etc. Rather, in real life, most of the time, our actions can flow from one to another." Thematic teaching, centered around a topical collection of children's literature, seeks integration of both learning activities and subject areas. In Ms. Long's self-contained classroom described above, she has the luxury of weaving the theme into *all* of her teaching throughout the day. Other teachers seek links between the reading/language arts area and the content areas of science, social studies, and mathematics. Yet another option is to use a theme to combine the pieces of reading, language arts, and literature, which historically have been more segmented. As teacher Tracie Willis pointed out, "Thematic teaching allows for the instruction of skills within the most logical of contexts: for example, grammar instruction during writing."

Components of Thematic Teaching

Thematic teaching seeks to paint a big picture—to look at the larger ideas embedded in our curriculum, the how and why of history, ecology, biology, and so on (Hepler, 1989). But where does one begin? Thematic units are a "multifaceted method of planning," "a dynamic process"; they have a broad enough scope to incorporate many types of books and materials but are not so broad that the connections within the topic are lost. They should have appeal to children as well as intellectual content. As with many aspects of teaching, it is often best to begin with something about which the teacher is personally enthusiastic—a special interest, a favorite children's book, even a hobby. In fact, the process of building a thematic unit is much like the workings of an avid collector gathering artifacts, reading up on this specialty, and sharing resources with other hobbyists.

The same kind of drive and motivation can be brought to bear on learning in school under a timely and interesting topic umbrella. The planning process itself can proceed in many different ways, through brainstorming or webbing. Many teachers plan together, bouncing ideas and related book titles off each other in an energetic generation of options. Some even involve students (and parents), who suggest possible topics, favorite books and other resources, and preferred activities. It is often the exciting, appealing, funny, or fascinating new children's book someone has just discovered that sets the process in motion. This is the literature foundation so fundamental to the success of thematic teaching.

1. Literature

Perhaps the topic of "Pets" seems particularly timely and interesting. What children's book titles come readily to mind which feature some kind of pet? *Koko's Kitten* by Francine Patterson (1985), an account of a gorilla and her pet cat? *Crictor* by Tomi Ungerer (1958), a story about a pet boa constrictor? Or maybe a more commonplace pet like the one in *Harry the Dirty Dog* by Gene Zion (1956)? Librarians can be tremendously helpful here in recommending titles from which to choose. More and more reference books and selection tools are now available for teachers to use in choosing books on themes and topics, including *Focus Units in Literature* (Moss, 1984), *Adventuring with Books* (Jensen & Roser, 1993), *Reading Ladders for Human Relations* (Tway, 1981), *The Horn Book Guide* (1989–present), *A to Zoo* (Lima, 1985), *Best Books for Children* (Gillespie & Naden, 1990), and *Children's Literature in the Elementary School* (Huck, Hepler, & Hickman, 1993). Some book companies even offer subject-matter computer searches of their database of books at no cost.

Having as many books on a topic as possible is best in order to meet the range of reading levels and interest areas the students will demonstrate as they pursue the topic in depth. Pappas, Kiefer, and Levstik (1990) suggest that the total collection of literature include at least four kinds of materials: books and other materials to read aloud (text that is relevant and interesting but that may be difficult for students' independent reading), materials for group activities (multiple copies, if possible, of fiction, nonfiction, magazines, newspapers), additional reading materials for personal exploration (series books, easy-to-read books), and primary source materials (originals or facsimiles of printed resources such as letters, journals, maps, photographs, advertisements, catalogs, and any other firsthand information). The general rule of thumb is that there can never be too many good books and materials, and a theme-related library within the classroom is ideal.

2. Integration

If the theme is "Pets," then perhaps the class might begin by sharing pet stories—pets the students have now or have had in the past, interesting stories about other people's pets, or speculation about what kinds of pets they might like to have. *Tight Times* by Barbara Shook Hazen (1979), a story about a family in financial difficulty that decides a stray cat (named "Dog") can stay with them despite the expense, might be a good first selection to read aloud. *A Dog Called Kitty* by Bill Wallace (1980) is a novel which could be read in chapters over several days. Next, students might enjoy working in groups to read about pet characters featured in several series books, such as Curious George the monkey, Clifford the big red dog, Harry the black-and-white border collie, or even Spot the puppy. Writing projects lead into science, where students can explore the life cycle of domestic animals by reading a book like *My Puppy Is Born* by Joanna Cole (1973) or into social studies, where the origins of various breeds of cats and dogs could be investigated. Even mathematics connections become apparent, as students poll and tabulate the number and kinds of pets their classmates have.

Literature leads the way into possible projects and content-area connections. Using a combination of whole-class, small-group, paired, and individual activities, the teacher sets the stage as the students enter into the world of "Pets." Planned integration occurs as books lead into activities in many areas, but often the children's choices and responses create the integration as well. Mindful of curricular objectives (sometimes externally imposed), the teacher balances what "needs to be covered" with what is naturally coming up on the topic of Pets. Flexibility is central, as teachers reconfigure the traditional scope and sequence of the curriculum in new ways. Now the subject-area textbooks are viewed as just another tool, rather than as the sole decision maker for instruction. The outcome, however, is generally a more comprehensive curriculum, filled with extensive learning experiences, rather than the former *minimal* content considered necessary for basic mastery.

Teachers vary greatly in how far they take the integration of their thematic units. Some teach *no* reading and writing in isolation. Instead, students read extensively about the topic (e.g., Pets) and write in a variety of formats that help them to better understand and explore the topic (e.g., a letter to a veterinarian, a research paper about guide dogs). The degree of integration depends somewhat on the logistics of scheduling within the school and somewhat on the individual style and interests of the teacher. But like a machine set in motion, integration takes on a life of its own, and everyone involved in thematic teaching looks for connections and finds them well beyond what was initially planned, making it a truly interdisciplinary approach. Without such integration, thematic teaching is simply a potpourri of lots of extra books—not bad, but not nearly enough.

3. Collaboration

Thematic teaching, it should be readily apparent, is labor-intensive. It takes extra time to replace lessons based strictly on textbooks or workbooks with something new. But as Pappas, Kiefer, and Levstik (1990) point out, all good teaching takes time. Teachers who plan thematic units together find that the workload is easier and the planning becomes more dynamic and satisfying. In fact, prepackaged units now on the market lack this personal connection. Though these sets may have excellent booklists and some good ideas and activity options, many teachers feel part of the pleasure of thematic teaching is the digging and searching and the finding and gathering of resources.

This also sets the stage for an aspect of thematic units that seems to occur spontaneously—people interact when they work together toward common goals and are surrounded with interesting materials and resources. Teachers do; children do. Thematic teaching is strongest in social classrooms where the teacher and students learn together by sharing and exchanging ideas with each other. All are encouraged and expected to share their backgrounds, prior knowledge, and individual interests for the common good: funny dog and cat stories from childhood, anecdotes about a parakeet or rabbit. Together, everyone researches the problem of unwanted pets and animal rights. Without such collaboration in thematic teaching, the emphasis shifts to a subtle competition, where each student works in secrecy to outdo the other with individual Pet projects, and then only for the academic prize of a good grade, rather than for the pleasure of discovering something new and interesting and telling someone about it.

4. Community Resources

Theoretically one could plan and teach an entire thematic unit without using community resources, but this component is vital in making yet another connection for students—the real-world connection. Parents can play an important role in sharing their experience and expertise. Businesses, organizations, museums, and so forth can offer rich resources that extend and enrich the unit by providing practical, concrete examples and applications. For example, in a unit on Pets, parents might be requested to bring family pets for classroom visits; a veterinarian or pet shop owner might be willing to talk to the class about pet care; the Society for the Prevention of Cruelty to Animals or local Humane Society might welcome the interest of a classroom seriously studying the topic. Here, also, a connection with concrete, physical objects, artifacts, or crafts can provide students with new firsthand experiences. How do you hold a hamster? Do most dogs really prefer to be stroked behind their ears? Media, too, add another dimension of learning through audiotapes, videotapes, photography, music, art, puppetry, and so forth. Children involved in thematic units are more apt to bring more to the field trip or outing—more information, more questions, more interest. A "culture of the topic" evolves, one of collective experience and participation. Students who learn that school is not the only place to learn things will say, "Remember that time we studied Pets, and. . . ."

5. Time It takes time to plan thematic units, and the units themselves generally last several weeks. Because the learning is integrated and collaborative, momentum builds and sustains motivation. Thus the topic can be explored both in its breadth and depth. During a sample study of Pets, one child's reading and research may lead into an extensive study of the rottweiler, piqued by fondness for the book *Good Dog, Carl* by Alexandra Day (1985), while another child might also share discoveries about Koko the gorilla and her new Manx kitten from reading *Koko's Kitten* by Francine Patterson (1985). Thematic teaching provides time for students to read many books because they are not reading just in "Reading" class. It also encourages a great deal of thinking because students are actively using that reading in real situations—whenever it comes up. There is greater continuity and less pressure since the topic is ongoing. Study can be picked up tomorrow where it was left off yesterday. Thus time—perhaps the "traditional" teacher's worst enemy—now becomes an ally. Finally, the passing of time allows students to develop a portfolio of varied activities, rather than the sameness sometimes provided by textbook-based instruction.

6. Empowerment Despite the fact that *empowerment* has become somewhat of a buzzword, it is a real factor in thematic classrooms where teachers have consciously chosen to teach in a new way. In particular, thematic teaching challenges both overreliance on textbooks and the compartmentalized school day and its subjects. Many teachers have long questioned this practice. They know the curriculum; they know their children. Who is better suited to decide how to teach them both? As teacher Martha Davidson commented: "The teacher can more readily develop a clearcut objective for the unit, since its structure is under her control. The activities chosen can be tailored to meet the objective and the students' needs . . . the teacher has the needed latitude with which to work." Pappas, Kiefer, and Levstik (1990) contend, "Teachers in integrated classrooms see themselves as professionals who own and develop their own programs" (p. 46). These are the same teachers who abdicate some of their traditional authority in the classroom to empower their students to take a more active role in *their* own learning.

Conclusion

Visit the classroom of someone involved in thematic teaching. Often one can hear the excitement in the hall, as talk about books and projects spills out the door. One place to start may be in collaborating with a teacher friend on an end-of-the-year thematic unit. A school in Texas devoted several weeks in May to a whole-school thematic unit on the topic of the "Frontier." All classrooms were involved with books and activities integrated around the theme. Then, as a culminating event, the entire school devoted a whole day to an indoor/outdoor Frontier fair at which parents dressed in costumes, cooked on outdoor grills, read aloud, and demonstrated crafts. These are the kinds of learning activities that children (and teachers, parents, and all involved) remember for years to come. As teacher Liz Lumpkins put it, "A successful thematic unit plants the seeds for continued investigation and further inquiry in students' minds that will grow into a lifelong yearning for knowledge."

References

Gillespie, J., & Naden, C. (Eds.). (1990). *Best books for children* (4th ed.). New York: R. R. Bowker.

Hepler, S. (1989). A literature program: Getting it together, keeping it going. In J. Hickman & B. Cullinan (Eds.), *Children's literature in the classroom: Weaving Charlotte's web.* Needham Heights, MA: Christopher-Gordon.

The Horn Book Guide (1989–present; issued biannually). Boston: Horn Book.

Huck, C., Hepler, S., & Hickman, J. (1993). *Children's literature in the elementary school* (5th ed.). San Diego: Harcourt Brace Jovanovich.

Jensen, J. M., & Roser, N. L. (Eds.). (1993). *Adventuring with books: A booklist for pre-K–grade 6* (NCTE Bibliography Series, 10th ed.). Urbana, IL: National Council of Teachers of English.

Lima, C. (1985). *A to zoo: Subject access to children's picture books.* New York: R. R. Bowker.

Moss, J. (1984). *Focus units in literature: A handbook for elementary school teachers.* Urbana, IL: National Council of Teachers of English.

Pappas, C., Kiefer, B., & Levstik, L. (1990). *An integrated language perspective in the elementary school.* White Plains, NY: Longman.

Tway, E. (Ed.). (1981). *Reading ladders for human relations* (6th ed.). Urbana, IL: National Council of Teachers of English.

Children's Books Cited

Branley, Franklyn M. (1985). *Flash, crash, rumble, and roll.* New York: Thomas Y. Crowell.

Bridwell, Norman. (1963). *Clifford the big red dog.* Illus. by Author. (Also see other books in the series.) New York: Scholastic.

Cole, Joanna. (1973). *My puppy is born.* New York: William Morrow.

Day, Alexandra. (1985). *Good dog, Carl.* Illus. by Author. New York: Simon & Schuster.

Hazen, Barbara Shook. (1979). *Tight times.* New York: Viking.

Hill, Eric. (1980). *Where's Spot?* Illus. by Author. (Also see other books in the series.) New York: G. P. Putnam's Sons.

Lund, Doris. (1966). *Attic of the wind.* New York: Parents Magazine Press.

Patterson, Francine. (1985). *Koko's kitten.* New York: Scholastic.

Rey, H. A. (1942). *Curious George.* Illus. by Author. (Also see other books in the series.) Boston: Houghton Mifflin.

Ungerer, Tomi. (1958). *Crictor.* Illus. by Author. New York: Harper & Row.

Wallace, Bill. (1980). *A dog called kitty.* New York: Holiday House.

Zion, Gene. (1956). *Harry the dirty dog.* Illus. by Margaret Bloy Graham. (Also see other books in the series.) New York: Harper & Row.

Zolotow, Charlotte. (1952). *The storm book.* New York: Harper & Row.

15 Making the Move from Basals to Trade Books: Taking the Plunge

Patricia L. Scharer
The Ohio State University at Lima

We wouldn't think of teaching our children to swim on dry land, but these children were being asked to learn to read from a desert of materials.

Charlotte Huck, *Children's Literature in the Classroom: Weaving Charlotte's Web*

A growing number of children's literature advocates are echoing Huck's beliefs that trade books must become a significant component of reading programs in elementary and middle schools. It is through interactions with real books, they argue, that children begin to learn literacy skills at a very early age and continue to grow as readers during formal schooling. Implementation of literature-based reading instruction, however, is more complex than simply exchanging basal reading materials for children's books. Teachers who have long relied on the step-by-step directions of basal manuals are often challenged by the professional demands of a change from basals to children's literature (Scharer, 1992). This chapter presents voices of teachers who have "taken the plunge" and increasingly use trade books as they plan literacy instruction. The teachers described have experienced both "sinking" and "swimming" sensations as they have struggled with difficult instructional decisions: How does such change take place? What brings it about? How is change facilitated and what gets in the way?

Voices of Teachers Who Have "Taken the Plunge"

Insight into these questions can be found in the stories of teachers' struggles and successes as they increase the use of children's books in their reading programs. The stories that follow are from eighty-four teachers who attended a one-day literature conference and responded to the following questions on a two-page survey:

1. What/who has helped you use literature in the reading program?
2. What difficulties/concerns have you encountered?

3. As you look back over the past five years, how has your reading program changed?
4. What was the easiest to change?
5. What was the most difficult to change?
6. What would you most like to change about your current classroom reading program?
7. If you were given $1,000 to spend on your reading program, what would you buy?
8. What hints would you share with a fellow teacher who wished to use more literature in his/her classroom?

Their voices are presented in this chapter in hopes that their stories will help other educators interested in making similar changes.

Motivation: Why Bother "Suiting Up"?

For some teachers responding to this survey, motivation for using children's literature for reading instruction was based on strong feelings about reading instruction during their own early school experiences. One teacher recalled "hating reading textbooks during my own student days in elementary schools and not becoming a reader until a sixth grade teacher let me borrow books from her personal library." Others claimed to be following their "instincts" and described a "gut level belief" that "an integrated curriculum is *the* best way to teach children so that all the pieces and parts come together in a meaningful way rather than isolating information, skills, etc."

Children's responses to reading instruction also were reported as motivating teachers during implementation. Observations of "children hating readers and workbooks" were sometimes coupled with teachers' descriptions of the basal series as "boring and repetitive" and were cited as sufficient cause for abandoning the basals. As the teachers observed the students' "excitement and sense of accomplishment," the enthusiastic responses of the children to literature then encouraged the teachers to continue.

"Sinking" Sensations: Difficulties during Implementation

Over one-third of the teachers listed evaluation as a troublesome issue concerning the use of literature to teach reading. Teachers were concerned, at the classroom level, with how to evaluate individual progress; at the district level, their concern was with external accountability pressures, particularly concerning standardized tests. Some expressed frustration as they tried to explain a child's progress to parents "who think you're not doing anything because no dittos go home." Others described a variety of mandates from administrators concerning the use of basal texts, end-of-level tests, the district's course of study, and standardized tests with "scores [that] become more significant than the learning taking place in a literature-based environment." One teacher asked, "How do you test using unfamiliar test structure without spending time on basal skill sheets, expect kids to achieve mastery and explain possible failure (that is, what the test says is failure) to administrators and parents?" An interesting solution for one teacher was "cheating on basal tests." How this was accomplished, however, was not explained on the survey instrument. Teachers' feelings concerning evaluation were aptly summed up by one teacher who wrote:

> [It] takes lots of planning to be sure you are incorporating skills required in the course of study and that are necessary to do well on tests. Evaluation is difficult to put down in percentages which is required by our school district.

The time needed for such planning was the second most frequently cited difficulty. Teachers needed time to get materials prepared, to work with individual children, to develop appropriate creative activities that extend children's understanding of the books, to integrate content-area subjects, and to organize a school day interrupted by recesses and special classes.

Teachers were equally concerned about the lack of support from parents, other teachers, and administrators. One teacher noted that she tried to "keep my head up while going against the constant 'logical' arguments of basal advocates." Some administrators were characterized as "resistant," "misunderstanding what I am about," or having "no idea what I'm doing."

The fourth difficulty most frequently expressed by teachers concerned acquisition and use of materials. The role of workbooks posed problems as teachers tried either to justify limited use of pages purchased by the parents or to shift funds from workbooks to library books. Lack of money for what teachers considered necessities for teaching reading was a significant problem for many. One teacher wrote that she spent over $500 of her own money to buy multiple copies of books for her class and then learned that she was being transferred to another grade where the books were clearly inappropriate.

When asked what they might buy for their reading program if given $1,000, nearly all teachers listed books they would purchase for classroom use including award-winning books, books that support various content areas, and recent selections, enabling teachers to "keep up" with the latest in children's literature. Other supporting materials on their "wish lists" included chart paper, markers, blank books and other bookmaking supplies, filmstrip-making kits, book racks, chart holders, carpet and comfortable seating for a library corner, and computer equipment, such as word processors and printers. Some teachers suggested using the money to sponsor an author visit to their school or to further their own education by taking university courses.

Some teachers reported easily changing their classrooms, decisions, and attitudes, while others reported much difficulty. One teacher wrote that she had to conquer "my feelings and insecurities about using whole language and not working solely on specific goals and objectives." For others, the pressures of faculty members who were less than supportive complicated their desire to implement literature-based reading in their classrooms. The desired changes seemed to go beyond replacing basal texts with children's books and included major shifts in the school day organization, the teacher's role, students' responsibilities, and classroom rules, such as children's movement within the room and the noise level tolerated. Such changes were not always made quickly or with ease.

Ways to Keep "Afloat"

The majority (70 percent) of teachers reported that taking courses at the university level assisted them in implementing literature-based reading instruction. Attendance at conferences followed closely, with 67 percent of the teachers reporting the importance of participating in inservice and professional meetings. Teachers also reported that they spent a great deal of time reading professional books and articles by such authors as Atwell, Calkins, Cullinan, Goodman, Graves, Holdaway, and Routman, which had a significant impact on their reading program.

University personnel and peers were the persons most frequently cited by teachers as assisting them in using literature in their reading program. Although principals and consultants were mentioned by only 10 percent of the teachers, appreciation for their support was clearly evident. One teacher wrote that she had the "pleasure of working in this type of program for 14 years under principals who were and remain dedicated to literature."

Over half of the teachers reported "using a lot more literature and integrating it across the curriculum." Teachers seemed to first experiment with using literature through reading aloud to their classes, having blocks of sustained silent reading, and developing classroom activities based upon literature selections. Books were often chosen for connections that could be made with topics discussed in science and social studies so that time spent reading children's books served the dual purpose of satisfying both language arts and content-area objectives. As the time for using literature increased, there appeared to be a gradual decrease in class time spent using basal materials, as teachers began to skip basal stories and workbook pages that seemed to be less valuable than lessons using trade books.

For many teachers, however, the decline of the basal text seemed to be quite rapid. When asked about the changes that were the easiest to make, the most frequent answer was to "totally put the basal readers on the shelf" and "get rid of stacks of worksheets to grade." Other easily made changes included reading more books aloud to their classes, facilitating book discussions, providing time for sustained silent reading, using books across the content areas, and "giving time for group extension projects based on the read aloud story."

Teachers' suggestions for other teachers included such imperatives as "Try it!" and "Get excited!" along with specific recommendations for interested peers. New literature-based teachers were cautioned to relax, "Do it slowly," and not allow others to mandate a time line for implementation. They were also encouraged to read professional books and journals, take courses, visit other classrooms, and ask for help from others.

Getting in the "Swim" of Things

The results of this survey begin to describe teachers who are working toward implementing changes within their classrooms that go beyond a shift in texts from basal readers to literature selections. Their willingness to complete a survey requiring them to respond thoughtfully in narrative form reflects both teachers' enthusiasm for using literature to teach reading and also their need to voice a variety of concerns. Their responses showed tension between experiencing excitement for teaching with children's literature and the pain of problems they encountered. Difficult decisions about materials, lesson plans, and evaluation of student achievement had previously been supported by suggestions in basal teachers' manuals. As they increasingly used trade books, however, teachers were now searching for answers to new questions that arose as they organized instruction to reflect a literature-based approach to literacy instruction.

Important implications for educators, based on the experiences of teachers completing this survey, may support others who are moving toward teaching with trade books. University personnel clearly played a significant, supportive role for teachers in this survey, and that role might be extended even further. For teachers wanting to remain current in the fluid world of children's books, universities can provide courses focusing on recent children's books and their uses in classroom settings. Continuation and expansion of educational opportunities such as seminars, inservices, and conferences dealing with literature-based reading instruction also seem appropriate. University personnel could further assist in the education of administrators who are working with teachers like those in this study. For many elementary school principals, reading methods courses are a distant memory. Growing interest in literature-based reading instruction, however, demands an administrator with greater understanding of current reading methodology, which might be fostered in university-based courses and seminars.

The description of administrators in this survey was mixed. The few teachers with supportive principals recognized and appreciated their contributions. But for a significant number of other teachers, the administration was simply another hurdle to overcome alone. Principals can support their teachers by listening to their needs, attending educational opportunities *with* teachers, and initiating dialogue that can result in increased mutual understanding. If the teachers in this survey could create the ideal administrator, they might describe a principal who secures funds for materials, applies for grant money from various sources, and sets up adult volunteer programs to free teachers from noninstructional duties. The ideal principal would also facilitate and encourage collaboration among the staff members by scheduling grade-level free periods or other opportunities that enable teachers to share ideas and plan together.

Both principals and university personnel could assist teachers with the troublesome issue of evaluation. Through courses, workshops, and in service sessions, teachers and administrators might discuss alternatives concerning testing and might better understand advantages and limitations of both formal and informal measures of literacy achievement. At the district level, principals can mediate the pressures resulting from standardized testing by lobbying with other administrators to schedule the bare minimum of districtwide formal tests. The manner in which such test results are analyzed will also have important implications for teachers. As part of a national study of the relationship between standardized testing and decision making, Scharer and Rogers (1989) describe a principal in a large urban district who, rather than focusing on scores at the level of the individual child or class, viewed scores in terms of patterns over the past several years. When examined in such a manner, the scores revealed that although the second-grade students scored below average, by the time they reached fifth grade their scores were typically two or three years above the national average. Viewing test scores in such a global manner assisted the principal in diffusing extensive pressure for program changes based upon initial low scores.

Administrators can also support their staff in determining ways to assess reading growth based upon observations of children engaged in authentic reading and writing tasks. Informal tools such as portfolios, reading logs, systematic observations, conference notes, informal reading inventories, and running records may be examined by the staff for possible classroom use (Clay, 1993). Other staff decisions might concern alternative reports to parents and explanation of such evaluations to parents.

Summary

Although most of the teachers who responded to this survey have enthusiastically "taken the plunge" by increasing the use of literature in their classrooms, major obstacles remain in the areas of evaluation, time management, and money. Teachers with support from universities and their administration are indeed fortunate. But many of the teachers in this survey have been using children's literature for literacy instruction without the support of either professors or principals. For those interested in literature-based reading instruction, participants in this survey would recommend that teachers read widely (both children's books and professional books and articles), ask questions of others, follow their own instincts, surround themselves with supportive educators, carefully observe students for affirmation of progress, and attend as many seminars, courses, workshops, and conferences as possible. Teachers who are making the move from basals to trade books and who participate in such opportunities for professional growth may experience excitement for their own learning that will create similar excitement about children's books in their classrooms.

References

Clay, M. M. (1993). *An observation survey of early literacy achievement.* Portsmouth, NH: Heinemann.

Huck, C. (1989). No wider than the heart is wide. In J. Hickman & B. Cullinan (Eds.), *Children's literature in the classroom: Weaving Charlotte's web* (pp. 251–62). Needham Heights, MA: Christopher-Gordon.

Scharer, P. L. (1992). Teachers in transition: An exploration of changes in teachers and classrooms during implementation of literature-based reading instruction. *Research in the Teaching of English, 26,* 408–45.

Scharer, P. L., & Rogers, T. (1989, December). *Assessment and decision-making in the schools.* Paper presented at the meeting of the National Reading Conference, Austin, TX.

16 Teaching and Learning Critical Aesthetic Responses to Literature

Patricia J. Cianciolo
Michigan State University

W hen teaching students to engage in critical thinking about literature, we are teaching them to think critically and respond aesthetically to literature. This type of thinking recognizes the value and inevitability of both *cognitive* and *affective* responses to literature. Both are inherent in critical thinking and aesthetic response and should be encouraged in any literature program, especially if we want to develop discriminating readers of literature who will turn to quality literature for lasting, memorable, and satisfying reading experiences.

Certain essential conditions must be acknowledged if a critical aesthetic response is to occur. First, the literary selection in and of itself is an independent and concrete object of art, with intrinsic characteristics, form, and structure. Second, aesthetic values do exist in literature; these characteristics or standards are determined by a society (a particular culture) over time, and they should be used to determine the worth or the quality of the literary art piece. Third, creativity is expressed by both the artist (author or illustrator) and the appreciator (reader) of the story.

At the first reading of a literary selection, children and adults tend to read for the plot of the story. Readers tend to react to the pace, mood, and the personalities and actions of the characters before becoming aware of the author's theme or argument, or the tone or style, and before concentrating on analytical and evaluative reading. It is at the second reading—or at least after readers have read a good portion of a selection, know the story, and have experienced the impact of the interrelationship of the literary elements cited above—that they can engage in critical thinking and evaluate the story as literary art.

Keep in mind that the background of experiences readers have had with literature tends to influence how they compare and contrast one story with another and new works by an author with his or her older works. Add to this the fact that readers need knowledge about literature: the elements of fiction (plot, characterization, setting, theme, mood, voice, tone, and style); the characteristics and structure of the various literary genres (e.g., historical fiction, traditional literature, modern fantasy, contemporary realistic fiction, mystery or adventure story, literary biography); and some knowledge and guidance about how to use techniques in critical thinking. During the second reading or during a time to reflect on what was read previously, readers can investigate why and what they liked or disliked about a particular book. Then they can define the qualities of the writing or the illustrations that either took them into the story or turned them away from it.

At this point with children, we may ask questions which foster development of their ability to engage in critical aesthetic response to the reading they have done. Students in the elementary grades may consider (in childlike, not childish, terms) aspects of character drawing, style, tone, voice, the point or theme of the story, effectiveness of the illustrations in an illustrated book or picture book, and so on.

A number of research studies concerning children's response to literature clearly demonstrate that the recognition of the cognitive element does not deny the importance of the emotional side of the aesthetic experience. Cognition and emotions are intrinsically related to aesthetic responses. The ways in which we understand a story influence our feelings, and our feelings guide our understanding of it. To a large extent, cognition shapes emotions and for this reason is a justified focus for analyzing and critiquing a literary work of art (Bogdan, 1986; Fox & Hammond, 1980; Parsons, 1979a, 1979b).

Questioning Techniques

Aside from teachers' knowledge about literature, the heart of this approach to literature is the ability to design questions that elicit aesthetic responses and also encourage children to advance developmentally in critical aesthetic responses to literature.

In this regard, the following points should be considered: (1) the approach to questioning should be based upon open-ended questions that focus readers' attention *into* the selection, not out of it; (2) the questions that teachers pose should be designed to move the learners along to more sophisticated ways of viewing and responding to literary works; and (3) students should be encouraged to ask themselves questions about the whys and hows of literature and their responses to it.

There seems to be a direct correlation between the syntax or level of thinking inherent in teachers' questions and the syntax or level of thinking evidenced in students' responses. Furthermore, teachers whose questions more frequently require divergent thinking produce more divergent thinking on the part of their students, in contrast to teachers who use more cognitive memory questions. Seldom, if ever, is one able to offer critical thinking–type questions without careful thought and planning. Likewise, seldom, if ever, can one respond to critical thinking–level questions without careful thought.

The syntactical structure of questions that one asks and the other statements that one makes about literature can model critical aesthetic response to literature and can help students to acquire new or more information or attitudes about literature, to compare and contrast this new information or their responses to it with what they already know or value, to draw meaningful relationships, and to apply or transfer those relationships when evaluating (judging) the quality of literary selections that they are rereading or on which they are reflecting.

Group work with individual monitoring and guidance by the teacher seems to be best for studying literature. Students should be helped to understand that teachers ask questions about their responses to literature in order to encourage their critical aesthetic response to literature. In addition, critical aesthetic response means higher-level cognitive and affective thinking in response to literature. Students should understand that the responsibility for critical aesthetic response to literature is theirs, that it is not only common but desirable for persons to respond differently to literature, that they may need time to realize what their own response to a literary selection is and why they responded in that manner, and that their response to literature can be changed with additional information about literature and experience with it.

One of the most challenging facets of effective questioning is to spontaneously follow up students' response to the higher-order thinking questions with questions that elicit critical thinking. This is especially true when discussing aspects of the selection that teachers and students do not already know from their reading. The discussion should further the students' understanding of the reading and their responses to it. Questions should be based on the students' responses to the selection and their explanation of or justification for their interpretations and responses to the reading by citing aspects of the selection itself. Questions should not be asked prior to the students' first encounter with the story or while reading it to them. In each case, the story should be read, first and foremost, for the pleasure it has the potential to offer each student and for the impact of the gestalt on the reader's involvement and identification with the literary elements. When questions are asked at the end of each chapter in a novel, these questions should not call for elaborate responses that lessen or destroy the intensity of involvement that has built up as the story advances.

The ultimate goal of posing questions that call for higher-order thinking about literature is to make it possible for students to actually experience critical aesthetic response and to help them understand their own role in responding to literature in this manner without suggestion or motivation from a teacher, so that they will acquire the habit of formulating their own higher-order thinking questions about the literature they read, discuss, write about, or interpret orally.

Questions designed to encourage critical aesthetic response to literature combine the affective (feelings and emotions) with the intellectual (cognitive). We found that such questions should be asked before introducing students to any other activities related to literature that is read to them or by them or should at least serve as the basis for designing the activities related to literature. The kinds of questions presented below seem to elicit the essence of critical aesthetic response to literature by children in kindergarten through grade five, although they may need to be reworded for use with kindergartners, especially at the beginning of the academic year. These questions are based on those recommended by Probst (1989), but they have been extensively reworded and adapted for use with students in the elementary grades. Obviously, one would not ask all of these questions during any one discussion or even about any one selection.

A. Initial affective and cognitive response to literature
   1. What did you notice about this story or poem?
   2. What do you think or feel about this story or poem?
   3. What ideas or thoughts come to mind due to (or were suggested by) this story or poem?
   4. Did you feel a part of this story or poem, or did you feel you were watching (observing) what was happening in the story or poem? Describe, explain, elaborate, etc.

B. Focusing on aspects of the story or poem or illustrations without ignoring the role of the reader while reading the selection
   1. What got your attention? What part of the story did you focus on (concentrate on)? What words, phrases, images, ideas, or illustrations do you think caused you to focus on that part of the story or poem?
   2. If you were to write (or tell someone) about this story, what would you focus on (emphasize)? For example, would you choose a memory or association it triggered,

an aspect (part) of the story, something about the illustrations, something about the author or illustrator, or something else about the selection? Describe, explain, elaborate, etc.

3. What in this selection (the story line, the illustrations, or your reading of it) pleased you? upset you? caused you the most trouble?

4. Do you think this is a good piece of literature? Why or why not?

5. If you were an illustrator, what aspect of the story would you select for illustration in order to interest someone in this book?

C. Direct attention to the context in which the selection(s) is (are) encountered—a context of other readers, other texts, and personal history

1. What memories do you have after reading this story or poem (memories of people, places, sights, events, smells, feelings, or attitudes)?

2. What sort of person do you think the author is? the illustrator?

3. How did your reading of this selection differ from that of your classmates or professional reviewers? How was your reading of it similar?

4. What did you observe (notice) about the others in the class as they read or discussed this story or poem?

5. Does this selection remind you of any other literary work—such as a poem, story, television program, or commercial film? If it does, what is the name of the other work? What connection do you see between the two works?

Teachers can evaluate students' questions by noticing the changes which occur over time in the quality of their responses to the literature they read independently or have read to them and in their ability to use critical thinking skills and strategies independently when reading new literary selections and new kinds of literature. Teachers should also observe the length of time during which the students engage in more thoughtful group discussions, characteristics of students' questions, and students' awareness of their own processes of and progress in critical aesthetic responses. Whether students are able to consistently respond at a more advanced level of critical aesthetic response to literature and to pay attention to, show interest in, respect, and appreciate others' points of view should also be noted.

Exemplary Instructional Practices

Specific learning experiences that successfully elicit critical aesthetic response to literature are described below. These activities might not appear unique, and admittedly many are not. What is crucial is that they did seem to direct the readers' attention *into* some aspect of the literary element of the story or some specific characteristics of its genre, not away from it. Collectively, these activities seem to help students to understand, evaluate, and appreciate aspects of an author's or illustrator's craftsmanship and talent, or lack thereof, and to recognize and express their responses to the literature they read or listened to. On some occasions, these activities seem to help students to understand what is within the selection itself that causes them to respond to it as they do. These activities encourage diverse responses to individual selections and also help students to understand more clearly why people respond so differently to some aspects of the same story and to respect and value these diverse responses.

Critical Aesthetic Response to Picture Books

Let us consider how one might contribute to students' understanding of literature as an art form, especially the interaction and interrelationship of the craftsmanship and techniques employed by the author and the illustrator of a picture book to develop the literary elements (e.g., action, characterization, setting, mood, tone). *The Lighthouse Keeper's Daughter*, written by Arielle North Olson and illustrated by Elaine Wentworth (1987), is a picture book for children ages five through eight and was used successfully to help third graders to understand and appreciate the roles played by the author and illustrator in developing the literary elements in a picture book. (Be advised that the children participated in these activities after they had read this book or listened to it be read aloud.) Combining incidents that actually happened along the Maine coast, the author has created a thoroughly credible and moving story about a young girl who kept the lighthouse lamps burning for weeks while a violent storm forced her father to remain ashore. The oversized full-color watercolor paintings provide beautiful scenes of the seascape, the inside of the lighthouse, and the family's home alongside the lighthouse on the rocky island.

To help readers focus on the literary aspects of this unique picture book, rather than just on how they would feel if they were this girl, her mother, her father, or the seamen caught in the winter storms (which is the type of question one usually finds in literature guidebooks), students were asked to record in their journals how they felt or what their thoughts and associations were while this picture book was being read to them. Then they were asked to write a series of journal entries detailing *the characters' responses* to the sights and incidents alluded to or depicted quite specifically by the author and the illustrator. In order to write the journal entries about the characters' responses, students had to reread the story and carefully reexamine the illustrations for the details that were depicted directly or inferred about the characters, setting, mood, and action by way of descriptive detail, tone, color, and style. To extend this activity, students might be asked to write a readers theatre script and dramatize it, or write editorials or human interest stories for the newspaper about aspects of this picture book; again, students would get their clues or ideas from the text and the illustrations.

Illustrations can be crucial to a story because of their potential to extend the text by adding an extra dimension to the literary elements of fiction that were established through the text. You might read or tell a story without showing the students the illustrations. Ask students to list orally the story clues that most encouraged mental pictures of each of the elements of fiction. Then ask students to illustrate some of the images they created in their minds as they listened to or read the story. Be certain to allow some time for students to compare their own illustrations with one another's as well as with the illustrations included in the book. These comparisons should focus on how diversely and effectively each student incorporated and extended the literary elements and the characteristics of the genre in his or her artwork rather than on the craftsmanship evidenced in the drawings or paintings. The following titles were used most successfully in this manner by some of the teachers participating in this study: *"More, More, More," Said the Baby: Three Love Stories*, written and illustrated by Vera B. Williams (1990), in kindergarten and grade one; *Chrysanthemum*, written and illustrated by Kevin Henkes (1991), in grades two and three; *Guess Who My Favorite Person Is*, written by Byrd Baylor and illustrated by Robert Andrew Parker (1977), in grade four; and *Harald and the Knight*, written and illustrated by Donald Carrick (1982), in grade five.

Regardless of the age of children with whom this activity was used, it alerted the children to at least three of the most basic characteristics of a picture book: (1) illustrations should support and extend the text; (2) illustrations should offer the reader new or different ways of interpreting the printed word; and (3) the illustrator's interpretations of the text are unique to him or her. Further, children were delighted to have a chance to explore what it is like to be a book illustrator.

I have found over the years in teaching literature, especially in my work with this literature study[1] (see Cianciolo, 1988), that we may enhance students' critical aesthetic responses to literature (especially to picture books) by informing them about the world of art, the social history reflected in the content and style of art, and the cultural traditions depicted in or applied to the illustrations. Children (as well as teachers and librarians) usually respond to this approach to illustration study with enthusiasm if it is not done too frequently and if they are not overloaded with information. Therefore, some direct instruction about various techniques used by illustrators is quite in order. It makes it possible for students to learn how to really "see" more of the details in the illustrations, which increase their awareness of what the illustrator did to help the reader appreciate, feel, and understand more fully the thoughts, needs, and emotions of the characters as they responded to one another and to the particular problem or conflict confronting them. This thorough examination also helps readers to take a closer look at setting and to gain a better understanding of time and place as factors which may establish or intensify the nature and parameters of the story's mood, and may even determine the character's response to the problem or conflict.

We wanted to demonstrate to second graders how illustrator Donald Carrick used a particular visual technique in *The Climb*, a picture book written by Carol Carrick (1981), to influence the mood or tone of the story and to develop the characters and setting in greater depth than was accomplished through the author's text alone. Transparency copies of the illustrations were shown on the overhead projector to demonstrate to second graders how successfully the illustrator built up suspense in this story by repeating the sequence of gradual shifts of focus from the panorama scene to a close-up of one of the characters, then back to the panorama scene, and gradually moving to a close-up again. During the discussion that followed the first reading of the story, students' comments indicated that they had little or no trouble understanding and identifying with the different kinds of fear each character displayed in this credible story: Brendan's fear of heights and Nora's fear when she thought she was stuck in a dark cave. But once students saw how Carrick used this clever, yet simple, visual technique of changing the focus in the illustrations from distant scenes of the terrain to close-up views of the characters, their responses to this story were even more enthusiastic. They understood more clearly why they responded to the story as they did. They understood how this visual technique increased the excitement and tension in the story and helped them to gain a more precise understanding of the role played by setting— namely, rugged mountains and the "cave," which, to a large extent, served as the basis for the story's action, motivated the characters, and shaped their behavior. Donald Carrick's technique enabled readers to closely observe the characters and thus be more inclined to identify with them, thereby experiencing (vicariously, of course) their feelings and dispositions and the effects of their personality traits in relation to one another and to their circumstances.

Occasionally during this literature study, I explained to the students (especially those in grade five) how an individual artist prepared his or her illustrations, and I even presented some information about the content of the illustrations. One lesson involved reading *The Flute Player*, an Apache folktale retold and illustrated by Michael Lacapa (1990), which depicts a *Romeo and Juliet* type of relationship begun when a boy and girl meet at a hoop dance. The second lesson focused on the illustrations in *The Dragon's Robe*, written and illustrated by Deborah Nourse Lattimore (1990), an original fairy tale that takes place in twelfth-century China during the Sung dynasty and that involves a young weaver who saves her people from drought and foreign invasion by weaving a robe for the imperial rain dragon.

The imagery in *The Flute Player* is based upon design elements typically found in western Apache coil basket designs. For example, in the first illustration, the river is represented by a zigzag formation, a design that is repeated and that has no beginning nor end. This design makes the statement that it is constant and represents "the river of life," which the Apaches consider eternal. In the night scene in which the boy and girl are at the hoop dance, a red and yellow zigzag pattern represents maleness (the red zigzag) and femaleness (the yellow). The combined zigzag pattern represents their "life spirit" in harmony. Throughout the book, the zigzag pattern is present in clothes worn by the boy and the girl, as well as on baskets. The zigzag motif is continued through the roots of trees. Again, the life force is represented by the ever present zigzag pattern, with the roots shown as the tree's life source. Cloud formations in each case are angular and made up of zigzag lines, but Lacapa's application of paint creates the impression of rounded cloud forms. In the death scene, zigzag designs are airborne and represent the girl's change from human to spiritual form; below the burden basket and the girl, the zigzag pattern no longer exists, indicating death. On the last page, the autumn landscape indicates the end of life, and the petroglyph of a circle and cross on the rock represents the burial site of the girl, for traditionally Apaches buried their dead in rock crevices. This illustration is identical to the beginning scene, but there the colors indicate life and death. Not only did students seem interested in and intrigued with how the illustrator used the basket designs to reinforce and enrich the story, but they also enjoyed learning more about the religious beliefs of the Apache people and the symbolism of designs woven in Apache baskets and on their clothes.

In *The Dragon's Robe*, Lattimore makes accessible to children an art style unusual to Western cultures. Her artistic authenticity indicates a definite and specific time and place for this story. Her use of a brush to make even the finest lines, the layout of each page, the color and textures in her illustrations, and the style of art are all typical of paintings done in China during the Sung dynasty (especially by the famous emperor and painter Hui Taung, who is still honored in China and throughout the world for his masterful painting). Lattimore's extensive study resulted in authentic depiction of all aspects of the particular culture and the time and place that were so basic to setting and action, to the characters' personalities and motivation, and to the tone of her story.

After students read *The Dragon's Robe*, I shared with them some information from Lattimore about her illustrations: how she did research in museums, special collections, and various published sources about the social history of China; the art of Emperor Hui Taung himself; and how she created the illustrations. In the past the Chinese often painted on silk, so each page in the book is stained to resemble faded silk. Although some of the true Chinese colors have been muted (probably so they would not look too bold for Western taste), they retain the original flavor of the traditional Chinese colors. Much in Lattimore's art indicates the era in which this story takes place: clothes (style and fabric design of the Imperial Robe and other Mongolian clothing), architecture, tile work, landscape scenes, and the layout of each page are true to traditions of the Sung dynasty and Emperor Hui Taung. The split-perspective architecture and inside-outside views of the world so noticeable in the illustrations focus all aspects of life on the same page: inside-outside, small and large, good and evil forces and forces of ethical diligence. This technique was originally used by Hui Taung and is now considered "typical" of the traditional Chinese way of illustration.

A comparison of the content, style of art, colors, and textures in Lattimore's illustrations with paintings done by Emperor Hui Taung and other artists during the Sung dynasty as shown and explained in *The Eastern Gate: An Invitation to the Art of China and Japan* (Moore, 1979) helped students to realize the authenticity of Lattimore's illustrations, without going into extensive detail about this style of art or historical facts about the Sung dynasty. Students enthusiastically participated in this comparative activity and were impressed with Lattimore's extensive knowledge of the Chinese people and their art and with her desire and ability to demonstrate this knowledge in an interesting and exciting picture book.

Critical Aesthetic Response to Novels

It was apparent during the reading of the 1990 Newbery Honor Book by Janet Taylor Lisle, *Afternoon of the Elves* (1989), that the fifth graders were caught up in this story of friendship between two girls. Nine-year-old Hillary comes from a happy home, has all of her material needs provided for, and has many friends at school; whereas eleven-year-old Sara-Kate is proud, independent, and an outcast, does poorly in school, is poorly dressed, and lives in a decrepit home with a weedy and trash-filled yard. Readers, like Hillary, were intrigued by Sara-Kate's village of elves and were shocked to discover that Sara-Kate cares alone for a mother who is severely mentally ill, penniless, and unable to provide the most basic physical and emotional necessities for herself or for Sara-Kate. Readers, like Sara-Kate, were devastated when Hillary's mother discovers the girl's miserable plight and when the authorities separate Sara-Kate from her mother, sending the mother to an institution and Sara-Kate to live with out-of-state relatives. After finishing this story, students thought about how the author actually crafted her story, about the techniques she used, for example, to portray the gradual development of each girl's influence on the other. They explained the role played by the elves' village (which served as the basis for much of the girls' play) in depicting the girls' personalities and needs and Hillary's change to a more imaginative, sympathetic, and caring person. Some students found it interesting to compare techniques, purposes, and effects of the imaginative play engaged in by the protagonists in *Afternoon of the Elves* with Katherine Paterson's *Bridge to Terabithia* (1977) and with Marilyn Sachs's *The Bears' House* (1971) and its sequel, *Fran Ellen's House* (1987).

One fourth-grade teacher used *The Bears' House* in an activity that focused on characteristics of an open-ended story. Students listed clues provided by the author and illustrator (directly or by suggestion) and used these clues to write an ending for this open-ended story. In other words, they engaged in logic (a specific kind of critical thinking) to formulate an hypothesis about how the story ended. The teacher read aloud the sequel, *Fran Ellen's House,* so that the children could compare their own endings with the author's.

It should be noted that seldom should children be asked to write another ending for a story when the author has already accomplished that in his or her writing. In most cases, children cannot (and should not) be expected to match the artistry of an acclaimed adult professional writer. Nor should they be asked to change the details of a well-crafted, professional artistic accomplishment evident in a published literary selection in order to create a new ending to a story merely because it did not meet their mind-sets or because they failed to notice the aspects of the story which logically led the author to create the actual ending of the story.

Janet Taylor Lisle's *Afternoon of the Elves*, Alison Cragin Herzig and Jane Lawrence Mali's *Sam and the Moon Queen* (1990), and Chris Van Allsburg's *Jumanji* (1981) are additional open-ended stories with which this kind of activity would work well.

After the novel *Sam and the Moon Queen* was read aloud to fifth graders, the students divided into small groups and created a sociogram to describe the major characters' relationships with each other and to discuss how and why each of these characters' relationships changed. This activity facilitated the students' interpretation of the novel and served as a preparation for creative dramatization of various episodes in this story. Also, to help students to further explore characters' motivations, actions, feelings, and attitudes, students selected a specific character in the book and created a list of questions to ask that character. Next, students divided into five groups. One person per group assumed the role of the interviewer, and the remaining students became their selected characters. The interviewer asked each character the particular list of prepared questions, to which the characters responded based upon the clues presented directly or by implication in the text and illustrations.

Meeting the Creators of Children's Books

During the course of this study we arranged visits by two award-winning creators of children's literature, author Carol Carrick and author/illustrator Pat Cummings. Throughout the month prior to each author's visit to the school, all of the teachers directed a critical study of her books. The students' application of knowledge and understanding of critical aesthetic response to literature was demonstrated in their responses to Carrick's and Cummings's books: the visual interpretive projects they created in response to each author's books, their engrossed attention during the authors' large-group presentations, the nature and quality of questions the students asked the authors, and the enthusiastic reading of the authors' books before and long after their visits to the school.

Conclusions: What Have We Learned?

This chapter discusses some of the aspects of an intervention study during which we aspired to improve the teaching and learning of literature in the elementary school, kindergarten through grade five, over two academic years. Our findings indicated that teachers experienced considerable growth in their knowledge and beliefs about the teaching and learning of literature and in their instructional practices.

It is evident that elementary school students, even those in kindergarten and first grade, are capable of learning how to respond critically and aesthetically to literature. We also have noticed that regardless of age or grade level, children who respond critically and aesthetically to one kind or aspect of literature do not necessarily respond to another kind or aspect of literature at the same level as they did the first. In fact, they may require more experience with the new genre or aspect of literature and direct and guided instruction concerning it.

We are convinced that some direct instruction about the structure of elements of a story, characteristics of each literary genre, or the structure or elements of illustrations has a place in teaching critical aesthetic response to literature in the elementary grades. The focus on evaluating how some of these aspects of literature are developed in a story rightfully belongs in an elementary school literature program. But none of this should precede or restrict reading a selection for the kind of literary experience or response that children are capable of making and inclined to make on their own (Cianciolo, 1988).

We acknowledge that it is crucial for teachers to recognize the value and inevitability of both *cognitive* and *affective* thinking when teaching critical aesthetic response to literature. Both kinds of thinking are inherent in responding to literature and should be encouraged in any literature program, especially one focusing on higher-order or critical thinking in response to literature.

We have learned from our own response to literature and by watching and listening to children's comments as we read aloud to them, or as they read on their own, that during the first reading of a literary selection one tends to read, first of all, for the story, for what happens next. Whatever form literature takes, readers tend to react to the pace, mood, and the personalities, actions, and interactions of the characters before becoming aware of the author's theme or argument, or the tone or style, and before concentrating on being analytical and evaluative in their reading. It is during the second reading—or at least after reading a good portion of a selection, becoming familiar with the story, and experiencing the interrelationship of literary elements—that readers can engage in critical thinking and evaluate a story as literary art.

Aesthetic development seldom occurs to any significant extent when literature is viewed primarily as a time filler or as a vehicle for learning skills or facts in some subject, such as history, reading, science, and health.

Notes

1. Funding for this study was shared by the Center for Learning and Teaching Elementary Subjects, Institute for Research on Teaching, Michigan State University, and by the Professional Development School project of the Michigan Partnership for New Education.

References

Bogdan, D. (1986). Virtual and actual forms of literary response. *Journal of Aesthetic Education, 20,* 51–57.

Cianciolo, P. J. (1982). Responding to literature as a work of art: An aesthetic literary experience. *Language Arts, 59,* 259–64.

———. (1988). *Critical thinking in the study of children's literature in the elementary grades* (Elementary Subjects Center Series No. 5). East Lansing: Michigan State University, Institute for Research on Teaching, Center for the Learning and Teaching of Elementary Subjects.

Fox, G., & Hammond, G. (Eds.). (1980). *Responses to children's literature.* Proceedings of the fourth symposium of the International Research Society for Children's Literature held at the University of Exeter, England, 9–12 September, 1978. New York: K. G. Saur.

Ingarden, R. (1973a). *The cognition of the literary work of art* (R. A. Crowley and K. R. Olsen, Trans.). Evanston, IL: Northwestern University Press. (Original work published 1968)

———. (1973b). *The literary work of art* (G. Grabawicz, Trans.). Evanston, IL: Northwestern University Press. (Original work published 1965)

McLennan, H. (1961). The books we read when we are young. *Canadian Library, 5,* 11.

Miller, B. (1981). *Teaching the art of literature.* Urbana, IL: National Council of Teachers of English.

Moore, J. G. (1979). *The eastern gate: An invitation to the arts of China and Japan.* New York: Thomas Y. Collins.

Parsons, M. J. (1979a). *How we understand art: A cognitive developmental account of aesthetic experience.* New York: Cambridge University Press.

———. (1979b). The place of a cognitive developmental approach to aesthetic response. *Journal of Aesthetic Education, 20,* 109–11.

Probst, R. (1989). Teaching the reading of literature. In D. Lapp, J. Flood, & N. Farnan (Eds.), *Content area reading and learning: Instructional strategies* (pp. 179–86). Englewood Cliffs, NJ: Prentice-Hall.

Russell, D. H. (1956). *Children's thinking.* Needham Heights, MA: Ginn.

Smith, F. (1984). *Learning to be a critical thinker.* Victoria, British Columbia: Abel Press.

Wolf, W., King, M. L., & Huck, C. S. (1967). *The critical reading abilities of elementary school children* (U.S. Office of Education Cooperative Teachers Project No. 2621). Columbus: The Ohio State University.

Children's Books Cited

Baylor, Byrd. (1977). *Guess who my favorite person is.* Illus. by Robert Andrew Parker. New York: Charles Scribner's Sons.

Carrick, Carol. (1981). *The climb.* Illus. by Donald Carrick. New York: Clarion Books.

Carrick, Donald. (1982). *Harald and the knight.* Illus. by Author. New York: Clarion Books.

Henkes, Kevin. (1991). *Chrysanthemum.* Illus. by Author. New York: Greenwillow Books.

Herzig, Alison Cragin, & Mali, Jane Lawrence. (1990). *Sam and the moon queen.* New York: Clarion Books.

Lacapa, Michael. (1990). *The flute player.* Illus. by Author. Flagstaff, AZ: Northland Press.

Lattimore, Deborah Nourse. (1990). *The dragon's robe*. Illus. by Author. New York: Harper & Row.

Lisle, Janet Taylor. (1989). *Afternoon of the elves*. New York: Orchard Books.

Olson, Arielle North. (1987). *The lighthouse keeper's daughter*. Illus. by Elaine Wentworth. Boston: Little, Brown.

Paterson, Katherine. (1977). *Bridge to Terabithia*. New York: Thomas Y. Crowell.

Sachs, Marilyn. (1971). *The bears' house*. New York: E. P. Dutton.

———. (1987). *Fran Ellen's house*. New York: E. P. Dutton.

Van Allsburg, Chris. (1981). *Jumanji*. Illus. by Author. Boston: Houghton Mifflin.

Williams, Vera B. (1990). *"More, more, more," said the baby: Three love stories*. Illus. by Author. New York: Greenwillow Books.

Guiding Children's Critical Aesthetic Responses to Literature in a Fifth-Grade Classroom

17

Renee Leonard
Averill Elementary School, Lansing, Michigan

M y fifth-grade classes and I have worked closely with Patricia Cianciolo in implementing the ideas she has described for teaching and learning critical aesthetic response to literature (see chapter 16). During a recent two-year period, I have focused on the following objectives:

1. To help children think about what they read
2. To encourage children's expression of feelings about what they read
3. To help children become aware of literary characteristics in general and characteristics of different genres in particular
4. To help children connect literature throughout the curriculum

Following is a discussion of these objectives with examples from the children's responses to three major language arts units: "Homelessness," " Multiculturalism," and "Children as Victims of War." Interestingly, and actually quite accidentally, each topic connected with the next in ways that I did not anticipate.

1. Thinking about Literature

Imaging

The first kind of response revealed children's thinking by describing pictures created in their minds when they read picture books and novels.

The novel *Monkey Island* by Paula Fox (1991) became the focal point for the "Homelessness" unit. Each day I read aloud a chapter or so from this contemporary realistic fiction novel about Clay, a boy who was abandoned by his parents and who lived in a park under

Guiding Children's Critical Responses to Literature

the protection of an elderly man, Calvin, and a young adult, Buddy. The children recorded their reactions in journals each day after I finished reading to them.

One day, after discussing a special moment between Buddy and Clay, Mike drew a poignant picture in his journal to express what he said was the most memorable part of the chapter. In response to another part of this story, Jennifer wrote:

> As you were reading and talking about the hospital, I was picturing it. I pictured the hospital [with] Clay on the bed, a railing sort of thing so that he doesn't fall off, and the other kid in the same room on the next bed and only a curtain in-between them.

In the "Children as Victims of War" unit, all the children read *The Upstairs Room* by Johanna Reiss (1972). This autobiographical novel set in the Netherlands during Nazi occupation depicts how Annie (author Reiss) and her sister were hidden in an upstairs room of the Oosterveld family's farm home. In response, Aaron wrote in her journal:

> I remember seeing the house from the inside and from the outside and what the characters looked like, what the hiding place [under the floor in the closet] looked like. It was like a movie playing in my head and I was reading.

Associations   As children formulate their own questions and associations about what they read, their thinking and understandings are stretched and become more individualized. After reading that Clay, the protagonist in *Monkey Island*, is in the hospital, Courtney wrote:

> Paula Fox did a good job describing the hospital room that Clay's staying in. About how the nurse was wearing a hat and Clay wanted to feel it. Paula Fox described the hospital bed or crib as Clay calls it. I have stayed in a hospital before and when they bring you your food they put the side down and have you hold your food on a tray. I know how it feels to have an I-V. It stretches when you move your hand and it really hurts to put an I-V in.

As the class studied units about the homeless, the immigration experience, and minority authors and illustrators as well as books about minorities and victims of war, it became apparent that students were making many associations about their learning.

Freedom Train by Dorothy Sterling (1954) tells about Harriet Tubman and hiding slaves on the Underground Railroad, which was compared to Annie's hiding in *The Upstairs Room*. Shirley's arrival in the United States and her first sight of the Statue of Liberty is described in Bette Bao Lord's *In the Year of the Boar and Jackie Robinson* (1984). This immigrant experience became more meaningful to students when they noticed that one of the illustrations in *C.L.O.U.D.S.*, written and illustrated by Pat Cummings (1986), shows this famous statue and when Cummings told them during her visit to our school that she is able to see the statue from her loft in Brooklyn. During our unit on immigration, children researched their own family's history. A number were surprised to find that some of their relatives fled Germany and Poland because of the war.

Judgments

A third approach prompted children's thinking to make judgments about the author's role by asking them, What would you have done differently if you were the author of this book? Two children responded to these questions after reading *Monkey Island*, a story in which not everyone lived happily ever after. Karen wrote in her journal:

> I am upset at the ending, because I don't like it when books leave you hanging. I would have changed it. I would have put in another chapter and wouldn't have the readers hanging at the end. I did like the book a lot. I wonder if there is a sequel to *Monkey Island*? I think this ending is very possible. A boy can be homeless, go to a foster home, and then find his mother. The reason I think it is possible is because my mother is a caseworker at the probate court. She works with neglected and abused children.

Jennifer wrote the following in her journal:

> I don't really like the way this story ended. I really wish Clay would had found his dad. This story just kind of left off just like if you stop in the middle of the book. If Paula Fox would had done one thing different I wish she would have made Clay find his dad and then his dad would find a job and they would move into a small house and live the rest of their lives happy. But, I really think that this was an excellent book! And I would like to read another book similar to this book.

Award-winning author/illustrator Pat Cummings visited our school in connection with our multicultural study. She told family stories about her past and present, drew pictures depicting her childhood experiences, and demonstrated how she has used these experiences in her writing and illustrations. Children's journal writings reflected their judgments about her as a person, as an author, and as an illustrator. Courtney's memories were expressed in the following narrative:

> How warm she is! She didn't get tense and knew what to say. The way she is open. She told things that she said that people told her not to tell. I liked her personal stories. They were very interesting.

> I will never forget her books. How realistic they are, so detailed. Like in *Clean Your Room, Harvey Moon* (1986), it's so much like a cartoon. She can make so many different faces. She doesn't draw a black man that looks white or a white man that looks black. I am so very glad that she came.

2. Expressing Feelings about Literature

Quality literature should not just help children to think about what they read; it should also evoke sincere emotional response on the reader's part. The questions that are asked should provide opportunities for children to express their feelings. A two-part question I have used frequently for journal writing is: How do you feel about what happened in the story today? Why do you feel that way? Kim's written response to this double question after we read a chapter in *Monkey Island* follows:

> Today I feel real bad for Buddy, Calvin, and Clay. Because Clay is very sick and Buddy and Clay both don't have enuf money put together to pay Clay and Calvin's hospital bill! And I shure do have to say I'm VERY thankful I'm not homeless and I feel bad for people who are. And when I grow up I will take home homeless people. How is Clay and Buddy going to pay the hospital bill?

Kelly wrote the following in her journal:

> I felt shocked! I never knew gangs went after homeless people! And calling Buddy a 'Nigger.' I was shocked! And where did Calvin go? Will Buddy save him if he got drunk? Does Buddy even care?

After listening to the picture book *Rose Blanche* by Roberto Innocenti (1985) and seeing the illustrations depicting a young German girl's discovery of a concentration camp, Matt said:

> I was feeling very sad for the children that were poor and living in the wooden houses [in the concentration camp]. It took a lot of courage and feeling to go each day and try to help those kids. Those kids were very unlucky. I know what he [the author] meant about the mayor getting fat, he was getting all the food.

Although these examples express a very somber and serious side, they also reflect the deep feelings that children are capable of having in response to literature.

3. Expanding Knowledge about Literature

By exposure to the general components of fiction (e.g., setting, characterization, plot, mood, theme, and style) and to the characteristics of each genre (e.g., modern realistic fiction, historical fiction, modern fantasy, biography, picture books, and informational books), children begin to recognize quality literature.

Believability   A "good" book is believable. The reader should believe that every-thing that happens in realistic fiction could have happened some-place in today's world or in the past.

After we finished reading *Monkey Island*, I asked students if they thought the ending was believable. Kathy wrote in response: "I think it's so believable that it sounds like it's her [Paula Fox's] life and like she puts Clay's name in instead of hers." But in contrast, Mike wrote, "I think this ending is not possible, because I don't think that Buddy would be able to get a job."

Style   The author's style and use of language is an important element to consider. It is through language that the author develops all the other components of fiction. Matt made the following comment about the writing style in *Monkey Island*:

> I liked the way Paula Fox describes Clay's feelings. He was feeling sad and you could tell that by the kid said he was going home, and Clay has no home to go to. You can also tell he was tired and weak by the way he was acting towards the other kid in the room.

As we prepared for the visit of African American author/illustrator Pat Cummings to our school during our "Multicultural-ism" unit, my class explored picture books about or by minorities. Using criteria to determine a picture book's quality, the children examined text and pictures in Sharon Bell Mathis's *The Hundred Penny Box* (1975), illustrated by Leo and Diane Dillon. The students identified an illustration in the book they particularly liked and explained reasons for their choices. Karen chose the picture in which Michael, the young protagonist, holds a penny, and his great-great Aunt Dew tells him what happened to her during the year engraved on that penny. Michael's mother is shown standing in the doorway watching Michael and great-great Aunt Dew. Karen indicated her reason for liking this illustration:

> It shows a lot of detail on how great-great Aunt Dew is so loving and caring and it tells a lot about the book. I think that the fading picture in the background tells not only about what she felt but that she remembers it so well that she can picture it. It also tells about the text and is done with cotton balls. It doesn't seem that it is done with cotton. It is done so well and neat.

Latoya chose the picture depicting Michael listening to great-great Aunt Dew singing her song. Her reason for choosing that picture follows:

> Michael and great-great Aunt Dew are together holding each other [and there are] hugs and kisses. Michael loves his Aunt Dew a lot because he stand up for her.

It is a very good picture. It has a lot of detail in it. She really looks old. Her face makes it look so realistic like a real aunt would look like. She or he [the illustrators, Leo and Diane Dillon] really put effort into this picture. You see all the weaknesses inside this picture and how Michael holds her in a loving way. I would give this book a red ribbon!

Impact of the Illustrations

After sharing the picture book *Let the Celebrations Begin*, written by Margaret Wild (1991) and illustrated by Julie Vivas, which was read as part of the "Children as Victims of War" unit, the class responded to what the illustrator did to help them understand the text in this story about women in a concentration camp sewing toys for the children. This focus helped students realize that in evaluating a picture book, they should reflect on its characteristics before writing their responses. After examining the surrealistic illustrations, Matt said, "the illustrations in this book told more than the book. They really showed the hurt and the pain. They also showed the happiness when they were rescued."

While most children focused on the dead flower on the barbed wire at the end of *Rose Blanche*, Mike chose to draw the mayor of the town seizing a Jewish child who had escaped from the truck on which he had been imprisoned. This demonstrates that readers may well vary in the aspects of a story on which they focus.

I Never Saw Another Butterfly, edited by Hana Volavková (1993), is a collection of poems and drawings created by children imprisoned in the concentration camp at Terezín, Czechoslovakia, during World War II and found in the camp after the war. While in some of the pictures children easily identified images described in the poems, there were others that were more abstract, such as a colorful watercolor picture painted on a sketchbook's grey cover, entitled *Fantasy* by its creator. As the class viewed this picture, we discussed what it might be about; however, I did not tell them its name. After seeing the bold splashes of yellow, red, orange, gray, and black, Jennifer remarked:

To me the picture looks like a concentration camp with little lights in the window. It looks like it was bombed by a huge fireball. The white looks like smoke coming up into the sky. The yellow at the top looks like the sun is lighting up the whole sky.

Tanika's interpretation of this illustration was quite different:

I think the picture is the gas chamber because it had smoke coming out of it and it looked like a building that they put Jews in to burn. They had so much red in it that I thought it had to do something with fire.

Comparing Literature on Comparable Themes

To help students identify characteristics of different genres, we compared books on the same topic, but of different genres. Examples of this kind of literary response are evident in two students' comments after I read *Let the Celebrations Begin* to the class. Jennifer stated:

> *The Upstairs Room* reminds me of *Let the Celebrations Begin* because in each one there was a lot of joy at the end because of the war ending. Each book had the characters changed to either defend themselves or to make it easier while in the concentration camp.

Matt compared *Let the Celebrations Begin* to two other books:

> This book reminds me of *Rose Blanche* and *The Upstairs Room*. It reminds me of those books because they're all similar in the way the war is changing lives: *Rose Blanche* because she risked her life to try and help people in the camps because everybody was getting thinner; *The Upstairs Room* and *Let the Celebrations Begin* both have the same quality of telling how [war] hurts people, like how people weren't getting enough exercise.

4. Connecting Literature throughout the Curriculum

Each year I facilitate integrated learning by connecting subject areas in the fifth-grade curriculum. Therefore, I plan activities that connect literature with social studies, art, music, and different kinds of writing.

In connection with the "Homelessness" unit, I arranged for the class to help at a soup kitchen operated in our city by one of the local churches. As we prepared for this visit, we shared our concerns and read aloud the picture book *Uncle Willie and the Soup Kitchen*, written and illustrated by DyAnne DiSalvo-Ryan (1991), to help students understand that their feelings about our forthcoming visit to the soup kitchen were not unusual. After the visit, students talked about the similarities between the activities and people they saw and those depicted in *Uncle Willie and the Soup Kitchen*. The children wrote about what they had learned from this visit and how they felt about it. Mike commented:

> I learned that people need food, shelter, friendly talks, friends, and family. Also they need lots and lots of love and fun, like they need you to tell them a joke or two.
>
> Before I went to the soup kitchen, I thought some people would smell. But when I got to the soup kitchen nobody smelled. I met a really nice guy. He taught me how to say "girl" in Spanish. I forget his name, but I'll always remember him. I also met another nice guy, and the way I met him was by pouring punch in his glass.

Ryan decided to use a poetic form to describe how he felt:

Ryan.
Scared, happy.
Praying, serving, saving,
Helping hungry, needy people.
Volunteer.

After children read several books of their own choice about
World War II and shared them informally in small-group discussions, they responded in writing to one book or to the theme of
"Children as Victims of War." Karen assumed the role of a child war
victim to write the following expressive journal entry:

Why?

I want to stay right here.
I like it here.
Why do we have to wear these stars on all our clothes?
Why do they hurt us so much?
Why can't I got to school?
Why are they taking us away?
Why are we gong to a camp?
Oh, because I'm Jewish!

Megan wrote the following poem in tanka form about the train ride
in *The Endless Steppe: A Girl in Exile* by Esther Hautzig (1968):

The Long Ride

It's been a long ride.
Many Jews are very ill.
Smell, overwhelming.
Families, separated.
I hope this ride ends real soon.

In response to *The Upstairs Room*, Matt assumed the role of Annie,
the young protagonist, in his verse:

I'm Stuck in This Room

I'm stuck in this room.
There is no way out of here.
I am so frightened.
I fear I will never get out of the endless war we have.

Conclusions

Perhaps the most valuable connection one can make with literature
is a firm foundation for a lifelong reading habit. As children study
literature and use it to expand their knowledge base, this habit of
lifelong reading is developing and is apparent in their lives. Kurt,
whose mother claims he hardly opened a book for pleasure at home
last year, not only reads constantly but has learned to discriminate in

the monthly paperback book selections he orders. Evan, who was also uninterested in reading, now reads every available moment in school and oftentimes at home; he also responds in detailed writing assignments to his reading. Megan, who always has been a reader, requests more books on our topic of "Children as Victims of War."

Furthermore, when children beg you to continue to read a story aloud, when they choose to reread the books you have read to them, and when they ask your help in choosing a book especially for them, you realize that you have helped lay invaluable foundations through activities that elicit critical aesthetic response to literature.

References

Parsons, M. J. (1989). *How we understand art: A cognitive developmental account of aesthetic experience.* New York: Cambridge University Press.

Probst, R. (1989). Teaching the reading of literature. In D. Lapp, J. Flood, & N. Farnan (Eds.). *Content area reading and learning: Instructional strategies* (pp. 179–86). Englewood Cliffs, NJ: Prentice-Hall.

Children's Books Cited

Cummings, Pat. (1986). *Clean your room, Harvey Moon.* Illus. by Author. New York: Lothrop, Lee & Shepard Books.

———. (1986). *C.L.O.U.D.S.* Illus. by Author. New York: Lothrop, Lee & Shepard Books.

DiSalvo-Ryan, DyAnne. (1991). *Uncle Willie and the soup kitchen.* Illus. by Author. New York: William Morrow.

Fox, Paula. (1991). *Monkey Island.* New York: Orchard Books.

Gallez, Christophe, & Innocenti, Roberto. (1985). *Rose Blanche.* Illus. by Roberto Innocenti. Mankato, MN: Creative Education.

Hautzig, Esther. (1968). *The endless steppe: A girl in exile.* New York: Thomas Y. Crowell.

Lord, Bette Bao. (1984). *In the year of the boar and Jackie Robinson.* Illus. by Marc Simont. New York: Harper & Row.

Mathis, Sharon Bell. (1975). *The hundred penny box.* Illus. by Leo & Diane Dillon. New York: Viking.

Reiss, Johanna. (1972). *The upstairs room.* New York: Thomas Y. Crowell.

Sterling, Dorothy. (1954). *Freedom train: The story of Harriet Tubman.* Garden City, NY: Doubleday.

Stolz, Mary. (1990). *Storm in the night.* Illus. by Pat Cummings. New York: Harper & Row.

Volavková, Hana (Ed.). (1993). *I never saw another butterfly: Children's drawings and poems from Terezín concentration camp, 1942–1944* (2nd ed.). New York: Pantheon.

Wild, Margaret. (1991). *Let the celebrations begin.* Illus. by Julie Vivas. New York: Orchard Books.

18 Literature in the Classroom: From Dream to Reality

Gloria Kinsley Hoffman
Eastern Elementary School, Lexington, Ohio

My preservice teacher education program at Ohio State University prepared me for whole language, literature-based instruction. However, the real world offered little incentive to put these ideals into practice. Support systems for nontraditional programs were few and far between, while teaching jobs were scarce and those seeking them plentiful.

I entered a unique position in midyear as part of a three-teacher team in a large open classroom housing three fourth grades. Getting my program going that first year was different from the planning I had done as a student, when I was responsible for developing only part of the lessons. Now that I was on my own, the program in place was seductive and safe. The basal had that "wonderful" guide showing exactly what to do and say, what questions to ask, and what the "right" answers should be. I was insecure even though my studies and undergraduate experiences had shown successful outcomes. How could I, a fledgling teacher, presume that my dreams were better than the ways of experts who had developed and written the texts, basals, and workbooks?

Still, I always have been fortunate to work with people who were willing to consider new ideas and programs and to adapt to change. While my principal willingly listened to my ideas, he felt that I should outline the reading program I planned to use. Writing my plan greatly helped me in organizing purposes and goals and in implementing ideas gleaned from various sources and courses.

Furthermore, my students were interested and involved in their learning. They showed excitement in being part of the planning process as well as in the execution of our plans. When the other teachers on my team saw what was happening, they became intrigued and decided to join our efforts.

Teachers on other teams, however, were critical of what was happening in the Pod (the nickname given our large room). Initial trickle-down comments from them shook my confidence even further. But when some teachers finally asked me if and how I dealt with grammar, spelling, and comprehension, I was able to explain my program. Their usual comment was, "I see, but isn't that a lot more work?" My reply to that continues to be, "Yes, but it's well worth it. Literature-based teaching and learning keep me and the students interested and involved. Innovation keeps us all thinking, learning, and protected from boredom or stagnation."

I have continued personal academic and professional growth through graduate study in university classes, attending seminars and conferences at the local, state, and national levels, and membership in professional organizations, such as the National Council of Teachers of English, International Reading Association, and Association for Supervision and Curriculum Development. These organizations and their publications offer many sound, research-based ideas for classroom practice.

Participating in an academic challenge internship program at Ohio State University for three years, and serving as a clinical faculty member there for another period of time, led to my teaching at the university level in addition to my elementary school. My academic and professional growth was furthered through interaction with other faculty members and education colleagues throughout the community.

My teaching dream has come closer to reality, but it has been gradual. My goal of an ideal classroom is evolving from each new concept applied and adapted. As new ideas emerge and research continues to support the advantages of literature use for students' learning, we all benefit from trying and sharing methods, strategies, and ideas. I learn daily from colleagues, students, and professors. While I pursue my dream, it keeps growing and changing as new realities emerge. What an exciting time to be in the field as a teacher!

19 Hear Ye, Hear Ye, and Learn the Lesson Well: Fifth Graders Read and Write about the American Revolution

Gail E. Tompkins
California State University at Fresno

Mrs. Ochs is a fifth-grade teacher at Jackson Elementary School, and her students use reading and writing as learning tools. In this chapter, I describe how Mrs. Ochs's students read and write during a theme cycle on the American Revolution. They relive history through reading and responding orally and in writing to stories, informational books, and poems. They write informally in learning logs and to create projects. While they are learning history, these fifth graders are developing reading and writing competencies.

Culminating Program

Mrs. Ochs steps onto the stage to welcome parents, the fourth- and fifth-grade classes, and friends to the special program culminating her students' month-long theme cycle on the American Revolution. She wears a colonial costume, as do most of her students, and she introduces one student, Melissa, as mistress of ceremonies. Melissa rings an old school bell and begins:

> Hear ye, hear ye, come forward one and all
> Americans who love liberty.
> Join with us to witness
> What happened more than 200 years ago
> in 1775, 1776, 1777 and year after year until 1783.
> The brave men and women who risked their lives
> for the freedoms we have today.
> Hear ye, hear ye, and learn the lesson well.

The students in Mrs. Ochs's class have assumed the roles of personalities from the Revolutionary War, and during this program they reenact scenes from that period, give speeches, recite poems they have written, and chorally read the Declaration of Independence. The performance includes the following acts:

- Two students reenact a conversation between Betsy Ross and George Washington about making the first American flag using five-pointed rather than six-pointed stars.

- A student portraying Martha Washington tells about herself and her life as George Washington's wife.

- A student in the costume of Amos, a mouse who has been to Carpenter Hall with Ben Franklin, recounts eavesdropping on events leading up to the Declaration of Independence. Amos shares gossip about what occurred behind closed doors at the Continental Congress and then gives a book talk encouraging the audience to read Robert Lawson's *Ben and Me* (1967) to learn more about his life with the famous inventor. Another child dressed as Ben Franklin joins Amos on stage to discipline him for gossiping to the audience.

- Several students role-play Washington and his troops crossing the Delaware on 24 December 1776. Then they show a print of Emanuel Leutze's *Washington Crossing the Delaware* and explain two inaccuracies in the painting.

- A student portraying Paul Revere tells about his famous ride, after which he and four classmates read an excerpt from Longfellow's poem "Paul Revere's Ride."

- A girl portrays Deborah Sampson in boy's clothes and reads an "I" poem she has written:

  I am Deborah Sampson
  a woman who dared to be an American patriot
  I was a soldier in the Massachusetts Regiment
  I pretended to be a boy
  I called myself Robert Shurtleff
  I am Deborah Sampson
  a woman who dared to be an American patriot.

- A small group of students recites a rap they have written about Bunker Hill, Cowpens, and other battles of the war.

- The entire class, led on stage by a red-headed boy playing the role of Thomas Jefferson, presents a choral reading of the Declaration of Independence.

Mrs. Ochs's Classroom

The twenty-eight students in Mrs. Ochs's classroom are a community of learners. These students, including several learning-disabled and emotionally disturbed class members, are responsible for and actively involved in learning activities. Students sit at tables arranged into five groups and often work collaboratively. Mrs. Ochs explains, "On the first day of school, I told the children that there are twenty-nine teachers and twenty-nine learners in the classroom. I can't be the only teacher. My students have developed a 'family' relationship, and I think it's because of my attitude."

The classroom itself is crowded with books, charts, maps and posters, science materials, and students' projects. A time line circles the room, just below the windows, bulletin board, and chalkboards. Several hundred books are organized on the shelves of the library center. One shelf is painted red and holds the books related to the current theme cycle. Beanbag chairs and a rocker are arranged for browsing. Other centers include listening, bookmaking, art materials for projects, and science, with several animals in aquariums and cages. A chalkboard section is available for student messages, and students have posted other signs around the classroom.

Planning for the Theme Cycle

Mrs. Ochs begins planning the theme cycle by setting goals and collecting materials. She consults school district goals and objectives to guide her teaching. She also reviews the social studies textbook adopted in her school district and decides what part of it, if any, she will use in the theme cycle. Her goals for students during the American Revolution theme cycle are the following:

- to understand the events of this time period and their effect on students' lives today
- to study the life of Paul Revere and one other person who lived during this period and to understand their sacrifices and contributions to our nation
- to read the Declaration of Independence and to understand the rights and responsibilities articulated within it
- to use reading and writing to learn about the Revolutionary War

Mrs. Ochs collects books, audiovisual materials, maps, and other materials related to the American Revolution. She organizes a special book display in her classroom. Some books come from her classroom library, and others she collects from the school and community libraries or from other teachers in the school. On the first day of the theme cycle, the class crosses the street to the public library, where the librarian has been saving books related to the theme. Students have library cards and check out books on the theme that interest them.

After preliminary planning, Mrs. Ochs consults the students and discusses what they would like to learn about the American Revolution. The topics and activities they suggest are battles, John Paul Jones, *Johnny Tremain* by Esther Forbes (1970) and Jean Fritz's biographies, the Boston Tea Party, George Washington, and period foods. They have studied the American colonies so they want to know more about Benjamin Franklin. They want to do a production at the end of the theme, read books with buddies, keep a learning log, make maps, dramatize battles, and draw murals.

With this input from students, Mrs. Ochs writes lesson plans for each week of the theme cycle, allowing for changes to reflect students' interests and other unplanned explorations. She uses three blocks of time each day for the theme cycle:

8:30–8:45	Opening
8:45–10:30	Block 1
10:30–10:45	Break
10:45–11:45	Math
11:45–12:30	Lunch
12:30–2:00	Block 2
2:00–2:15	Break
2:15–3:00	Block 3
3:00–3:15	Cleanup and Dismissal

Block 1 includes daily guided and shared reading and response activities; Block 2 calls for reading aloud to students and mini-lessons; and in Block 3 students do independent reading and project work.

Next, Mrs. Ochs makes plans to assess students' learning. She identifies the activities that she will grade and prepares an Assessment Checklist that she copies and distributes to students (see Figure 19.1). Mrs. Ochs is a "kidwatcher" (Goodman, 1985). She observes students and writes anecdotal notes as they read, write, and work on projects. She takes these notes on small, self-adhesive slips of paper that she inserts into a file folder for each student. The students also write self-evaluations at the end of the theme cycle to reflect on their learning, work habits, and effort. Mrs. Ochs determines students' grades from these three sources of information.

Mrs. Ochs also prepares theme folders, notebooks, maps, and copies of the Declaration of Independence to distribute to students on the theme cycle's first day.

Week 1 of the Theme Cycle

To begin the theme cycle, Mrs. Ochs constructs a K-W-L chart (Ogle, 1989) on butcher paper with three columns labeled as follows: "K—What We *Know*," "W—What We *Want* to Learn," and "L—What We *Learned*." Students fill in what they already know about the American Revolution in the first column and list questions and things they want to learn in the second column. During the cycle, they add more questions to the second column and fill in what they have learned in the third column.

Figure 19.1.
Assessment checklist for the American Revolution theme cycle.

Name _____   Beginning date _____

                                                                    Ending date _____

1. Keep a learning log with:

    _____ notes about Paul Revere   _____

    _____ log for Johnny Tremain

    _____ log for *The Fighting Ground*

    _____ notes about the Second Continental Congress

    _____ notes about the battles

    _____ other notes

2. Make chart to compare Paul Revere and Johnny Tremain   _____

3. Make a time line of the period   _____

4. Read 4 books   _____

    _____ *And Then What Happened, Paul Revere?*

    _____ *Declaration of Independence*

    _____ _____

    _____ _____

5. Biography project   _____

    _____ simulated journal

    _____ life line

    _____ portrait

    _____ I poem

    _____ something else _____

6. Revolutionary War project title: _____   _____

    _____   _____

7. Sharing   _____
    _____ share a book

    _____ share bio project

    _____ share project

8. Help with program   _____

9. Research and report about battle   _____

10. Choral reading   _____

11. Self-evaluation of theme   _____

12. Something else: _____   _____

Students help Mrs. Ochs hang another sheet of butcher paper for a word wall. During the theme cycle, Mrs. Ochs and her students write words that are interesting, technical, or historical on the wall. Sometimes Mrs. Ochs writes the words, and at other times, students do. Mrs. Ochs often reviews the words, asking students to compose a word riddle or to find five words on the wall that relate to one historical personality.

Mrs. Ochs introduces books about the American Revolution in a special section of the classroom library. She has a wide variety available, including those listed in the text set at the end of this chapter. Students choose from these books, those they checked out of the community library, or others they have brought from home for independent reading. They spend thirty-five to forty-five minutes reading each day. Some students read independently while others read with a partner or in a small group. After reading, students write in their learning logs, noting the title, author, their general reaction, and information learned. Students use the last fifteen minutes of independent reading to share the books they are reading and what they are learning. Some students talk about a book, while others read excerpts, read from their logs, or report information they have learned.

During the rest of the first week, Mrs. Ochs concentrates on Paul Revere and the events in Boston that led to firing "the shot heard 'round the world." Over twelve days, she reads aloud *Johnny Tremain*, Esther Forbes's (1970) story of an apprentice silversmith caught up in Boston's pre–Revolutionary War crisis. Mrs. Ochs stops at key points, such as when Johnny burns his hand, to reenact the scene. Students assume the roles of the characters and dramatize the scene, with Mrs. Ochs prompting as needed. Students reflect on the book in their learning logs and participate in "grand conversations" (Eeds & Wells, 1989), book discussions in which students share their reactions and interpretations rather than answer a series of teacher-designed questions.

Mrs. Ochs has fifteen copies of Jean Fritz's *And Then What Happened, Paul Revere?* (1973), which students read with buddies, predicting each time the text says, "And then what happened?" Next, they follow in their books as Mrs. Ochs reads aloud. After-wards, Mrs. Ochs talks about heroes. "American heroes like Paul Revere seem larger than life—too good to be true," she explains. "How does Jean Fritz portray Paul Revere?" Students identify parts of the book that show Revere as a real person and parts that show him as a hero, and they brainstorm lists of *real person* and *hero* examples. Then Mrs. Ochs asks students to quickwrite about these two aspects of Paul Revere. Seth writes:

Paul Revere is a hero because of his ride to warn the patriots that the British are coming but he is more too. He was a dad and a husband and his job was to make silverware and stuff. He was a regular man but the war made him special. If there were no British soldiers in Boston nobody would remember him today. Except his family and grandchildren. You have to be a regular person and then maybe you will become special but it depends on what happens when you live. Sometimes wars and other things make you do something brave. Then people remember you for 200 years and maybe for 2,000 years.

Mrs. Ochs also shares her Paul Revere bio-box with the class. Her box is covered with aluminum foil because Revere was a silversmith. Included inside are a life line of Revere, a map of his famous ride, a copy of Longfellow's poem "Paul Revere's Ride," an advertisement for Revere cookware (made with the process Revere invented for putting copper onto another metal), a magazine picture of John Singleton Copley's famous Revere portrait, a silver teaspoon, and a tracing of a political cartoon Revere made of a skull and crossbones between the king's crown and a patriot's cap. Explanations on cards are attached to the items. Mrs. Ochs suggests that students may make their own bio-boxes as projects.

The next day students add words from *And Then What Happened, Paul Revere?* to the word wall. They also change the name of their learning logs to *day books* after Paul Revere's term for his log. To focus on vocabulary, Mrs. Ochs lists twenty words from the word wall and duplicates copies for the five groups of students. She asks students to put a plus by words that relate to Paul Revere and a minus by words that do not. Students reread portions of the book, hunting for a word and deciding whether it relates to Revere. The connection is clear for words such as *sloppy* and *artificial teeth,* but other words cause student disagreement. It is not important to Mrs. Ochs whether the words relate to Revere; she wants her students to think about the words.

On Thursday, Mrs. Ochs shares the picture book version of Longfellow's poem "Paul Revere's Ride" illustrated by Ted Rand (1990). This leads to a grand conversation, discussing the poem, Revere's bravery, and the vivid watercolor illustrations. Students also mention Longfellow's language and their favorite lines in the poem. Mrs. Ochs notes that Longfellow wrote the poem around the time of the Civil War, long after Revere's ride, and asks students if they find any inconsistencies between the two versions of the event. She also displays a print of Grant Wood's painting *Paul Revere's Ride,* and they compare Wood's surrealism to Rand's more realistic illustrations. On Friday, Mrs. Ochs reads *Jack Jouette's Ride* by Gail Haley (1973), a book about another American patriot riding for liberty.

Students compare this ride to Longfellow's account of Revere's ride. In small groups they construct charts to compare the two works.

Each day Mrs. Ochs teaches a mini-lesson. Some lessons deal with social studies (e.g., causes of the American Revolution), others with language arts (e.g., how to write simulated journals), and sometimes the two are integrated (e.g., how to interpret political cartoons). In each lesson, Mrs. Ochs presents information and provides opportunities for students to read or write in small groups or together as a class. Students write notes about the mini-lesson in their learning logs.

Week 2 of the Theme Cycle

Mrs. Ochs devotes the second week to the Second Continental Congress and the Declaration of Independence. Students choose a person from this historical period to role-play and for a biography project. The class begins a list of patriots and loyalists. Melissa notes that almost all the interesting people were men and boys. Mrs. Ochs explains that even though men played a prominent role, girls and women were important, too. She shares books on Martha Washington, Deborah Sampson, Abigail Adams, Betsy Ross, and Molly Pitcher. She also points out books about Crispus Attucks and Benjamin Banneker, two free African Americans of the period.

Students read informational books to learn about the Second Continental Congress and the Declaration of Independence. Mrs. Ochs has eight copies each of Dennis B. Fradin's *The Declaration of Independence* (1988) and Norman Richards's *The Story of the Declaration of Independence* (1968). (The books are similar, but Fradin's version is easier to read.) Mrs. Ochs briefly introduces the books, and students choose one to read. After reading, students discuss the Second Continental Congress and add words to the class word wall, but they raise more questions than answers.

To provide a more vivid picture of events at the Congress, Mrs. Ochs shows excerpts from a videotape of the musical *1776*. Students are enthralled as the people and events come to life in the movie. They watch the excerpts several times and pick personalities to role-play. Students quickly assume the roles of these characters. They call themselves by their new names and begin wearing colonial-style clothes. Several students set small candles and quill pens on their desks.

During their independent reading time, students search for information for their biography projects. Mrs. Ochs asks them to find three sources of information, in what she calls the "triangle approach." Most students read a biography (source 1), check information in an encyclopedia (source 2), and find a reference to the person in an informational book (source 3).

Mrs. Ochs's mini-lessons focus on the biography project. She discusses the genre, phase biographies like Fritz's *And Then What Happened, Paul Revere?* and complete biographies such as Aliki's *The Many Lives of Benjamin Franklin* (1988), and activities for the project. One activity is simulated journals in which students write as though they were a historical personality. Mrs. Ochs reads excerpts from *The Winter at Valley Forge* by James Knight (1982) to model the approach. Students make special journals with grocery sack covers, crumpled and torn (rather than cut), to look authentic. Here is one student's entry, written as Martha Jefferson:

> King's Head Inn
> Philadelphia
> July 8, 1776
>
> Dearest Diary,
>
> Tom has been so irritable and hard to talk to. It really hurt his feelings that the delegates changed so many of his beautiful words in the declaration he wrote. But today was a very important day for him. Tom read the Declaration of Independence out loud to the people of Philadelphia. I was there! Bells were ringing! I could see Tom's red hair over the crowd and I heard his brave voice reading the words "When in the course of human events . . ." King George thinks we are traitors but I know we are patriots.

On Friday morning students role-play the events they read about and watched on the video. Their classroom becomes a room in Carpenter Hall, and their desks become the delegates' desks. One child assumes the role of John Hancock and sits at Mrs. Ochs's desk. Students role-play the event, and Mrs. Ochs plays the role of a loyalist delegate (a role no one wants to play!). She stops the dramatization several times to challenge students to think more deeply about the seriousness of the situation.

Students also read the Declaration of Independence. They follow along as Mrs. Ochs reads it aloud once and then mumble along as she reads it a second time. Next, students decide how they will read the document chorally—that is, which lines to repeat as a chorus. The class reads the document several times. Two boys hum "Yankee Doodle" for background music as Mrs. Ochs tape-records their final choral reading.

Week 3 of the Theme Cycle

The focus during the third week is on the war's events. Mrs. Ochs and the students brainstorm a list of battles, including Lexington and Concord, Bunker Hill, Trenton, Quebec, Bennington, Long Island, Yorktown, and John Paul Jones's sea battles. Students decide what to learn about each battle: date, location, generals on each side, number of deaths, outcome, and other interesting information; and Mrs.

Ochs writes these items on a chart. Students divide into teams to explore a particular battle. As each group reports to the class later, students record the battle information on a class chart and note the battle's location on a large map of the thirteen colonies. Students write about the battles in learning logs and mark maps in their theme folders.

After one team reports on the Americans' surprise attack on the Hessians and their victory at Trenton, Mrs. Ochs hangs a print of Emanuel Leutze's painting *Washington Crossing the Delaware.* She asks students to examine it and to compare the report on the battle of Trenton to the painting. Mark, role-playing George Washington, comments, "Well, I would not be so stupid and stand up in a boat, especially in the middle of winter." Several students agree. Mrs. Ochs reminds students that the crossing occurred on 24 December 1776. Kristen, portraying Betsy Ross, notes a second inconsistency: the flag. She explains that "she" did not make the first American flag until six months after Washington crossed the Delaware.

Mini-lessons are taught each day this week. On Monday, Mrs. Ochs describes life lines (a time line of a person's life), and students make life lines as part of their biography projects. On Tuesday and Wednesday, she explains political cartoons and how to interpret them. She shares copies of Ben Franklin's famous "Join, or Die" cartoon of a snake cut into pieces with each piece identified as a colony. They discuss the literal meaning and the information Franklin added so readers would understand the political message. She shares other cartoons from the Revolutionary War, and some students create their own political cartoons, like Aaron's cartoon featuring King George as a dog, shown in Figure 19.2.

After Mrs. Ochs finishes reading *Johnny Tremain,* she begins reading aloud *The Fighting Ground* by Avi (1984), an account of thirteen-year-old Jonathan's experiences as a soldier on 3 April 1778. Chapters in this book are labeled with times, and Mrs. Ochs asks students to give an appropriate title to each chapter. Students also react to the book in their learning logs and participate in grand conversations.

Week 4 of the Theme Cycle

During the fourth week, students work on projects and prepare for the Friday program. In the morning block, some students meet in writing groups for feedback on their compositions, some draw murals and posters, some write poems, and some rehearse skits for the program. Others construct dioramas and tabletop scenes of battles, copy "quotable quotes" in calligraphy with a parent volunteer's assistance, or confer with Mrs. Ochs.

Figure 19.2.

 On Wednesday, students make a "quilt" with quotes related to the theme. Their patriotic pattern of white-construction-paper stars glued onto a red-and-blue-striped background contains well-known quotes from the period, such as "Give me liberty or give me death!" On Thursday morning, students gather to tape-record a read-around, during which students take turns reading memorable sentences from the book and Mrs. Ochs contributes favorite sentences from *Johnny Tremain*. The tape will be played at the following day's program.

 This week Mrs. Ochs finishes *The Fighting Ground*, and students have a grand conversation comparing it with *Johnny Tremain* and discussing historical fiction. Some students compare the fictional characters in these stories to the subjects of their biography projects. Other students relate the universal themes of these books to other books they have read. They compare Johnny Tremain and Jonathan to James in *James and the Giant Peach* by Roald Dahl (1961), Willy in *Stone Fox* by John Reynolds Gardiner (1980), and Kit in *The Witch of Blackbird Pond* by Elizabeth George Speare (1958).

Mini-lessons are included this week, too. The class discusses the menu for their Revolutionary War lunch, to be held on Friday. Mrs. Ochs shares information about foods and recipes from *Slumps, Grunts, and Snickerdoodles: What Colonial America Ate and Why* by Lila Perl (1975). Then students decide their menu: ham sandwiches, apples, snickerdoodles, corn bread and honey, and ginger ale (the only ale Mrs. Ochs will permit). Notes go home to parents about needed foods, cooking equipment, and parent helpers.

One day, students review the format of an invitation and, in groups, write program invitations that are sent to the fourth- and fifth-grade classes, the principal, and other interested persons. On Thursday, Mrs. Ochs reviews self-evaluations with the class and asks students to write theirs, reflecting on their learning during this theme cycle, their reading and writing experiences, their projects, and their work habits and effort.

Friday is a special day. Students wear their costumes. In the morning they rehearse their program and prepare their lunch. Several students share their projects with the rest of the class. After lunch, Mrs. Ochs and the class complete the K-W-L chart begun on the theme cycle's first day, and students submit their theme folders and completed activities. Then they present their program to demonstrate and celebrate their learning during the theme cycle.

Guiding Principles

Mrs. Ochs teaches from a holistic perspective and believes in children's power as learners. This theme cycle on the American Revolution demonstrates many of the reading and writing principles that guide her teaching and how they are translated into learning outcomes. Four of the most important principles are discussed below.

Teach with Literature

Mrs. Ochs uses literature—stories, informational books, poems, and historical documents—rather than social studies textbooks to teach history. Her students benefit as they do the following:

- read about the American Revolution from a variety of genres
- focus on one genre—biography—and read and write about one person from the era
- compare the contributions of stories, informational books, biographies, and other genres in painting a picture of the historical era

Involve Students

In Mrs. Ochs's classroom, students are involved in learning and making choices about reading and writing activities in which they are engaged. Her students develop their reading and writing processes and assume responsibility for their learning. Specifically, the students perform the following tasks:

- help plan the theme cycle
- select books they want to read
- write in learning logs
- choose projects they will pursue
- plan and present a culminating program

Do Authentic Activities

Mrs. Ochs's students are involved in reading and writing activities of real literacy and social studies value, rather than workbooks that are completed, collected, and graded. Students do authentic activities, such as the following:

- assume the role of a Revolutionary War personality
- research a Revolutionary War battle and share information with classmates
- plan, create, and share projects with classmates
- read authentic historical documents
- share learning at the culminating program

Integrate the Language Arts

Mrs. Ochs's students read and write to learn about the Revolutionary War. Not only are the language arts connected with each other, but they are connected across the curriculum. Specifically, the students do the following:

- connect reading and writing in learning logs, charts, and projects
- focus on theme-related words through reading and writing activities
- use drama to enrich their reading and learning interpretations
- read political cartoons critically and create cartoons as political statements related to the historical period or current events

Conclusion

Through this theme cycle on the American Revolution, Mrs. Ochs's students have had many more learning opportunities than they would have had in a traditional classroom. Her instructional methods allowed her fifth graders to "learn the lesson well." Researchers have documented that reading and writing enhance learning (see Shanahan, 1990). Mrs. Ochs's students experienced reading and writing as constructive processes (Tierney & Pearson, 1983) and learned about literary genre and writing forms (Tompkins, 1990). Also, students expanded their reading and writing competencies and learned political uses of literacy. The culminating program described at the beginning of this chapter documents students' enhanced learning through this theme cycle and the power of connecting reading and writing across the curriculum.

References

Eeds, M., & Wells, D. (1989). Grand conversations: An exploration of meaning construction in literature study groups. *Research in the Teaching of English, 23,* 4–29.

Goodman, Y. (1985). Kidwatching: Observing children in the classroom. In A. Jaggar and M. Smith-Burke (Eds.), *Observing the language learner.* Newark, DE: International Reading Association.

Ogle, D. M. (1989). The know, want to know, learn strategy. In K. D. Muth (Ed.), *Children's comprehension of text: Research into practice* (pp. 205–23). Newark, DE: International Reading Association.

Shanahan, T. (1990). Reading and writing together: What does it really mean? In T. Shanahan (Ed.), *Reading and writing together: New perspectives for the classroom* (pp. 1–18). Norwood, MA: Christopher-Gordon.

Tierney, R. J., & Pearson, P. D. (1983). Toward a composing model of reading. *Language Arts, 60,* 568–80.

Tompkins, G. E. (1994). *Teaching writing: Balancing process and product* (2nd ed.). New York: Macmillan.

Children's Books Cited

Aliki. (1988). *The many lives of Benjamin Franklin.* New York: Simon & Schuster.

Avi. (1984). *The fighting ground.* New York: Harper & Row.

Dahl, Roald. (1961). *James and the giant peach.* Illus. by Nancy Burkert. New York: Alfred A. Knopf.

Forbes, Esther. (1970). *Johnny Tremain: A story of Boston in revolt.* Boston: Houghton Mifflin.

Fradin, Dennis B. (1988). *The Declaration of Independence.* Chicago: Children's Press.

Fritz, Jean. (1973). *And then what happened, Paul Revere?* Illus. by Margot Tomes. New York: Coward, McCann & Geoghegan.

Gardiner, John Reynolds. (1980). *Stone fox.* Illus. by Marcia Sewall. New York: Harper & Row.

Haley, Gail. (1973). *Jack Jouette's ride.* Illus. by Author. New York: Viking.

Knight, James E. (1982). *The winter at Valley Forge: Survival and victory.* Mahwah, NJ: Troll Associates.

Lawson, Robert. (1976). *Ben and me.* Boston: Little, Brown.

Longfellow, Henry Wadsworth. (1990). *Paul Revere's ride.* Illus. by Ted Rand. New York: E. P. Dutton.

Perl, Lila. (1975). *Slumps, grunts, and snickerdoodles: What colonial America ate and why.* New York: Clarion Books.

Richards, Norman. (1968). *The story of the Declaration of Independence*. Chicago: Children's Press.

Speare, Elizabeth George. (1958). *The witch of blackbird pond*. Boston: Houghton Mifflin.

Text Set of Books on the American Revolution

Stories

Avi. (1984). *The fighting ground*. New York: Harper & Row.

Benchley, Nathaniel. (1969). *Sam the minuteman*. Illus. by Arnold Lobel. New York: Harper & Row.

———. (1977). *George the drummer boy*. New York: Harper & Row.

Brady, Esther W. (1988). *Toliver's secret*. New York: Crown.

Collier, James Lincoln, & Collier, Christopher. (1976). *The bloody country*. New York: Scholastic.

———. (1983). *Jump ship to freedom*. New York: Delacorte Press.

———. (1983). *War comes to Willy Freeman*. New York: Delacorte Press.

———. (1984). *Who is Carrie?* New York: Delacorte Press.

Forbes, Esther. (1970). *Johnny Tremain: A story of Boston in revolt*. Boston: Houghton Mifflin.

Gauch, Patricia Lee. (1974). *This time, Tempe Wick?* New York: Coward, McCann & Geoghegan.

Haugaard, Erik Christian. (1983). *Adventures of John Paul Jones*. Boston: Houghton Mifflin.

Lawson, Robert. (1953). *Mr. Revere and I*. Boston: Little, Brown.

———. (1967). *Ben and me*. Boston: Little, Brown.

Monjo, F. N. (1973). *Poor Richard in France*. New York: Dell.

Rappaport, Doreen. (1988). *The Boston coffee party*. New York: Harper & Row.

Roop, Peter, & Roop, Connie. (1986). *Buttons for General Washington*. Minneapolis: Carolrhoda Books.

Informational Books

Adler, David A. (1989). *A picture book of George Washington*. New York: Holiday House.

———. (1990). *A picture book of Benjamin Franklin*. Illus. by John & Alexandra Wallner. New York: Holiday House.

Aliki. (1988). *The many lives of Benjamin Franklin*. New York: Simon & Schuster.

Carter, Alden R. (1988). *The American Revolution: The darkest hours*. (M. Kline, Ed.). New York: Franklin Watts.

Clapp, Patricia. (1977). *I'm Deborah Sampson: A soldier in the war of the Revolution*. New York: Lothrop, Lee & Shepard Books.

D'Amato, Anthony, & D'Amato, Janet. (1975). *Colonial crafts for you to make*. New York: Julian Messner.

David, B. (1976). *Black heroes of the Revolution.* New York: Harcourt Brace Jovanovich.

Evans, Elizabeth. (1975). *Weathering the storm: Women of the American Revolution.* New York: Charles Scribner's Sons.

Felton, H. (1976). *Deborah Sampson: Soldier of the Revolution.* New York: Dodd, Mead.

Ferris, Jeri. (1988). *What are you figuring now: A story about Benjamin Banneker.* Minneapolis: Carolrhoda Books.

Fisher, Leonard Everett. (1988). *Monticello.* New York: Holiday House.

Forbes, Esther. (1974). *America's Paul Revere.* Boston: Houghton Mifflin.

Foster, G. (1970). *Year of independence, 1776.* New York: Charles Scribner's Sons.

Fritz, Jean. (1973). *And then what happened, Paul Revere?* New York: Coward, McCann & Geoghegan.

———. (1974). *Why don't you get a horse, Sam Adams?* Illus. by Trina Schart Hyman. New York: Coward, McCann & Geoghegan.

———. (1975). *Where was Patrick Henry on the 29th of May?* New York: Coward, McCann & Geoghegan.

———. (1976). *What's the big idea, Ben Franklin?* New York: Coward, McCann & Geoghegan.

———. (1976). *Will you sign here, John Hancock?* New York: Coward, McCann & Geoghegan.

———. (1977). *Can't you make them behave, King George?* New York: Coward, McCann & Geoghegan.

———. (1981). *Traitor: The case of Benedict Arnold.* New York: Viking.

Gibbons, Gail. (1986). *From path to highway: The story of the Boston Post Road.* Illus. by Author. New York: Thomas Y. Crowell.

Holbrook, Stewart H. (1954). *America's Ethan Allen.* Boston: Houghton Mifflin.

Knight, James E. (1982). *Boston Tea Party: Rebellion in the colonies.* Mahwah, NJ: Troll Associates.

———. (1982). *Seventh and Walnut: Life in colonial Philadelphia.* Mahwah, NJ: Troll Associates.

Leckie, Robert. (1973). *The world turned upside down: The story of the American Revolution.* New York: G. P. Putnam's Sons.

Loeper, John J. (1973). *Going to school in 1776.* New York: Atheneum.

Marrin, Albert. (1988). *The war for independence: The story of the American Revolution.* New York: Atheneum.

McDowell, Bart. (1980). *The Revolutionary War: America's fight for freedom* (4th ed.). Washington, DC: National Geographic Society.

Millender, Dharathula H. (1965). *Crispus Attucks: Black leader of colonial patriots.* New York: Aladdin Books.

Perl, Lila. (1975). *Slumps, grunts, and snickerdoodles: What colonial America ate and why.* New York: Clarion Books.

Quackenbush, Robert. (1989). *Pass the quill, I'll write a draft: A story of Thomas Jefferson.* Illus. by Author. New York: Pippin Press.

Stevenson, Augustus. (1959). *George Washington: Young leader.* New York: Aladdin Books.

———. (1983). *Benjamin Franklin: Young printer.* New York: Aladdin Books.

———. (1983). *Molly Pitcher: Young patriot.* New York: Aladdin Books.

Wagoner, Jean B. (1986). *Martha Washington: America's first first lady.* New York: Aladdin Books.

Weil, Ann. (1983). *Betsy Ross: Designer of our flag.* New York: Aladdin Books.

Poems

Bangs, Edward. (1989). *Yankee Doodle.* New York: Four Winds Press.

Benet, Stephen Vincent, & Benet, Rosemary. (1961). *A book of Americans.* New York: Henry Holt.

Fisher, Leonard Everett. (1976). *Liberty book.* New York: Doubleday.

Hopkins, Lee Bennett. (1977). *Beat the drum: Independence Day has come.* New York: Harcourt Brace Jovanovich.

Longfellow, Henry Wadsworth. (1990). *Paul Revere's ride.* Illus. by Ted Rand. New York: E. P. Dutton.

20 Supporting Children's Learning: Informational Books across the Curriculum

Evelyn B. Freeman
The Ohio State University at Newark

D inosaurs—insects—colonial America—the Civil War—money! These common topics studied in elementary classrooms are found in science, social studies, or math textbooks. Yet to ensure that those topics are interesting to children, comprehensive in content, and varied in perspective, teachers know they must supplement the textbook with other resources and learning experiences. Children's literature can support these and other topics in all content areas and provide an invaluable resource for learning across the curriculum. Huck (1977) points out that:

> No textbook in social studies or science can begin to present the wonder, the excitement, the tragedy of man's discoveries and mistakes as the biographies, stories, and informational books that are available for children today. Not to use them is to deny children their right to participate in the drama of the making of our civilization. (p. 368)

While all genres of literature can support the elementary school curriculum, this chapter focuses specifically on informational books. As used here, informational books refer to those classified as nonfiction under the Dewey decimal system, excluding poetry and folklore. This genre traditionally has received less attention from teachers than fiction or picture books. With the increase in the number and quality of informational books being published, more teachers are turning to nonfiction to enhance their curriculum. Informational books support children's learning in the elementary curriculum in at least three ways: they can expand and deepen children's content knowledge; they can support specific aspects of children's development such as critical thinking, social development, and writing; and they can support children's interests and their motivation for reading.

Knowledge in Content Areas

Children's literature is now available on a wide range of topics in all areas of the elementary curriculum. Children's books provide knowledge that extends information found in content-area textbooks. Literature expands and deepens children's knowledge by presenting specific facts and concepts about a topic as well as various points of view. In addition, books may reflect an inquiring spirit by exploring the process by which individuals discover and investigate the world. In contrast, textbooks do not provide coverage depth or topic detail; nor do they usually reflect on the human experience and feelings involved in the topic.

Many avenues exist for teachers to integrate children's literature in content-area studies. Books can be shared by teachers reading them aloud as well as through independent student reading. Teachers may also read aloud only select sections of a book, or they may share and discuss illustrations and what can be learned from them. Teachers should collect books on a given topic and have them available in the classroom for children's specific research and reference, for individual and group projects, and for perusal. Children can discuss books and respond to them through projects in art, writing, drama, movement, music, or cooking.

Money Sense

In math, money is studied in primary and intermediate grades. *If You Made a Million* by David M. Schwartz (1989) elucidates the concept of money through text, and Steven Kellogg's colorful, humorous illustrations are appropriate for all ages. The world of money is introduced in a way no mathematics textbook can, as Marvelosissimo the Mathematical Magician leads us to explore pennies, nickels, dimes, quarters, and dollars and how we can increase our resources by accumulating interest in the bank. An author's note provides more in-depth information about banks, interest, checking accounts, and loans. Many abstract concepts become clarified in this delightful book. Students also will enjoy the companion book by Schwartz and Kellogg, *How Much Is a Million?* (1985).

Dinosaurs

Dinosaurs is a popular unit in the elementary grades. While myriad dinosaur books are available, *The News about Dinosaurs* by Patricia Lauber (1989) provides a unique perspective. It enables the reader to identify with the spirit of inquiry so essential to the generation of new knowledge. The book's format juxtaposes currently held beliefs about dinosaurs with new scientific evidence that dispels what we previously thought was fact. For example, "Scientists began to think they had discovered nearly every kind of dinosaur that ever walked the earth. THE NEWS IS: The work was far from finished. Today new kinds of dinosaurs are found all the time" (p. 7). "THE NEWS IS," printed in bold red letters, emphasizes how knowledge continues to change. The scientific process is elucidated, and the continued search for new knowledge is valued.

Travel the Globe

Geography and "map skills" have received much public attention in recent years. A unit on maps can be enhanced by *My Place* by Nadia Wheatley and Donna Rawlins (1987). This book travels back in time by ten-year intervals to describe a tract of land and the changes it has undergone. For each decade, a map has been drawn by the child narrating that page. Children could easily use the book as a model for constructing maps about their own streets and community and as a resource to understand the importance of maps in establishing location.

Books take children to places they may never visit in person and introduce them to cultures unlike their own. *Sahara: Vanishing Cultures* by Jan Reynolds (1991) provides a personalized account of the Tuareg, tribal people who live in the Sahara desert. The book is written from the perspective of a young boy named Manda, and the people's culture and daily life are revealed through text and color photographs taken by the author. Students may discuss how their lives and Manda's are alike and different. They may investigate specific aspects of desert life, the Sahara, or the Tuareg. Children certainly gain multicultural awareness and understanding through this book. *Himalaya: Vanishing Cultures,* also by Jan Reynolds (1991), follows a similar format in introducing children to a young Sherpa girl.

Stereotypes about the Eskimo are dispelled through reading *Arctic Memories* by Normee Ekoomiak (1990), *In Two Worlds: A Yup'ik Eskimo Family* by Aylette Jenness and Alice Rivers (1989), or *Eskimo Boy: Life in an Inupiaq Eskimo Village* by Russ Kendall (1992). We learned that *Eskimo,* which means "people who eat raw fish," was a term used by the Cree Indians to describe their neighbors. Eskimos refer to themselves as *Inuit,* which means "people." We further discover that several individual cultures comprise Alaskan Native Americans, such as the Yupiks, the Inupiaqs, or the Aleuts. A rich, comprehensive picture of Inuit life both past and present is found in this trio of books. Kendall lived in the Inupiaq Eskimo village of Shismaref, a little island off Alaska's northwest coast, for nearly ten months. His magnificent color photographs present a vivid picture of Native Alaskan life from a seven-year-old boy's perspective. Primary teachers will find this book appropriate to share with young children. In *Arctic Memories,* we are exposed to Inuktitut, the language of the Inuit, through bilingual text written in both English and Inuktitut. The book, written by an Inuk who illustrated his text with paintings and embroidered wall hangings, informs readers about his people's heritage and traditions. Changes that have occurred in the Native Alaskan culture are described through text and photographs in *In Two Worlds: A Yup'ik Eskimo Family.* We meet Alice and Billy Rivers, who live in Scammon Bay, Alaska. Through them and their family, the life of the Yup'ik Eskimos today and long ago is revealed.

Accentuate the Arts

The fine arts are also supported through children's literature. Children read about famous artists both past and present in such books as *Linnea in Monet's Garden* by Christina Björk (1985) and *Inspirations: Stories about Women Artists* by Leslie Sills (1989). In *Inspirations,* students meet Faith Ringgold, the artist who wrote and illustrated the award-winning picture book *Tar Beach* (1991), based on her original story quilt. Through the eyes of young Linnea, in *Linnea in Monet's Garden,* we travel to France to explore the life and art of the famous artist Claude Monet. In these books, many art styles and varied media in which artists work are presented. Students may experiment with their own illustrations, using different styles and materials. Music, dance, and drama may also be explored in such books as *A Very Young Musician* by Jill Krementz (1991), *I Feel Like Dancing* by Steven Barboza (1992), and *Theater Magic: Behind the Scenes at a Children's Theater* by Cheryl Walsh Bellville (1986).

Children's Development

Literature can also enhance children's development in many areas. The books discussed below promote critical thinking, social development, and writing.

Critical thinking can be fostered by children's books. One recent and controversial topic has been the focus on Christopher Columbus and his "discovery" of the Western Hemisphere. The many books about Columbus provide children with an opportunity to examine this controversy by comparing and contrasting "facts," questioning their previously held ideas about Columbus, and reaching their own conclusions about the contributions of this historical figure. For instance, Milton Meltzer in *Columbus and the World around Him* (1990) immediately dispels some long held myths about Columbus: "When historians tell us that Columbus 'discovered' America, what do they mean? Surely not that no one knew America was there. . . . These Native Americans knew where they were. It was Columbus who didn't know where he was" (p. 9). Children can compare Meltzer's book with that by Nancy Smiler Levinson, *Christopher Columbus: Voyager to the Unknown* (1990). Students may investigate similarities and differences in the information presented and compare each author's point of view. Are the authors objective, or do the children feel they are biased in some way? What new perspective on Columbus is provided in *I, Columbus, My Journal, 1492–3*, edited by Peter and Connie Roop (1990)? Do we gain any new insights about Columbus by reading these translated excerpts from his actual diary? Children may also explore how illustrations influence readers' understanding and impression of content. Children can discuss this issue as they share *Christopher Columbus: From Vision to Voyage* (1991), a photobiography with text by Joan Anderson and color photographs by George Ancona. Costumed members of the Spanish National Opera were photographed in Spain for the book. These photographs could then be compared with the beautiful paintings by Peter Sis in *Follow the Dream* (1991). These books, presented in various formats, include divergent perspectives and plentiful information, enabling readers to reach their own conclusions about Columbus and his contributions.

Books also can awaken children's social conscience, sensitivity to others' needs, and empathy for those whose life situations may be very difficult. For example, many children are concerned about the homeless in America. Several recent children's books have addressed this issue and provide children with broader understanding. The picture book *Fly Away Home* by Eve Bunting (1991), the novel *Monkey Island* by Paula Fox (1991), and the information book *No Place to Be: Voices of Homeless Children* by Judith Berck (1992) can be used together to offer factual information about the homeless and also to convey the feelings and human relationships involved. These books can lead to community-based projects in which children may become involved with homeless shelters or soup kitchens in their communities.

Informational books can support children's writing in the content areas. As children read varied books on social studies and science topics, they learn to appreciate how authors research topics, organize data, and write a stimulating, enjoyable book that maintains readers' interest. For example, Cynthia Rylant relied on her personal experiences to create *Appalachia: The Voices of Sleeping Birds* (1991), which is written in a narrative, lyrical style. On the other hand, Walter Dean Myers consulted books, journal articles, and historical documents and photographs in researching *Now Is Your Time! The African-American Struggle for Freedom* (1991). Hope Ryden traveled to Kenya to research and photograph the animals that appear in her book *Wild Animals of Africa ABC* (1989).

Freeman (1991) provides a detailed framework for using informational books in report writing. As children select topics, locate their sources, collect and record data, and determine the organization and format for their reports, informational books can serve as important models. For example, children may want to present their reports in an ABC format such as *Ashanti to Zulu: African Traditions* by Margaret Musgrove (1976), or in chronological order like *Volcano: The Eruption and Healing of Mount St. Helens* by Patricia Lauber (1986), or more conceptually such as *Immigrant Kids* by Russell Freedman (1980). Salesi (1992) discusses how informational books assist children in becoming more aware of text and language structures in expository writing. For example, she notes how Aliki in *The King's Day: Louis XIV of France* (1989) introduces French terms by using the definition or synonym in apposition.

Interests and Motivation

Literature can support children's interests and can motivate them to want to read. Teachers can develop a reading interest inventory to determine the main areas of children's interests, or they can interview children about their feelings and the topics and issues about which they want to learn. Even the most reluctant reader may be tempted to read a book if it is of interest. For example, many children are fascinated by aviation and flying. Books can build upon that curiosity and help children pursue the topic in more depth. *Flight: The Journey of Charles Lindbergh* by Robert Burleigh (1991) uses suspense, poetic language, and heightened emotions to let the reader travel across the Atlantic with Charles Lindbergh. Readers identify with Lindbergh and his thoughts during his flight and are eager to find out what happens to him: "He repeats over and over to himself: I must not sleep, I must not sleep. Here, high above the churning ocean, To sleep is to die!" As children's interest in early flight is piqued, they can explore the topic further by reading about how Wilbur and Orville built their plane in *The Wright Brothers: How They Invented the Airplane* by Russell Freedman (1991).

Another area of interest to students is animation. Many are curious about how cartoons on television and animated movies are created. In the book *Look Alive: Behind the Scenes of an Animated Film* by Elaine Scott (1992), readers learn about how the animated film version of *Ralph S. Mouse* by Beverly Cleary (1982) was made. This book describes all the steps necessary to transform an award-winning children's novel into an award-winning film. After reading the book, students may attempt their own animation of a favorite book or original story, using *Make Your Own Animated Movies and Videotapes* by Yvonne Andersen (1991) as a reference.

Humor in children's books helps to spark the interest of somewhat reluctant readers and to encourage their involvement with books. *The Magic School Bus* series (1986 to the present), written by Joanna Cole and illustrated by Bruce Degen, has used the humorous adventures of Ms. Frizzle and her class to introduce science and health topics to children. Readers follow Ms. Frizzle's class to the water works, inside the earth, inside the human body, into the solar system, on the ocean floor, and back to the time of the dinosaurs. Each book contains a wealth of information for children to respond to and extend in various ways.

Conclusion

Whatever the topic or the interest of students, a book can be found to expand and deepen children's knowledge. Through using children's literature across the elementary curriculum, students have the opportunity to gain facts and processes, develop critical thinking skills and empathy, see models of expository writing, and satisfy their curiosity about the world. Like a good friend, a good book supports the learning and living of all children.

References

Freeman, E. B. (1991). Informational books: Models for student report writing. *Language Arts, 68,* 470–73.

Huck, C. (1977). Literature as the content of reading. *Theory into Practice, 16,* 363–71.

Salesi, R. A. (1992). Reading and writing connection: Supporting content area literacy through nonfiction trade books. In E. B. Freeman & D. G. Person (Eds.), *Using nonfiction trade books in the elementary classroom: From ants to zeppelins* (pp. 86–94). Urbana, IL: National Council of Teachers of English.

Children's Books Cited

Aliki. (1989). *The king's day: Louis XIV of France.* Illus. by Author. New York: Thomas Y. Crowell.

Andersen, Yvonne. (1991). *Make your own animated movies and videotapes.* Boston: Little, Brown.

Anderson, Joan. (1991). *Christopher Columbus: From vision to voyage.* Photographs by George Ancona. New York: Dial Books.

Barboza, Steven. (1992). *I feel like dancing.* Photographs by Carolyn George d'Amboise. New York: Crown.

Bellville, Cheryl Walsh. (1986). *Theater magic: Behind the scenes at a children's theater.* Minneapolis: Carolrhoda Books.

Berck, Judith. (1992). *No place to be: Voices of homeless children.* Boston: Houghton Mifflin.

Björk, Christina. (1985). *Linnea in Monet's garden.* Illus. by Lena Anderson. New York: R & S Books.

Bunting, Eve. (1991). *Fly away home.* Illus. by Ronald Himmler. New York: Clarion Books.

Burleigh, Robert. (1991). *Flight: The journey of Charles Lindbergh.* Illus. by Mike Wimmer. New York: Philomel Books.

Cleary, Beverly. (1982). *Ralph S. Mouse.* Illus. by Paul O. Zelinsky. New York: William Morrow.

Cole, Joanna. (1986). *The magic school bus at the water works.* Illus. by Bruce Degen. New York: Scholastic.

———. (1987). *The magic school bus inside the earth.* Illus. by Bruce Degen. New York: Scholastic.

———. (1989). *The magic school bus inside the human body.* Illus. by Bruce Degen. New York: Scholastic.

———. (1990). *The magic school bus lost in the solar system.* Illus. by Bruce Degen. New York: Scholastic.

———. (1992). *The magic school bus on the ocean floor.* Illus. by Bruce Degen. New York: Scholastic.

———. (1994). *The magic school bus in the time of the dinosaurs.* Illus. by Bruce Degen. New York: Scholastic.

Ekoomiak, Normee. (1990). *Arctic memories.* Illus. by Author. New York: Henry Holt.

Fox, Paula. (1991). *Monkey Island.* New York: Orchard Books.

Freedman, Russell. (1980). *Immigrant kids.* New York: E. P. Dutton.

———. (1991). *The Wright brothers: How they invented the airplane.* New York: Holiday House.

Jenness, Aylette, & Rivers, Alice. (1989). *In two worlds: A Yup'ik Eskimo family.* Boston: Houghton Mifflin.

Kendall, Russ. (1992). *Eskimo boy: Life in an Inupiaq Eskimo village.* New York: Scholastic.

Krementz, Jill. (1991). *A very young musician.* New York: Simon & Schuster.

Lauber, Patricia. (1986). *Volcano: The eruption and healing of Mount St. Helens.* New York: Bradbury Press.

———. (1989). *The news about dinosaurs.* New York: Bradbury Press.

Levinson, Nancy Smiler. (1990). *Christopher Columbus: Voyager to the unknown.* New York: Lodestar Books.

Meltzer, Milton. (1990). *Columbus and the world around him.* New York: Franklin Watts.

Musgrove, Margaret. (1976). *Ashanti to Zulu: African traditions.* Illus. by Leo & Diane Dillon. New York: Dial.

Myers, Walter Dean. (1991). *Now is your time! The African-American struggle for freedom.* New York: HarperCollins.

Reynolds, Jan. (1991). *Himalaya: Vanishing cultures.* San Diego: Harcourt Brace Jovanovich.

———. (1991). *Sahara: Vanishing cultures.* San Diego: Harcourt Brace Jovanovich.

Ringgold, Faith. (1991). *Tar Beach.* Illus. by Author. New York: Crown.

Roop, Peter, & Roop, Connie (Eds.). (1990). *I, Columbus, my journal, 1492–3.* Illus. by Peter E. Hanson. New York: Walker.

Ryden, Hope. (1989). *Wild animals of Africa ABC.* New York: E. P. Dutton.

Rylant, Cynthia. (1991). *Appalachia: The voices of sleeping birds.* Illus. by Barry Moser. San Diego: Harcourt Brace Jovanovich.

Schwartz, David M. (1985). *How much is a million?* Illus. by Steven Kellogg. New York: Lothrop, Lee & Shepard Books.

———. (1989). *If You Made a Million.* Illus. by Steven Kellogg. New York: Lothrop, Lee & Shepard Books.

Scott, Elaine. (1992). *Look alive: Behind the scenes of an animated film.* New York: William Morrow.

Sills, Leslie. (1989). *Inspirations: Stories about women artists.* Niles, IL: Albert Whitman.

Sis, Peter. (1991). *Follow the dream.* Illus. by Author. New York: Albert A. Knopf.

Wheatley, Nadia, & Rawlins, Donna. (1987). *My place.* Long Beach, CA: Australia in Print.

21 Keeping the Reading Lights Burning

Peter Roop
McKinley Elementary School, Appleton, Wisconsin

When Anna, one of my second graders said, "Mr. Roop, where *do* you get all of these neat ideas?" I laughed. Her puzzled look allowed me to explain how good her comment made me feel, not only as coauthor of the book we were reading, *Keep the Lights Burning, Abbie* (Roop & Roop, 1985), but also as her teacher. She was responding to our book and to the activities I hoped would expand her experience with it.

As a third/fourth-grade teacher, I had been reluctant to share with my students the books Connie and I had written. I knew they would respond favorably to Beverly Cleary, E. B. White, or Jamie Gilson. But what if they did not like our books?

Connie, my wife and coauthor, who teaches experimentally based science classes, helped me overcome this obstacle. Reading fiction is a cornerstone of her science teaching. To get an A in her class, one has to read quality books with an environmental or science theme. Scott O'Dell's *Island of the Blue Dolphins* (1960), Jean Craighead George's *Julie of the Wolves* (1972), and Theodore Taylor's *The Weirdo* (1993) are just three of more than forty books on her science reading list.

Connie also encourages her students to write. One of her most successful projects is when her students examine an animal's life cycle and write a story or a poem, incorporating into their texts what they have learned in their reading. As a model for this approach, she uses our book *Seasons of the Cranes* (Roop & Roop, 1989) in which we followed the life of a fictional whooping crane family through a year. By using a structure similar to ours, many students found their writing improved when they presented information as a story or poem. Not only did the project promote students' conceptual learning, but they also became more successful writers.

Taking these cues from Connie, I brought our coauthored books into my third/fourth-grade class. We discussed characters, setting, and plot. I fielded questions. But somehow just sharing did not seem enough. Something more was needed.

The answer came one day in a writing lesson. "Why do we have to write a second draft?" Gary complained. I tried explaining that almost every author writes two, three, maybe twenty drafts. Reflecting on Gary's comment, I decided not just to tell the students about rewriting, but to *show* them. Armed with multiple drafts of *Keep the Lights Burning, Abbie*, I set out to convince Gary and his colleagues of the necessity of rewriting.

In planning this lesson, I thought back to the stages Connie and I had experienced from idea to writing through rewriting to publication. Then I guided my students through the process, explaining how we first got the idea while researching an article on Maine's islands, how the book began as fiction but evolved into nonfiction, how we wrote and rewrote *Abbie* ten times to get the thousand words just right, and how the book was published. Then I read the story to them.

Their reaction made me regret not having shared the book before. From then on, whenever we wrote stories, there was never a complaint about rewriting! I have since refined the lesson, retaining parts that appealed to the students and dropping parts that added little to their understanding.

When the opportunity to teach a combination first/second-grade class came along, I took it. Changing grade levels meant creating new lessons and invigorating my teaching through a literature-based approach to reading. I involve my students with books in reading, science, math, and social studies. Each day I read a book aloud to them and use every opportunity to link books with what we are studying. Our room is awash in books: current, theme-related books line the chalk rail; our "book castle" is overloaded with books to the point of collapsing; our counters are often covered with books; books fill our rolling library cart; desks are crammed with "missing" books.

A Teaching Unit for First/Second Graders

Creating a teaching unit for *Keep the Lights Burning, Abbie* helped me learn how to fashion other such units. In addition to using *Abbie* as a writing lesson, I wanted to expand my students' knowledge of islands, lighthouses, and life long ago. I wanted to incorporate other reading experiences, poetry, and art as we enjoyed *Abbie* together. Like every unit I create, this one evolves each year as I reflect on its success, receive feedback from students, and gain input from other educators.

Our class brainstorms before every in-depth book experience because I want to assess what the students already know and gear my teaching to incorporate this prior knowledge. Brainstorming helps us focus on and think about the topic. We develop a wall chart of topical words, which serves the additional purpose of allowing us to record new vocabulary we encounter. We also use the chart as a spelling aid when we write.

In preparation for reading *Abbie,* we inventoried all we knew about lighthouses. I had drawn a large lighthouse outline on white paper, which we filled with lighthouse words: *tall, shiny, white, saves ships, rocky, flashing, strong, bright, stairs, windows, ocean, see, sea, height, burning, lonely, powerful, night, foggy, storm.*

Then I read *Beacons of Light: Lighthouses* by Gail Gibbons (1990), which gave us insights into the uses of lighthouses and provided images of the different types of lighthouses. We added new words to our lighthouse word chart and discussed what life might have been like for those living in and taking care of lighthouses.

The following day I brought *Keep the Lights Burning, Abbie* and took my readers through the book's creation. They especially enjoyed the "sloppy copy" drafts. I then read the book, and we compared it with what we already knew about lighthouses and their caretakers.

The third day proved to be one of the unit's highlights, when students brought in flashlights for making their own lighthouses. I had planned for students to first learn a lighthouse poem; then we would build the model lighthouses. But the temptation to play with flashlights quickly altered my plans as soon as the first one "accidentally" switched on. Seizing the opportunity for a memorable lesson, I quickly turned off the overhead lights and let all the students turn on their flashlights. Within seconds the walls, ceiling, and children were covered with dancing beacons. Their excitement was almost as bright as the flashing lights. Now I had their attention (and their lights) focused on the poem hanging on the chalkboard: Rachel Field's (1957) "I'd Like to Be a Lighthouse."

I'd Like to Be a Lighthouse

I'd like to be a lighthouse
    All scrubbed and painted white.
I'd like to be a lighthouse
    And stay awake all night
To keep my eye on everything
    That sails my patch of sea;
I'd like to be a lighthouse
    With the ships all watching me. (p. 91)

Throughout the year we had memorized other poems related to topics we were studying, yet learning this one under wiggling flashlight beams added a new dimension, one which I hope will help them remember the poem all their lives.

Kyle suggested, "Let's blink our lights off and on like we learned in the lighthouse book." We quickly established our own lighthouse signal: two long flashes, followed by two short ones. In fact, we so enjoyed the poem and the flashlights that I had to postpone what I had perceived as the lesson's focus (making miniature lighthouses) until later that day. I still chuckle remembering my children chanting, "I'd Like to Be a Lighthouse," down the hall as they went to lunch.

We eventually made the lighthouses, after one more session with the lights and the poem. Later, using our lighthouse chart for words, we created a class lighthouse poem for a model before writing individual poems. We began with the word *lighthouse* and then selected five or six words to describe it, ending the poem with *lighthouse*. We then drafted our first copies on lined paper before writing our final versions on lighthouse-shaped paper. Kelly, a first grader, wrote the following poem:

> Lighthouse
> burning
> bright
> light
> at night
> white
> Lighthouse

The morning of the fourth day I began by rereading *Abbie* as all the children followed along in their own copies. I specifically asked the readers to spot things they had not seen before. It could be a detail from the story, the illustrator's perspective, a question about a character. I was flooded with responses: "Why is Abbie's boat called the *Puffin*?" "Could they have caught fish to eat?" "Why are Abbie and her sisters dressed that way?" "What disease did Abbie's mother have?" "Was the storm like the one we just had that blew down trees in my yard?" "How did you know what the lights looked like?" "Did Abbie have a flashlight like we do?" "Why are some pictures in color and others in black-and-white?"

With their questions and my answers still fresh, we turned to our next activity, writing letters to Abbie. We brainstormed what it would be like to get mail only twice a year and what we might write to Abbie if we were her friends.

On chart paper, I wrote the date and the year, *May 15, 1856,* for a model. I let each child pick a date for his or her letter (most picked their own birthdays). I had wondered just what my students' reactions would be in trying to think about someone who lived 150 years ago, knowing their sense of time is usually based on recess and lunch. As usual, they surprised me. Some enjoyed the time element, even figuring just how old they would be today if they really had been Abbie's friend in 1856 (144, Anna figured). Others expressed their concern over Abbie's mother or Abbie's lack of sleep during the lighthouse vigil. They all added their own questions for Abbie: "Do you make your bed?" "Can you come visit?" "How many books are in your library?" "Do you like to read? I do!" Did you get scared when your father went away?" "Do you use 'playdo'?" "Did you invent 'skool'?" "What was it like eating all those eggs? Was it good or was it 'grose'?" "How could you stay awake all night and watch the lighthouse?" One student, Jenny, wrote the following letter:

May 27, 1856

Dear Abbie,

How are you? I am fine. We get to go to school. Did your mother die? Why didn't you eat the chickens? What did it feel like eating eggs for a long time? How did your mother get sick? Vanessa, my sister would like to play with Mahala. Vanessa all ready knows her A,B,C's and she knows how to read too. Does Mahala have a favrite book?

Your friend

Jenny

With our letters completed (and photocopied), we addressed envelopes to Abbie Burgess, Matinicus Rock Lighthouse, Maine, and "mailed" them.

Capitalizing on the success of the letter writing, we then wrote in our journals that afternoon, pretending that Abbie was a friend and that we were writing about her.

Another highlight of the unit came on the fifth day, when it rained so hard we could not go out for recess. Jenny, Cathy, and Anna asked if they could borrow a copy of the book for a "project" they were doing. It was clear that they wanted to create a surprise. They worked on the "project" whenever they had spare time during the day, and before we went home they treated the class to a lights-out, lighthouse performance of the chicken scene from the book. They had even incorporated a singing version of "I'd Like to Be a Lighthouse," getting the tune from the music teacher.

The sixth day we discussed the key scenes from the book in order to write our own "circle" stories. As we decided which scenes were the most important, I wrote them on the board. We cut large circles and folded them to get eight "pizza pie" triangles. At the edge of each triangle we wrote one of the sentences and then illustrated each scene.

Our study of *Keep the Lights Burning, Abbie* concluded with our viewing the *Reading Rainbow* program that featured the book. As an educator and an author, I find that seeing the involvement of my own students with *Abbie* reinforces my belief in the value of rich literary experiences in keeping those reading lights burning brightly in young readers.

Now I might even bring more of our books into my classroom!

Children's Books Cited

Field, Rachel. (1957). "I'd like to be a lighthouse." In *Poems*. Illus. by author. New York: Macmillan.

George, Jean Craighead. (1972). *Julie of the wolves*. New York: Harper & Row.

Gibbons, Gail. (1990). *Beacons of light: Lighthouses*. Illus. by Author. New York: William Morrow.

O'Dell, Scott. (1960). *Island of the blue dolphins*. Boston: Houghton Mifflin.

Roop, Peter, & Roop, Connie. (1985). *Keep the lights burning, Abbie*. Illus. by Peter E. Hanson. Minneapolis: Carolrhoda Books.

———. (1989). *Seasons of the cranes*. New York: Walker.

Taylor, Theodore. (1993). *The weirdo*. New York: Avon.

22 "Joyful Noises" across the Curriculum: Confessions of a Would-Be Poetry Teacher

Joel D. Chaston
Southwest Missouri State University

"Why do we have to study poetry?" It was my second week of student teaching, and I had just announced to a group of high school seniors that we were about to embark on a poetry unit. I had become very excited when my cooperating teacher told me that I was to cover modern British poetry. After all, I had taken graduate courses in British literature and had aspirations of becoming a poet. It never occurred to me that I might have to explain why poetry was important to my students—it just was.

The student asking the question planned on going into business. What good would it do for him to study British poetry, he wanted to know. I suggested that one can learn about language from reading poetry, that poetry deals with important human emotions, and that it helps readers see the world in new ways, and so we proceeded. We wrote poems in the school courtyard and read T. S. Eliot's "The Hollow Men," discussing its possible allusions to Guy Fawkes Day and *The Wizard of Oz.* But in the long run, I am afraid that I never managed to convert my students to the value of reading poetry.

A couple years later, I found myself teaching sixth and seventh graders in a middle school. I was still convinced that my students ought to have a good dose of poetry. Poetry was a required subject; the district guidelines mandated computerized pretests and posttests to assess students' knowledge of poetic terms. I should have been prepared for the reception I received when I announced we would be reading poetry. "Why do we have to study poetry again?" the class complained. "We studied poetry last year. Our teacher even made us write haikus—yuch!" My approach this time was to suggest that poetry was "fun," and during the next few weeks we *did* have fun. We wrote collaborative poems and read Shel Silverstein's *A Light in the Attic* (1981), which many students already knew and loved, and *Reflections on a Gift of Watermelon Pickle, and Other Modern Verse,* a collection compiled by Stephen Dunning, Edward Lueders, and Hugh Smith (1967).

During the years since I first tried to teach poetry, I have never given up the notion that it is important. The question is, however, how can I help my students feel that poetry is meaningful to them? I can still remember the first time I read William Wordsworth's frequently quoted definition of poetry. Poetry, he explains, is "the spontaneous overflow of powerful feelings" which are "recollected in tranquility." It seems to me that a key to teaching poetry is to help students experience some of these powerful feelings.

Armed with books as diverse as *The Way to Start a Day* by Byrd Baylor (1978), *Sing a Song of Popcorn: Every Child's Book of Poems,* compiled by Beatrice Schenk de Regniers and others (1988), and *Goodnight Moon* by Margaret Wise Brown (1947), I have worked with students, helping them to discover that poetry is valuable and meaningful whether they plan on becoming truck drivers, accountants, or English professors. In using these books in the classroom, there are a few principles that I now try to keep in mind. First, students should be helped to see how poetry relates to their personal experiences, to other forms of literature, and to all areas of the curriculum. Second, children and young adults need to be exposed to poetry of all kinds and varieties. At the same time, they should be helped to appreciate the language and music of poetry. Finally, students should be encouraged to respond to poetry in a variety of ways, through music, drama, art, and dance as well as literature.

Relevance of Poetry

As I found out when I tried to teach poetry while student teaching, children and young adults often feel that reading poetry is like deciphering hieroglyphics. Poetry, they sometimes say, is written only by dead people and has nothing to do with them personally. Besides, it is only about flowers and lovesick goons. Unfortunately, many students have not been exposed to poetry dealing with subjects that concern them. Several years ago, my college class in adolescent literature was discussing poetry after reading from Richard Peck's *Sounds and Silences: Poetry for Here and Now* (1970), an anthology divided into topics such as "Childhood," "Isolation," "Dissent," and "Pain." Each student had been asked to find a poem in the book that he or she liked and then to discuss it with the class. That particular day just happened to be the morning after the Gulf War began. One after another my students chose poems and songs like "Where Have All the Flowers Gone?" "Naming of Parts," and "Of Bombs and Boys," poems about war and peace, poems that suddenly became meaningful in the context of current events.

Poetry, of course, also relates to readers in less dramatic ways. When my son, Brad, was younger, his favorite book was Margaret Wise Brown's *Goodnight Moon* (1947), a picture book poem in which a rabbit says goodnight to all of the objects in his bedroom. Like countless other readers, Brad found great comfort in imitating the rabbit in the book, bidding goodnight to everything around him and repeating the book's last line, "Goodnight noises everywhere." Something about the ritual in the poem helped Brad go to sleep. Similarly, many of my current students enjoy the sense of security suggested by a more recent picture book poem, *Owl Moon* (1987) by Jane Yolen, which celebrates one moment of closeness when a father and daughter go owling.

Poetry in Children's Books

A number of poetry books seem perfect for helping students see that poetry is relevant to their lives and concerns. In the last few years, several illustrated anthologies have been produced that feature poems grouped together by theme or topic. For example, *The Random House Book of Poetry for Children* (1983), edited by Jack Prelutsky, presents groups of poems about nature, holidays, animals, food, childhood experiences, family relationships, fantasy, and the alphabet. It includes many old standbys, such as Robert Louis Stevenson's "Windy Nights" and "From a Railway Carriage" and Eugene Field's "The Duel," as well as contemporary verses about pizza, television westerns, homework, skateboarding, skyscrapers, and freeways. Nearly every one of the 572 poems in the volume is accompanied by a small drawing by Caldecott medalist Arnold Lobel.

Since the publication of this book, several similar anthologies have appeared. Among the best is a revised version of *Poems Children Will Sit Still For* (1969), now titled *Sing a Song of Popcorn: Every Child's Book of Poems* (compiled by Beatrice Schenk de Regniers et al., 1988). Newly illustrated by nine Caldecott medalists, it has sections of poems about weather, the supernatural, nonsense, animals, people, and the senses, as well as others featuring long narrative poems and very short verses. While these books are geared toward older readers, two similar anthologies are excellent introductions for very young children. *Read-Aloud Rhymes for the Very Young* (1986), edited by Jack Prelutsky and illustrated by Marc Brown, and *Talking Like the Rain: A First Book of Poems* (1992), edited by X. J. Kennedy and Dorothy M. Kennedy and illustrated by Jane Dyer, also are divided into thematic sections with short poems that reflect the experience and emotions of young children.

There are also a number of exceptional picture book versions of single poems. These books help young readers visualize the events or ideas described in the poems, in many cases heightening a poem's appeal through illustrations. One of my favorite book poems is Susan Jeffers's version of Robert Frost's *Stopping by Woods on a Snowy Evening* (1978), a book whose illustrations reflect the mysterious nature of the original poem. Similarly effective is illustrator Ed Young's treatment of Robert Frost's *Birches* (1988). Other well-known poems that have become picture books include an edition of Lewis Carroll's classic *Jabberwocky* illustrated by Jane Breskin Zalben (1977), Longfellow's *Hiawatha* (1983), illustrated by Susan Jeffers, and Longfellow's *Paul Revere's Ride* (1963), illustrated by Paul Galdone.

Of course, narrative poems are the basis of some of the most popular and enduring picture books for younger readers. Children are attracted to stories and narrative poems that link fiction and lyric poetry, oftentimes engaging the reader in the joy of language. Dr. Seuss's many books of nonsense verse are, of course, still popular. However, I have successfully used with kindergartners and first graders an even older picture book, Wanda Gág's *Millions of Cats*. First published in 1928, this story still appeals to children, particularly with its repeated poetic refrain and suggestion that seemingly insignificant creatures really may be the most "beautiful" ones. When I have read this book in elementary schools, the children invariably chant along, and the book promotes discussion of pets and animals.

Extending Poetry into Content Areas

In the classroom, it seems important to help readers see that poetry relates to other content areas. Several years ago, I periodically visited a first-grade classroom in Conway, Missouri, for six weeks as part of an attempt to integrate reading and writing into science instruction. Eventually, the project focused on meteorology. The class read books about weather forecasters, thunderstorms, snow, the water cycle, and so forth. The children wrote stories and reports, including personal accounts of the effects of a tornado in their town. Several times, however, we concentrated on poetry. I brought in poems about rain and wind, including Rhoda Bachmeister's "Galoshes" and Christina Rossetti's "Who Has Seen the Wind?" The children clearly liked the poems we read; they chanted repeated lines and gathered favorite words from the poems for use in writing their own poems. Eventually, our efforts were "published" in a class magazine.

Several books by award-winning children's poets have treated topics related to areas of science besides meteorology. Traditionally, animals have been favorite topics of poetry for the young. Paul Fleischman's *I Am Phoenix: Poems for Two Voices* (1985) treats a variety of birds, while his *Joyful Noise: Poems for Two Voices* (1988) celebrates insects. "Chrysalis Diary," in the latter book, which won the 1989 Newbery Medal, portrays the transformation of a caterpillar into a butterfly from the insect's point of view. "Honey Bees" explores the life of bees from two perspectives, that of a worker and a queen, while "Book Lice" portrays two insects with distinct literary tastes. Jack Prelutsky's *Zoo Doings: Animal Poems* (1983) presents a humorous look at various animals.

Poetry can also be easily integrated into social studies. Several anthologies highlight poems from various countries and cultures. *Zero Always Makes Me Hungry: A Collection of Poems for Today* (1976), edited by Edward Lueders and Primus St. John, is an excellent collection of poems for high school students, containing several translated from other languages. I have used *I Never Saw Another Butterfly: Children's Drawings and Poems from Terezín Concentration Camp, 1942–1944*, edited by Hana Volavková (1993), after teaching Lois Lowry's World War II novel, *Number the Stars* (1989). The title poem, "The Butterfly," clearly reveals pain associated with life in a concentration camp. Byrd Baylor's *When Clay Sings* (1972), which introduces children to the stories depicted on Native American pottery, and *The Way to Start A Day* (1978), which describes how people from different cultures greet the sunrise, effectively combine illustrations and text. Eloise Greenfield's *Honey, I Love, and Other Love Poems* (1978) and Nikki Giovanni's *Spin a Soft Black Song* (1985) both highlight the experience and feelings of being African American in the United States.

A number of historical events have also been turned into verse. For example, Arnold Lobel's *On the Day Peter Stuyvesant Sailed into Town* (1971) is a comical introduction to life and politics in New Amsterdam of the 1600s. Alice Provensen's *The Buck Stops Here: The Presidents of the United States* (1991) presents each president in a short counting rhyme accompanied by portraits that illustrate his accomplishments and failures. The customs surrounding many holidays and cultural events are frequent topics of children's poetry. *The Family Read-Aloud Christmas Treasury* (1989), edited by Alice Lowe and illustrated by Marc Brown, features traditional carols as well as poems by writers as diverse as Christina Rossetti, John Updike, and Langston Hughes. Jack Prelutsky has mined American holidays for humor in books such as *It's Halloween* (1977), *It's Christmas* (1981), *It's Thanksgiving* (1982), and *It's Valentine's Day* (1983). Myra Cohn Livingston's *Celebrations* (1985) includes poems for virtually every major American holiday.

Mathematics, too, sometimes finds its way into poetry for children and young adults. For example, "Arithmetic," a frequently anthologized poem by Carl Sandburg, captures the frustrations that children sometimes feel when "numbers fly like pigeons in and out of [their] head" (in the Dunning et al. collection, 1966, p. 58). Numbers, of course, are an integral part of many folk rhymes, such as those collected in Alvin Schwartz's *And the Green Grass Grew All Round: Folk Poetry from Everyone* (1992).

Illustrated poems about colors and artists could supplement art lessons. One of my favorite poetry books, Mary O'Neill's *Hailstones and Halibut Bones*, which first appeared in 1961, still remains popular and was republished with illustrations by John Wallner in 1989. This book includes poems for virtually every color. For example, "What Is Green?" gives the definition of the color through words, objects, and feelings, such as coolness, spring, jade, olives, pickles, water trickles, peppermint, meadows, fuzz, ivy, and shade. Nancy Willard's *A Visit to William Blake's Inn: Poems for Innocent and Experienced Travelers* (1981) and *Pish, Posh, Said Hieronymus Bosch* (1991) provide readers with humorous introductions to British painter and poet William Blake and Dutch painter Hieronymus Bosch. Kenneth Koch and Kate Farrell have edited a superb collection of poetry, *Talking to the Sun: An Illustrated Anthology of Poems for Young People* (1985), which is illustrated with paintings and artifacts from the Metropolitan Museum of Art. This collection emphasizes poetry that will appeal to young readers from poets representing many countries and cultures. A number of poems are also accompanied by brief comments that help the reader understand their poetic qualities.

The topics of poetry for children and young adults are endless. Food is the subject of a number of collections, as in Arnold Adoff's *Eats: Poems* (1979) and his more recent *Chocolate Dreams* (1989). The latter contains forty-nine poems about chocolate, including "Let the Biter Beware," about the dangerous caramel centers of some chocolates, and "I Raise My Voice Most High, This Night," which celebrates Milk Duds. Sports and games, too, are frequent subjects of anthologies, including Adoff's *Sports Pages* (1986) and R. R. Knudsen and P. K. Ebert's collection of verse for older students, *Sports Poems* (1971). School itself is the subject of Mel Glen's *Class Dismissed: High School Poems* (1982), a collection of vignettes from young adults' points of view. Kali Dakos's *If You're Not Here, Raise Your Hand: Poems about School* (1990), for younger readers, features humorous poems about substitute teachers, messy desks, forgotten homework, and endless worksheets.

I have also discovered that nonfiction books can help students generate ideas for poetry. A former colleague, Connie Weaver, introduced me to Tomie dePaola's *The Popcorn Book* (1978), with which she has led students to write poems about popcorn. While both Connie and I generally believe in encouraging children to choose their own topics for writing, books of all varieties can generate background material useful in creating poetry.

I do not mean to suggest, however, that poetry should be used mechanically as part of lesson plans. Poetry should be enjoyed for its own sake, and much of its pleasure comes from its music and language. A year ago, a group of my college students worked through Nancy Larrick's *Let's Do a Poem: Introducing Poetry to Children* (1991), in which poems are grouped that lend themselves to singing, chanting, choral reading, dance, and drama. In her excellent commentary in the book, Larrick suggests that "the modern Child's love of poetry depends largely upon hearing the poems read aloud and then becoming actively involved in the musical language of the poems" (p. 2). In her first chapter, Larrick provides a bibliography of song books for children, all useful for introducing poetry and its music to young readers.

The words of poetry are also part of its pleasures. Nonsense poems that play with language, including works by Carroll and Lear, are available in many editions. Ogden Nash's *The Adventures of Isabel* (1991) has been reissued with cartoon-like illustrations by James Marshall that effectively complement the text. Shel Silverstein's and Jack Prelutsky's collections of humorous verse are best-sellers, dispelling the notion that poetry is completely unpopular. Interestingly, Ann Terry's (1974) study of children's poetry preferences argues that children's favorite poems are both humorous and musical.

Many poems can be related to other forms of literature and might be read along with them. When I have students read Mollie Hunter's *A Stranger Came Ashore* (1975), we also read "The Selchie's Midnight Song" and "Ballad of the White Seal Maid" from Jane Yolen's *Neptune Rising* (1982). Like Hunter's novel, Yolen's poems explore the tension between land and sea, the pastoral and the industrial, and also feature "selchies," seals who come to shore and take human form.

Although I could continue listing poetry books for children and young adults, the point is that many good books help dispel stereotypes about the inaccessibility and irrelevance of poetry. These books can help students discover a variety of poetic forms and genres, fostering personal experience and close reading that will keep poetry alive. Hopefully, teachers will not be dismayed by students' preconceptions about poetry and will help them discover what Paul Fleischman describes as the "Joyful Noise" of contemporary poetry for children and young adults.

References

Terry, A. (1974). *Children's poetry preferences: A national survey of upper elementary grades.* Urbana, IL: National Council of Teachers of English.

Children's Books Cited

Adoff, Arnold. (1979). *Eats: Poems.* Illus. by Susan Russo. New York: Lothrop, Lee & Shepard Books.

———. (1986). *Sports pages.* Illus. by Steve Kuzma. New York: J. B. Lippincott.

———. (1989). *Chocolate dreams.* Illus. by Turi MacCombie. New York: Lothrop, Lee & Shepard Books.

Baylor, Byrd. (1972). *When clay sings.* New York: Charles Scribner's Sons.

———. (1978). *The way to start a day.* New York: Macmillan.

Brown, Margaret Wise. (1947). *Goodnight moon.* Illus. by Clement Hurd. New York: Harper & Row.

Carroll, Lewis. (1977). *Jabberwocky.* Illus. by Jane Breskin Zalben. New York: Frederick Warne.

Dakos, Kali. (1992). *If you're not here, please raise your hand: Poems about school.* New York: Macmillan.

dePaola, Tomie. (1978). *The popcorn book.* Illus. by Author. New York: Holiday House.

de Regniers, Beatrice Schenk, Moore, Eva, White, Mary Michaels, & Carr, Jan (Comps.). (1988). *Sing a song of popcorn: Every child's book of poems.* New York: Scholastic. (Original work published 1969 as *Poems children will sit still for*)

Dunning, Stephen, Lueders, Edward, & Smith, Hugh. (Eds.). (1967). *Reflections on a gift of watermelon pickle, and other modern verse.* New York: Lothrop, Lee & Shepard Books.

Fleischman, Paul. (1985). *I am phoenix: Poems for two voices.* New York: Harper & Row.

———. (1988). *Joyful noise: Poems for two voices.* New York: Harper & Row.

Frost, Robert. (1978). *Stopping by woods on a snowy evening.* Illus. by Susan Jeffers. New York: E. P. Dutton.

———. (1988). *Birches.* Illus. by Ed Young. New York: Holt, Rinehart & Winston.

Gág, Wanda. (1928). *Millions of cats.* Illus. by Author. New York: Coward-McCann.

Giovanni, Nikki. (1985). *Spin a soft black song* (Rev. ed.). Illus. by George Martins. New York: Hill & Wang.

Glen, Mel. (1982). *Class dismissed: High school poems.* New York: Clarion Books.

Greenfield, Eloise. (1978). *Honey, I love, and other love poems.* New York: Harper & Row.

Hunter, Mollie. (1975). *A stranger came ashore*. New York: Harper & Row.

Kennedy, X. J., & Kennedy, Dorothy M. (Eds.) (1992). *Talking like the rain: A first book of poems*. Illus. by Jane Dyer. Boston: Little, Brown.

Knudsen, R. R., & Ebert, P. K. (1971). *Sports poems*. New York: Dell.

Koch, Kenneth, & Farrell, Kate. (1985). *Talking to the sun: An illustrated anthology of poems for young people*. New York: Metropolitan Museum of Art/Henry Holt.

Larrick, Nancy. (1991). *Let's do a poem: Introducing poetry to children*. New York: Delacorte.

Livingston, Myra Cohen. (1985). *Celebrations*. Illus. by Leonard Everett Fisher. New York: Holiday House.

Lobel, Arnold. (1971). *On the day Peter Stuyvesant sailed into town*. Illus. by Author. New York: Harper & Row.

Longfellow, Henry Wadsworth. (1963). *Paul Revere's ride*. Illus. by Paul Galdone. New York: Thomas Y. Crowell.

———. (1983). *Hiawatha*. Illus. by Susan Jeffers. New York: E. P. Dutton.

Lowe, Alice. (1989). *The family read-aloud Christmas treasury*. Illus. by Marc Brown. Boston: Little, Brown.

Lowry, Lois. (1989). *Number the stars*. Boston: Houghton Mifflin.

Lueders, Edward, & St. John, Primus. (Eds.). (1976). *Zero always makes me hungry: A collection of poems for today*. New York: Lothrop, Lee & Shepard Books.

Nash, Ogden. (1991). *The adventures of Isabel*. Illus. by James Marshall. Boston: Little, Brown.

O'Neill, Mary. (1989). *Hailstones and halibut bones* (Rev. ed.). Illus. by John Wallner. New York: Doubleday.

Peck, Richard. (Ed.). (1970). *Sounds and silences: Poetry for now*. New York: Delacorte.

Prelutsky, Jack. (1977). *It's Halloween*. Illus. by Marylin Hafner. New York: Greenwillow Books.

———. (1981). *It's Christmas*. New York: William Morrow.

———. (1982). *It's Thanksgiving*. Illus. by Marylin Hafner. New York: Greenwillow Books.

———. (1983). *It's Valentine's Day*. Illus. by Yossi Abolafia. New York: Greenwillow Books.

———. (1983). *Zoo doings: Animal poems*. Illus. by Paul O. Zelinsky. New York: Greenwillow Books.

Prelutsky, Jack (Ed.). (1983). *The Random House book of poetry for children*. Illus. by Arnold Lobel. New York: Random House.

———. (1986). *Read-aloud rhymes for the very young*. Illus. by Marc Brown. New York: Alfred A. Knopf.

Provensen, Alice. (1991). *The buck stops here: The presidents of the United States*. Illus. by Author. New York: HarperCollins.

Schwartz, Alvin. (1992). *And the green grass grew all around: Folk poetry from everyone*. Illus. by Sue Truesdell. New York: HarperCollins.

Silverstein, Shel. (1981). *A light in the attic*. Illus. by Author. New York: Harper & Row.

Volavková, Hana (Ed.). (1993). *I never saw another butterfly: Children's drawings and poems from Terezín concentration camp, 1942–1944* (2nd ed.). New York: Pantheon.

Willard, Nancy. (1981). *A visit to William Blake's inn: Poems for innocent and experienced travelers*. Illus. by Alice & Martin Provensen. New York: Harcourt Brace Jovanovich.

———. (1991). *Pish, posh, said Hieronymus Bosch*. Illus. by the Dillons. San Diego: Harcourt Brace Jovanovich.

Yolen, Jane. (1982). *Neptune rising: Songs and tales of the undersea folk*. New York: Philomel Books.

———. (1987). *Owl moon*. Illus. by John Schoenherr. New York: Philomel Books.

23 Literary Tapestry: An Integrated Primary Curriculum

Peggy Oxley
St. Paul School, Westerville, Ohio

When my thirty-five second-grade students and I gather on the carpet to start each day, we discuss our current unit themes and what contributions each individual can make. As we share books and information in this daily class meeting, we see our investigations grow. My literature-based reading and writing program has evolved over the last ten years into a tapestry of themes. The curriculum now is woven of units consonant with our district courses of study and enriched by fine literature integrated throughout all subject areas. Although I begin each school year with an outline of topics we will cover, the children and I plan and expand the themes together.

Our varied themes include many disciplines—social studies, science, literature, and language arts. Frequently, one study dovetails nicely into the next, demonstrating relationships among subject areas in school as in life. For example, a recent theme was "Strangers in a Strange New Land," a study of migrations. Migrants included people, plants, and animals living in changed locations for natural, scientific, or historic reasons. Our largest focus was on people: Native Americans, pioneers, and immigrants from many lands. Literature for our study included such books as *When Africa Was Home* by Karen Lynn Williams (1991), *Watch the Stars Come Out* by Riki Levinson (1985), *Babushka's Doll* by Patricia Polacco (1990), and *The Potato Man* by Megan McDonald (1991). Multiple copies of such books as *Molly's Pilgrim* by Barbara Cohen (1990) and *The Long Way Westward* by Joan Sandin (1989) allowed for small-group discussions centered on specific immigrant experiences. We also invited people who had journeyed to America from other lands to visit us and share their memories of adjusting to a new country.

Animal and plant migrants provided a second focus for study. *City Geese* by Ron Hirschi (1987) and other books illustrated migrations of animals continually adapting to new surroundings. Books like *The Comeback Dog* by Jane Resh Thomas (1984) about stray animals that have involuntarily changed homes were shared and became the basis for much poignant writing by the children. Even plants that have invaded new areas—such as the California poppy, now threatening to replace some of Washington State's native flora—were investigated.

Based on this study, the class created a "Strangers in a Strange New Land" mural, which filled the wall outside our classroom. Their centerpiece was a collage representation of a scene from *When Africa Was Home* shown with pride to Floyd Cooper, the book's illustrator, when he visited our school. Surrounding the center were brightly colored reproductions of covers from many of the books in our study and the children's written and artistic responses to those books. A display of stray animal stories explained each piece's relevance to our theme. As the children reported their findings and cooperated with each other on our mural's creation, they slowly assimilated material from their studies and from the source books to which they returned for help.

After concluding "Strangers in a Strange New Land," we were ready to discover through a "Then and Now" unit how our early immigrant pioneers settled this new land, and to compare life in times long gone to our ways of life today. Background for small-group discussions was supplied through multiple copies of *Bread and Butter Journey* by Anne Colver (1970), *Pioneer Cat* by William H. Hooks (1988), and *Wagon Wheels* by Barbara Brenner (1978). *Aurora Means Dawn* by Scott Russell Sanders (1989), *Yonder* by Tony Johnston (1988), *Going West* by Jean Van Leeuwen (1992), and *My Prairie Christmas* by Brett Harvey (1990) were four books used by the whole class for our study. From these books we gained rich information and a feel for the strength and courage it took to establish a new life in lands far from home.

Several smaller, adjunct studies connected with these two major themes. So much of our study had concerned rural life that we felt it appropriate to compare farms and farming then and now. Some of the books we used were *Farming* by Gail Gibbons (1988), *Heartland* by Diane Siebert (1989), *On Granddaddy's Farm* by Thomas B. Allen (1989), and *The Midnight Farm* by Reeve Lindbergh (1987). From the books and from discussions of our own experiences, we built an awareness of both the joys and frustrations of farming, and of its importance to us all. Raising our own windowsill garden further strengthened our understanding and led to our reading books such as *Linnea's Windowsill Garden* by Christina Björk (1978) and *Bugs* by Nancy Winslow Parker and Joan Richards Wright (1987), which helped explain why such creatures are so important to farmers.

Throughout all our studies, we noticed the importance of weather and the cycle of changing seasons. As our interest in these phenomena grew, we developed related thematic units on weather, climate, and seasons as they have affected life in America. We were aided in our understanding by well-crafted books such as *Weather Words* by Gail Gibbons (1990), *The Cloud Book* by Tomie dePaola (1975), *Storms* by Seymour Simon (1989), and *Tornado* by Arnold Adoff (1977). Video cassettes, observations, and discussions of personal experiences increased our awareness of weather's importance, along with Ron Hirschi's seasonal books: *Spring* (1990), *Summer* (1991), *Fall* (1991), and *Winter* (1991). We focused part of these studies on our "class tree" actually growing outside our window. Visiting, observing, and discussing the tree through the changing weather and seasons gave us concrete experience with the effects of these elements. The children each wrote about the tree and represented it in various artistic media throughout the year, creating several classroom displays of their work. At year's end, they collected their individual writings and illustrations into books for their own future rereading. Outstanding books are available to help study trees, such as *Tree Trunk Traffic* by Bianca Lavies (1989), *Tree* by David Burnie (1988), *The Gift of the Tree* by Alvin Tresselt (1992), *Once There Was a Tree* by Natalia Romanova (1985), and *A B CEDAR: An Alphabet of Trees* by George Ella Lyon (1989).

In our classroom, one thematic study leads to and blends with the next, providing connections between and among subjects. These overlapping links make clear the interdependence of events in history and in our lives, and demonstrate that disciplines are not fragmented units but rather parts of a universal whole. These studies are embedded with literature, which provides experiences that endure and enrich our lives. Indeed, we are building a literary tapestry of understanding.

Children's Books Cited

Adoff, Arnold. (1977). *Tornado! Poems*. New York: Delacorte Press.

Allen, Thomas B. (1989). *On granddaddy's farm*. Illus. by Author. New York: Alfred A. Knopf.

Björk, Christina. (1978). *Linnea's windowsill garden*. Illus. by Lena Anderson. Stockholm: R & S Books.

Brenner, Barbara. (1978). *Wagon wheels*. Illus. by Don Bolognese. New York: Harper & Row.

Burnie, David. (1988). *Tree* (Eyewitness series). New York: Alfred A. Knopf.

Cohen, Barbara. (1990). *Molly's pilgrim*. Illus. by Michael J. Deraney. New York: Bantam Books.

Colver, Anne. (1970). *Bread and butter journey.* Illus. by Garth Williams. New York: Avon Books.

dePaola, Tomie. (1975). *The cloud book.* Illus. by Author. New York: Scholastic.

Gibbons, Gail. (1988). *Farming.* Illus. by Author. New York: Holiday House.

———. (1990). *Weather words.* Illus. by Author. New York: Holiday House.

Harvey, Brett. (1990). *My prairie Christmas.* Illus. by Deborah Kogan Ray. New York: Holiday House.

Hirschi, Ron. (1987). *City geese.* Illus. by Galen Burrell. New York: Dodd, Mead.

———. (1990). *Spring.* Illus. by Thomas D. Mangelsen. New York: Cobblehill Books.

———. (1991). *Fall.* Illus. by Thomas D. Mangelsen. New York: Cobblehill Books.

———. (1991). *Summer.* Illus. by Thomas D. Mangelsen. New York: Cobblehill Books.

———. (1991). *Winter.* Illus. by Thomas D. Mangelsen. New York: Cobblehill Books.

Hooks, William H. (1988). *Pioneer cat.* Illus. by Charles Robinson. New York: Random House.

Johnston, Tony. (1988). *Yonder.* Illus. by Lloyd Bloom. New York: Dial Books.

Lavies, Bianca. (1989). *Tree trunk traffic.* New York: E. P. Dutton.

Levinson, Riki. (1985). *Watch the stars come out.* Illus. by Diane Good. New York: E. P. Dutton.

Lindbergh, Reeve. (1987). *The midnight farm.* Illus. by Susan Jeffers. New York: Dial Books.

Lyon, George Ella. (1989). *A B Cedar: An alphabet of trees.* Illus. by Tom Parker. New York: Orchard Books.

McDonald, Megan. (1991). *The potato man.* Illus. by Ted Lewin. New York: Orchard Books.

Parker, Nancy Winslow, & Wright, Joan Richards. (1987). *Bugs.* Illus. by Nancy Winslow Parker. New York: Greenwillow Books.

Polacco, Patricia. (1990). *Babushka's doll.* Illus. by Author. New York: Simon & Schuster.

Romanova, Natalia. (1985). *Once there was a tree.* Illus. by Gennady Spirin. New York: Dial Books.

Sanders, Scott Russell. (1989). *Aurora means dawn.* Illus. by Jill Kastner. New York: Bradbury Press.

Sandin, Joan. (1989). *The long way westward.* New York: Harper & Row.

Siebert, Diane. (1989). *Heartland.* Illus. by Wendell Minor. New York: Thomas Y. Crowell.

Simon, Seymour. (1989). *Storms.* New York: William Morrow.

Thomas, Jane Resh. (1984). *The comeback dog.* Illus. by Troy Howell. New York: Bantam Books.

Tresselt, Alvin. (1992). *The gift of the tree.* Illus. by Henri Sorensen. New York: Lothrop, Lee & Shepard Books.

Van Leeuwen, Jean. (1992). *Going west.* Illus. by Thomas B. Allen. New York: Dial Books.

Williams, Karen Lynn. (1991). *When Africa was home.* Illus. by Floyd Cooper. New York: Orchard Books.

VI Collaborating

Collaborating with Children on Theme Studies

Linda Lamme
University of Florida

s Shannon Jones's second-grade class walked to their new portable classroom, students came upon a nest of abandoned baby rabbits whose home had been displaced by preparation for new school construction. Examining the nest, they saw that one rabbit already had died, but two little ones remained alive. Immediately the students discussed how to save the rabbits. They brainstormed where they could find information about the care of baby rabbits. Some students searched for books about rabbits in the media center. Others telephoned a local veterinarian for information. They asked the librarian to purchase some suitable food at a nearby feed store. For three weeks the class nursed these baby rabbits, read every book they could find about rabbits, wrote about rabbits, drew rabbits, sang rabbit songs, and generally immersed themselves in the study of rabbits. When the babies were released to the wild, the students felt as though they really had accomplished something.

How different Shannon's theme study on rabbits evolved compared to many theme studies totally planned in advance by teachers. When teachers plan units, find the resources, design the learning experiences, and schedule the field trips or activities, they own the resulting instruction. Children participate in it and in most cases enjoy it, but their learning is classified as "schoolwork," with assignments completed to please the teacher. Teachers never know whether the skills learned can be applied to real-life information quests. It is not every day that we come upon rabbits in an abandoned nest, creating an authentic need for information and study, but if we build our thematic studies with children, we can replicate Shannon's experience and give children a sense of curricular ownership. We can teach strategies for finding resources and compiling information that will be more authentic and usable when students need to apply those strategies to learning situations that occur at home.

This chapter addresses how teachers can collaborate with children in planning and teaching literature-based studies. It is written in response to several practices prevalent in schools today where teachers spend hours, even days, planning thematic studies, coming up with objectives, activities, resources, and evaluation strategies. When teachers collaborate with children, not only is the job easier, but children gain partial ownership in the curriculum and thereby become more seriously engaged in learning.

Why Collaboration?

Why is it important for students to have opportunities to collaborate and not just work as individuals or as a whole class under direct teacher instruction? Collaboration is a key factor in the social-constructivist approach to learning. Newman (1991) explains that "collaboration is at the heart of any enterprise-based curriculum" (p. 96). When children collaborate, they have many opportunities to test what they are learning and how they are learning with their peers. They typically remember and apply at length information discovered through interactions with their peers. Learning is more permanent because students have a broader context with which to link their own knowledge and to construct their own learning that makes sense to them.

Collaboration provides students with support they need when they are confronted with moderately challenging tasks. Within a group, some students can help others right at the point where that help is most needed and appreciated. Helping others validates one's own knowledge, so collaboration helps both the provider and the receiver. Negotiation and consensus building help determine the social value of an individual's knowledge. They help children make sense of learning.

A Collaborative Model of Curriculum Planning

In literature-based theme studies, it is appropriate to let children help select topics that interest them. Topics related to current events, to happenings in their lives, and to children's interests immediately generate more enthusiasm than preselected curricular topics. While it is important to balance studies over a year, it is often possible to give children choices of themes within a broad category.

Some school districts predetermine theme studies so that children do not study the same topic repeatedly in elementary school. These district-level mandates deprive both children and teachers of curricular ownership; and when teachers feel powerless, they become less than enthusiastic about what they are teaching. The alternative is to record in portfolios or curriculum folders the units that have been explored in depth each year. Thus an upper-grade teacher can easily check whether a topic has been studied.

Advantages often cited for teacher-generated theme units are that themes can be chosen in advance, materials can be ordered, and teachers can avoid the possibility of children studying dinosaurs during every year of elementary school, while omitting study of other important topics. These concerns are valid. One way to compromise is to partially control students' selection of topics. For example, if a theme explored last year went well, share the interesting experiences of that class in order to encourage this year's children to study the same topic.

If the children appear eager to study a topic, first survey their previous knowledge of the topic. Brainstorm a list of everything they already know about the topic. If they already know much about the topic, chances are they have studied it previously and have little need for further information. If, however, they know only a moderate amount about the topic, this one is appropriate to explore.

Brainstorm all of the questions students have about the topic, again recording these on a chart. It is best to leave this chart up on the wall for several days, or even throughout the unit, so new questions can be added as they arise. Sometimes children will go home and return with new questions after discussing the topics with their parents. The children's questions then become the focus of the study. Of course, teachers can add questions to the list as well, but these should be genuine questions, not ones added because you think it would be good for the children. Modeling your curiosity tells children that learning is a lifelong activity, not just something we do in school.

After questions have been generated, they can be grouped into meaningful categories for ease in finding appropriate resources to answer them. At this point, some teachers group children according to the questions in which they are most interested so that each subcategory becomes a mini-unit. Other teachers work with the whole class on exploring answers to the questions; still others let children sign up individually or with buddies to find the answer to a question. The question list is posted until the end of the unit, since evaluation will involve seeing how well the questions were answered.

Planning with children has many pragmatic advantages. It takes less teacher time. It provides twenty-five to thirty ideas instead of just one or a few. Planning with children has educational advantages as well. It allows the teacher to model curiosity about learning and strategies for finding information. It gives children major curricular ownership and authentic reasons to read and write.

Collaboration in Finding Resources

Collaborative learning encourages children to brainstorm resources in which they might find answers to their questions. Generating possible resources empowers children to then use that same skill when they have questions of their own at home. Of course, the library will be the first place to which children turn, but they soon learn that the library is not the only source of information. Local expertise and parents become vital adjuncts to a literature-based curriculum and expand the collaborative model. Children can write a note to parents informing them of the new unit of study and asking for any resources available—books on the topic, artifacts, slides, photographs, and other sources of information. Since at home children turn to parents when they seek information, involving parents from the beginning of a study demonstrates to children that learning is authentic, not just something you do in school. Parent participation in literature-based studies creates exciting home-school relationships because both students and parents feel ownership in the curriculum.

Knowing *how* to use literature is as important as selecting the best. Books that not only recommend literature but also suggest how to incorporate it into the curriculum are especially helpful. One technique many teachers use is webbing a book or a theme with children in order to brainstorm all the topics and related literature that might support theme studies. Bromley's *Webbing with Literature: Creating Story Maps with Children's Books* (1990) is an especially helpful resource for mastering the webbing technique. Moss (1990) and Gamberg (1988) each share ways to construct focus units with literature as a base.

Finding current high-quality literature on thematic topics can be a challenge. The teacher's role is to ensure that the best literature is included in the study. Fortunately, there are some excellent selection aides that can be useful. Three books merit special attention. Two R. R. Bowker publications, *A to Zoo! Subject Access to Children's Picture Books* (Lima & Lima, 1989) and the *Subject Guide to Children's Books in Print* (issued annually) list books by topic. *Eyeopeners: How to Choose and Use Books about Real People, Places, and Things* (Kobrin, 1988) makes book recommendations and also offers guidelines for selecting quality nonfiction titles. *Literature-Based Social Studies: Books and Activities to Enrich the K–5 Curriculum* (Laughlin & Kardalett, 1989) and *Science through Children's Literature* (Butzow & Butzow, 1989) are two other sources for special content-area studies. Also, periodicals such as *Science and Children, Social Education,* the *CLA Bulletin,* and *Language Arts* provide the outstanding "picks of the year" in their curriculum area.

Collaboration in Learning Content

As resources become available, their use becomes critical. Several models are described here. In one model, a kindergarten teacher reads to her class every day from fiction, nonfiction, and poetry selections related to her theme studies when possible. After reading each selection, children tell her what information they want to remember, and she records this on a chart. Each day, the previous day's information is read. By the end of the month, these charts are lengthy, and the results as reflected in children's writings are astounding. Their discussions during other parts of the day and their written work are full of interesting information, and no two pieces of writing are alike.

In another model, which evolved in a second-grade classroom, each child decides what aspect of life in Nigeria he or she wants to explore. Various books and reference materials are placed on the tables, with children selecting what they want to read. As they learn something, the children write down the information on an index card, using one card for each piece of information they find. At the end of the reading time, children decide under which category their information fits, label the card, and sign their names to it. Then the cards are distributed to the person who is researching information in that category. Children write reports from the information on the collected index cards. The teacher and a volunteer circulate among children as they read and take notes, helping children who are emergent readers, especially early in the study when much of the vocabulary is new. Later in the week, many of the words have become more familiar, and children are able to help each other. In some cases children work in pairs, with experienced readers reading aloud to the less experienced ones, who often become the recorders of information. While they are writing, children frequently conference with each other to interpret these information notes. The resulting reports, compiled into a book for the classroom library, are amazingly detailed and informative.

A third model is for children to break into groups according to the subcategories of information generated. In this scenario, children within the group brainstorm the questions they would like answered on each child's topic. The children within each group make a list of sources of information and help each other find it. For example, on a transportation unit, six groups are generated on six different aspects of transportation: inventors of transportation, animals used for transportation, aviation, trains, boats, and land transportation. The students in the "inventors group" decide that each of their reports will contain the following information: how the inventor got the idea for the invention, what inventions preceded the transportation invention, how the inventor gained financial backing to develop the transportation, who first used the transportation, how old the inventor was when he or she created the invention, why the inventor created the invention, and the impact of the invention on the person's later life. Seeking parallel information about different individuals gives everyone an opportunity to share sources of such information and ideas for presenting well-organized reports that will be easy to read.

The "animal transportation" group includes Tibetan yaks, Egyptian camels, Spanish donkeys, and Alaskan huskies. In each case the children are curious about how much weight the animal can carry or pull, how far the animal can travel in a day, why the animals are used for transportation, what kinds of cargo the animals haul, how the animals are cared for, and the value of the animals to the culture.

As individuals in each group gather information, they write rough drafts of their reports and then share the drafts with their collaborative group. Since the other children contribute questions to the writer, they have a vested interest in the contents of the report. After revision, support groups help each other edit and finally present the information in polished form. Because the other groups have studied other topics, there is an authentic reason to read each other's reports and share information.

In any one of these models where there is collaboration in learning content, children must be taught many useful strategies for acquiring information. As they try to find information in books, they will appreciate learning how to use a table of contents, an index, and bibliographic resources. Typically the school librarian joins the teacher in the media center as children decide which resources will be most beneficial to their group. A good time for a mini-lesson on using bibliographic resources is just prior to finding materials in the library. Mini-lessons on using indexes and tables of contents will be useful when each group has found a number of books that might include information on the topics they are investigating. When the reasons for learning these strategies are real and when the strategies are part of learning information that the children themselves have chosen to learn, the lessons on these strategies are welcomed. Students see the purpose behind them. Working collaboratively helps students learn the strategies better because they can ask each other questions as they work toward a collaborative end.

Once they have found books containing information that might be of use, children need to learn how to skim texts for information they need. Each group might brainstorm key words to look for in their books, and then children could take turns skimming the headings and the material to find these key words. As they find good information, they need to take notes. Several note-taking strategies might be tried. One child might read while the others take notes; then at the end of a section, the children can decide which notes they want to use in developing their report. As the one student reads aloud, the other members of the group could decide collectively which information they wanted to record. One teacher had her students use adding machine tape for taking notes so that students would learn to copy key words, not whole sentences of information. Students then cut the adding machine tape, with one note on each slip of paper. The students grouped the notes by topic to write their report. Other teachers, like the one mentioned earlier with the Nigeria unit, have students take notes on index cards.

Another strategy useful in most theme studies is interviewing experts on a topic as a way of gathering information. A group of students can plan what information they want to gather from the individual, can design the questions they want to ask, and can decide how they will record the information. If they tape-record the interview, they can listen jointly and decide which information they want to use in their report.

Students within the group might divide the notes up into logical topics (a strategy for organizing the writing) and then write portions of the report. Since all the students collaborate on finding the information and taking notes, they all share in determining if the written parts include the needed information. Issues like the report's audience and the writer's voice can be discussed by the group as each individual shares his or her sloppy copy. Working together demonstrates to students that good writing is almost always a collaborative event. After the content is revised, children can edit their pieces and, using their sources of information as models, can learn how to prepare a bibliography or footnotes.

Collaboration in Sharing Information

When much work has gone into finding information, children enjoy sharing it with varied audiences. One teacher has the children dictate what they have learned about their topic for a weekly newsletter that is sent home to parents. Another has the children themselves write and "publish" the most important information they learned for a parent newsletter. If the children are in groups, each group might contribute a page to the newsletter. Parents are a perfect audience.

Children in other classes in the school become another audience. A third grade, in a unit on birds, collected bird nests to examine from several other classes in the school. When two children learned what kind of bird made each nest, they returned the nest to the class from whom it was borrowed and orally shared this information. Classes can trade books they have written during their theme studies, or children can read from their reports to younger reading buddies. Individuals who contribute information to the project enjoy reading the final reports.

Collaboration in Evaluating Theme Studies

Several aspects of collaborative learning need to be assessed as the theme study progresses, not just at the end of the unit. The process of acquiring and learning information needs ongoing assessment. Students can spend five minutes at the end of each group session responding to the following questions:

1. Did everyone in our group participate?
2. How did the session make me feel?
3. Were the members of the group supportive and not critical?
4. What strategies worked well?
5. What strategies do we want to change for our next meeting?

During the theme study, each child might keep a day book in which he or she responds to these questions: What did I learn during this session? What did I feel best about during our group meeting?

At the end of the unit of study, children return to their original list of questions about the topic and explore the extent to which they found the information they sought. As groups share their reports, children can mark the questions that were answered. It is good to have some unanswered questions or questions that arise during the sharing of information so that the students can continue to think about the topic after the formal study of it has concluded. Students will return weeks later exclaiming about how they heard something on the radio or read something that resolves a previously unanswered question.

Evaluation of the process is as important as evaluation of the product. The group can discuss the following questions and report back to the teacher:

1. How many resources did we use to find our information?
2. Which resources were the most useful and important to our report?
3. Which books did we enjoy the most and why?
4. What strategies that we used for gathering information, organizing information, and sharing information worked best and why?

Students might be provided with a checklist on which they would respond to the following questions:

1. Which experts did we use to find information?
2. What types of literature did we use?

3. What information did we get from our peers?

4. What information did we get from our parents?

5. Which reference books did we use on our topic?

Children need to assess the quality of their own work. Was their work on this project better than their work on previous projects? Why or why not? As children share their work, it is important for other students and the teacher to contribute reasons why the work is valuable or well done. Students need to be taught what constitutes good work.

Summary

Giving children ownership of thematic studies empowers them to be active seekers of information and provides authentic reasons to share that information. It makes the manner in which they learn more like how they learn in life outside school. Our goal is to make children avid lifelong learners, not just students who perform well on school assignments. Teachers who collaborate with children in the design and implementation of literature units learn along with their students. That model of adult learning is powerful. It makes the classroom a true community of learners.

References

Bromley, K. D. (1991). *Webbing with literature: Creating story maps with children's books.* Boston: Allyn & Bacon.

Butzow, C., & Butzow, J. (1989). *Science through children's literature.* Englewood, CO: Libraries Unlimited.

Gamberg, R. (1988). *Learning and loving it: Theme studies in the classroom.* Portsmouth, NH: Heinemann.

Kobrin, B. (1988). *Eyeopeners: How to choose and use children's picture books about real people, places, and things.* New York: Penguin Books.

Laughlin, M. K., & Kardalett, P. P. (1989). *Literature-based social studies: Books and activities to enrich the K–5 curriculum.* Phoenix, AZ: Oryx Press.

Lima, C. W., & Lima, J. A. (1989). *A to zoo! Subject access to children's picture books* (3rd ed.). New York: R. R. Bowker.

Moss, J. F. (1990). *Focus on literature: A context for literacy learning.* Katonah, NY: Richard C. Owen.

Newman, J. (1991). *Interwoven conversations: Learning and teaching through critical reflection.* Portsmouth, NH: Heinemann.

Subject guide to children's books in print. (issued annually). New York: R. R. Bowker.

25 Teachers Encouraging a Love for Literature

Charles A. Elster
Purdue University

Tammy Younts
Purdue University

Mary Lee Webeck
Monticello, Indiana, Public
Schools and Purdue University

Melissa Reed
Purdue University

Teachers Encouraging a Love for Literature (TELL), a local support group consisting of both university and public school educators, grew out of dissatisfaction with the status quo in reading and language arts programming. TELL promotes literature-based activities, particularly literary studies, in elementary-grade classrooms.

Since 1990, teachers and administrators from public schools in Tippecanoe County, Indiana, have worked with professors and students from Purdue University in after-school literary study groups and half-day weekend workshops. TELL's goals are to develop greater knowledge of literary theory, strategies for using literature in classrooms, and materials for their own use and for dissemination to professional colleagues.

TELL's members are committed to bringing quality literature and literary studies into the heart of the reading/language arts curriculum, rather than supporting textbook-based learning. They have read and discussed articles on literary theory and curriculum, tried varying strategies for teaching reading and language arts with literature, shared classroom experiences, and established basic definitions and grade-level proposals.

The TELL Contract

During 1991–92, the TELL group used a common core of children's picture books in their K–6 classrooms. TELL teachers agreed to try the books in their classrooms, to attend semimonthly after-school meetings where they would discuss literary theory and share their classroom experiences, and to complete lesson summaries and book evaluation forms, which included a six-point scale rating each book's appropriateness for their classroom and space for comments.

The TELL board (consisting of two professors, two administrators, and four teachers) selected the books to be shared, provided a copy of each book for each TELL teacher, chose and distributed professional and scholarly articles to go along with the books, and copied and distributed teachers' lesson summaries and summaries of book evaluations. They arranged four half-day Saturday workshops featuring children's authors and literacy educators. TELL group members also shared their insights and experiences through media presentations of their classroom work. Finally, they published and distributed a quarterly newsletter that provided links between literary themes, exemplary teacher lessons, and published language arts guidelines.

Literary Studies

TELL teachers themselves pursued a course of literary studies in preparing to implement such study in their classrooms. Their focus was on (1) how literature is made, including story structures, author styles, illustrations, and techniques such as irony; (2) what the content of literature is, including common literary themes, such as the hero's journey, and the cultural-historical content of literature; and (3) what effects literature has on readers, exploring issues of aesthetic and efferent reader response (Rosenblatt, 1990; Zarrillo, 1991). The teachers also looked at curriculum models: for example, the one in which literary themes "spiral" across grade levels (Stott, 1987).

The Picture Books

The TELL board's goal was to choose recent high-quality picture books that (1) would challenge teachers and children to explore the imaginative potential of stories told in words and pictures, (2) dealt with cultures and lifestyles that differed from those found in Indiana, and (3) reflected some of the literary study and curriculum themes pursued by the group, particularly the pattern of "The Hero's Journey." The eight books chosen for 1991–92 were *Ruby* by Michael Emberley (1990), *Foolish Rabbit's Big Mistake* by Rafe Martin and Ed Young (1985), *The Orphan Boy* by Tololwa M. Mollel (1990), *Lizard's Song* by George Shannon (1981), *The Sandman* by Rob Shepperson (1991), *The Story of Jumping Mouse* by John Steptoe (1989), *Rainbow Crow: A Lenape Tale* by Nancy Van Laan (1989), and *Tuesday* by David Wiesner (1991). (Annotations of these books appear at the end of the chapter.)

Assessment of the Project

At the end of the school year, a TELL assessment team was formed to look at what the group had done. The university-based team, made up of a professor, an instructor, a graduate student, and an undergraduate student, examined and analyzed the teachers' book evaluations, lesson summaries, and midyear evaluations of the TELL program. The team's goals were to find evidence of teachers' knowledge and use of literary studies themes and to document patterns in the teachers' responses, beliefs, and classroom practices. The team found much consistency in the way teachers used particular books. That is, the character of a book dictated to some extent the kind of activities and talk which occurred with that book in classrooms across the K–6 grade levels.

The most prevalent type of classroom activity for literary studies was comparing and contrasting different literary works, whether different versions of the same tale, different examples of a common genre, or stories with common themes, motifs, or cultural content. This compare-contrast technique bridges questions of content and form (how books are made). Almost all of the classes compared *Ruby* to at least one other version of *Little Red Riding Hood;* one fourth-grade teacher helped children chart salient features of eighteen versions of the tale. Some classes compared *Foolish Rabbit's Big Mistake* to *Chicken Little*. Some teachers reported that students as young as kindergartners spontaneously made comparisons on their own after several months of literary studies activities.

Many of the classes studied Native American literature and cultures in connection with *Rainbow Crow* and *The Story of Jumping Mouse*, both Native American legends. Analysis of illustrations and visual art activities were a natural focus for many classes when reading *Foolish Rabbit's Big Mistake, Tuesday,* and *The Sandman*, which contain extraordinary illustrations. And several classes wrote their own text to the largely wordless *Tuesday*.

Text genre was a common focus of classroom literary studies. For example, teachers linked *Rainbow Crow,* a Lenape tale of how the crow became black, to other Native American tales and to *pourquoi* tales from cultures other than Native American. Then they could "spiral" back to Native American themes and the *pourquoi* genre when studying *The Tale of Jumping Mouse*. A media specialist helped fifth graders to see the links between *Foolish Rabbit's Big Mistake* and the fables of Aesop.

In their genre studies, TELL teachers helped children to link literary forms with literary content and cultural origin. Often children were able to go beyond genre to recognize and explore common literary themes treated in diverse styles. For example, *The Sandman, Tuesday,* and *The Orphan Boy* all portray fantastic events that could be interpreted as dreams, and many classes discussed this possibility, linking their experience and understanding of these three books, as well as other "night fantasy" books like *Where the Wild Things Are* by Maurice Sendak (1963). Children also had opportunities during discussion to make connections between "quality

Elster, Younts, Webeck, and Reed

literature" and popular culture. When discussing *Tuesday*, a kinder-gartner remarked, "Look at the one with the cape. He is just called Super Frog now" (lesson summary). When discussing *The Sandman*, several children made a connection between the title character and the 1950s song "Mr. Sandman," which appears in the movie *Back to the Future.*

In many TELL classrooms, "The Hero's Journey" was a central theme in the curriculum "spiral." A third-grade teacher compared the journey in *Ruby* with the journey in *The Jolly Postman* by Janet and Allan Ahlberg (1986), which also allowed her to link the children's knowledge of fairy tale characters. Another third-grade teacher made "Journey" a part of many of her literature activities. For example, children illustrated the character's journey in *Rainbow Crow* (lesson summary).

As TELL teachers explored the content of the picture books, they became aware of the resources needed for literature-based instruction. For example, while sharing *Rainbow Crow*, a third-grade teacher wrote in a book evaluation: "I would like more resources about Indian art and picture representations from them."

Teachers also learned to tie literary content to students' needs and to mandated curriculum goals. For example, when sharing *Lizard's Song*, one first-grade class "discussed different types of homes that people and animals live in" (lesson summary), while students in one fifth-grade class linked the book to their study of vertebrates and invertebrates: "The students could search for 'homes' of chosen animals and insert the names of these in the song they created about the animal" (lesson summary). A teacher of learning-disabled children discussed concepts about *Ruby* which she felt were appropriate to her students' needs. Before reading, she introduced story vocabulary and background knowledge necessary for comprehending the story (e.g., traditional relationships between cats and dogs and what intercom systems are). After reading, she helped the students chart characters and what they had said in the story, reinforcing comprehension, recalling story dialogue, and encouraging group participation.

A third-grade teacher used a classroom study of *Ruby* and other versions of *Little Red Riding Hood* to fulfill the goal of distin-guishing realism and fantasy as outlined in the adopted basal. This type of linkage between literary content and mandated program goals is important for teachers who wish to move from textbook-based to literature-based programs.

Giving children opportunities and strategies for responding to literature personally and aesthetically (Zarrillo, 1991) was a recur-ring focus in TELL lessons. For example, when sharing *The Sandman*, teachers capitalized on story elements to which children respond personally—going to sleep, dreaming, believing in mythical characters, and messing up one's room. In the lesson summary, one teacher wrote about *Tuesday*:

> I have been trying to build a classroom [where] children feel safe to voice their thoughts about books. This book was wonderfully free for interpretation. It could be so many things. There was not right or wrong to worry them. They could simply express what they felt.

Illustrations were an important interest for children at all grade levels. For example, when discussing *The Story of Jumping Mouse,* children in fifth grade noticed that background colors reflected the character of different animals. Children at all levels explored story details in *The Sandman* and *Tuesday*.

Some teachers struggled with how to balance aesthetic and efferent responses to literature. Commenting about *The Sandman*, a teacher wrote in a book evaluation:

> The challenge is to enhance literature without turning it into a chore. Writing can be a drawback if that is all we attempt to do when literature [is] in a short time span. . . . Over-journalizing can kill the joy in reading.

By providing the elements necessary for personal response—time, choice, and trust—teachers supported children's personal-aesthetic responses. Then they helped children choose modes of efferent response; for example, they tied the dream-journey themes to illustrations used in storytelling.

One of the most gratifying changes in teacher attitudes and practices was the acceptance of picture books by upper elementary teachers as appropriate materials for their classes. A media specialist for grades 5 and 6 wrote in her book evaluation of *Ruby*:

> I had serious doubts about using this book with fifth or sixth graders. After all, *Ruby* is merely a picture book and based on the babyish tale about Little Red Riding Hood. I feared being laughed out of my room. Out of obligation to the TELL project I decided to stick my neck out and give it a try.

After sharing the book and having the children write their own versions of a traditional tale, she wrote in her lesson summary:

> The excitement of the class was rejuvenating for me. I could not contain them. I also learned that it is very possible, even beneficial, to use carefully chosen picture books with fifth graders.

This change in attitude, begun with the first shared picture book, reflected the teacher's broadened understanding of reader response and of the thematic depths present in fairy tales and other archetypal literature.

Likewise, teachers examined the relationship of book format (how books are made) and reader response (the effect books have on readers). After sharing *The Sandman,* a sixth-grade teacher wrote in a book evaluation: "The book was wonderful. However, the detail did not make it a book easily shared in a group setting. I need to discover ways to bring books like this into the classroom on an individual basis."

Teachers work hard to help children deepen their responses to literature. Commenting on her class's experience with *Lizard Song,* one teacher wrote in her lesson summary:

> The students are following on physical journeys but not making much connection with the emotional changes that characters are making. I will be discussing this with them more each week. They need to still make the leap to seeing the physical and emotional journeys as being connected.

One kindergarten teacher indicated in her midyear evaluation that she and her students were developing a more cohesive and sustained approach to literary studies:

> I have discovered that my kindergartners think much more about illustrations, about characterization, about comparison of stories from the past, from the present—how the pattern of the story is alike or different—the thread of theme that surfaces over and over—the predictability. . . . I realize now that in the past, when I used good literature with students, I really did so in "isolation"—wasn't *that* a good story? What did you like about *that* story? What did you notice about *that* character?—and then I would go on to something else. But that was before I "jumped over the moon."

In their semimonthly meetings, teachers became more sophisticated students of literature and literature-based instruction. By the end of the school year, they were discussing cultural and literary components, connections between illustrations and texts, and connections between texts with similar themes with a sophistication not apparent at the beginning of the school year.

Conclusions

Teachers who participated in the TELL program adopted literary studies themes in their classroom activities and linked TELL books to other areas of the curriculum. Commonalities and differences in teachers' use and response to literature extended across books, grade levels, and teachers. While teachers adopted a core set of literary themes in their book-sharing activities, they also adapted the use of picture books to their own grade-level needs and instructional and personal agendas. The TELL program did not impose a single agenda on all teachers but allowed them to pursue their own journeys as teachers and learners.

TELL teachers also broadened their literary understanding and appreciation through sharing with peers their classroom experiences and personal reactions to children's literature. Upper-elementary teachers came to appreciate picture books as appropriate for their students. Teachers at all levels expanded their appreciation of picture book aesthetics and their understanding of thematic linkages between books.

The TELL program has demonstrated that educators at all levels can collaborate to plan "grassroots" changes in English/language arts/reading instruction, creating a program that encourages lifelong learning for teachers as well as children. A fourth-grade teacher wrote in a midyear evaluation:

> The thing that I have enjoyed the most with the TELL group is the opportunity to gather ideas from others who are out there in the trenches. I'm not always original, but I can take someone else's idea and modify and enhance it until I have a product that works for me. I look forward to those sharing times.

TELL has also shown that collaboration between university and public school systems in implementing literary studies is a fruitful approach. It is a program that could be emulated in other areas of the country. But teachers must create a program and curriculum that match the needs of teachers, administrators, and children in their area and that support shared goals and objectives. Honest, persistent collaborative work among teachers, children, and those who back their efforts is required if teachers and children are ever to "jump over the moon" from textbooks to literature-based learning.

References

Rosenblatt, L. (1990). Literature—SOS! *Language Arts, 68,* 444–48.

Stott, J. (1987). The spiralled sequence story curriculum: A structuralist approach to teaching fiction in the elementary grades. *Children's Literature in Education, 18*(3), 148–62.

Zarrillo, J. (1991). Theory becomes practice: Aesthetic teaching with literature. *The New Advocate, 4*(4), 221–34.

Children's Books Cited

Ahlberg, Janet, & Ahlberg, Allan. (1986). *The jolly postman; or, Other people's letters.* Illus. by Authors. Boston: Little, Brown.

Emberley, Michael. (1990). *Ruby.* Boston: Little, Brown.

Kellogg, Steven. (1985). *Chicken Little.* New York: William Morrow.

Martin, Rafe, & Young, Ed. (1985). *Foolish rabbit's big mistake.* New York: G. P. Putnam's Sons.

Mollel, Tololwa M. (1990). *The orphan boy.* Illus. by Paul Morin. New York: Clarion Books.

Sendak, Maurice. (1963). *Where the wild things are.* Illus. by Author. New York: Harper & Row.

Shannon, George. (1981). *Lizard's song.* Illus. by Jose Aruego & Ariane Dewey. New York: Greenwillow Books.

Shepperson, Rob. (1991). *The sandman.* Illus. by Author. New York: Farrar, Straus & Giroux.

Steptoe, John. (1989). *The story of jumping mouse: A Native American legend.* Illus. by Author. New York: William Morrow.

Van Laan, Nancy. (1989). *Rainbow Crow: A Lenape tale.* Illus. by Beatriz Vidal. New York: Alfred A. Knopf.

Wiesner, David. (1991). *Tuesday.* Illus. by Author. New York: Clarion Books.

TELL Program Books

Emberley, Michael. (1990). *Ruby.* Boston: Little, Brown.

> A droll modern urban retelling of *Little Red Riding Hood* with animal characters.

Martin, Rafe, & Young, Ed. (1985). *Foolish rabbit's big mistake.* New York: G. P. Putnam's Sons.

> Based on a traditional Buddhist tale, this story of how Rabbit spreads the word that the earth is breaking up has similarities to *Chicken Little.* Brightly colored chalk drawings reflect the emotions of the story.

Mollel, Tololwa M. (1990). *The orphan boy.* Illus. by Paul Morin. New York: Clarion Books.

> An African tale of an old herdsman who is befriended by a mysterious and magical boy during a drought.

Shannon, George. (1981). *Lizard's song.* Illus. by Jose Aruego & Ariane Dewey. New York: Greenwillow Books.

> In this modern fantasy, Lizard composes a song about his home. Bear cannot learn that song until he creates a song about his own home. The author's theme of forgetting is drawn from traditional African tales.

Shepperson, Rob. (1991). *The sandman.* New York: Farrar, Straus & Giroux.

> A fantasy of what happens when the sandman visits a boy who has trouble falling asleep. Dynamic, detailed illustrations extend the minimal text.

Steptoe, John. (1989). *The story of jumping mouse: A Native American legend.* Illus. by Author. New York: William Morrow.

> This Native American tale about a mouse's heroic journey to a far-off land has realistic black-and-white illustrations.

Van Laan, Nancy. (1989). *Rainbow crow: A Lenape tale.* Illus. by Beatriz Vidal. New York: Alfred A. Knopf.

> A Native American tale of a brave crow who loses his bright colors when he brings fire from heaven to earth.

Wiesner, David. (1991). *Tuesday.* Illus. by Author. New York: Clarion Books.

> A largely wordless fantasy about an invasion of frogs. Dynamic, surreal illustrations carry the story.

VII Assessing

26 Assessment in a Literature-Based Classroom

Linda J. Fenner
Daniel Wright Elementary School, Dublin, Ohio, and The Ohio State University at Columbus

I have been interested in literacy assessment for at least ten years, four of which were spent as a language arts consultant in a state education agency. During these four years, I began to understand that the most important work in education, particularly for those who are interested in educational reform, was taking place, not in discussions of policy or curriculum, but with children in classrooms.

Most recently, I have returned to teaching fifth grade and am shaping the theories I used to read about into a studio-like workplace for my students and me. I have pondered what constitutes "authentic" literacy experiences for my students at their particular stage of development and have addressed, from a teacher's perspective, critical measurement issues such as *reliability*, making consistent judgments about literacy, and *validity*, focusing assessment on the processes and behaviors critical to literacy development.

Reinventing Assessment in the Classroom

When I returned to the classroom, I simply struggled to survive. My curriculum development and consulting work should have provided me with an adequate theoretical framework for my teaching. More than anything, however, I was a first-year teacher—for the second time in my life. Events moved so quickly that I seemed to spend all of my time reacting to what was happening. I had little time to reflect and make sense of what I was doing. I was startled to find myself acting atheoretically. Eventually I discovered a strategy that helped me recapture my theoretical framework. By using metaphors as shorthand versions of theories, I found that I could keep important classroom images at the forefront of my thinking and interactions with children.

While considering assessment, I evolved into thinking about "taking soundings." Knowing that a student's cognitive map, like the ocean floor, is full of topographical surprises, I sensed that sometimes I was plumbing the depths and sometimes I had completely missed a significant feature. I learned to keep sweeping across the terrain, however, until I could get a reasonably full picture of the peaks and valleys of a student's literacy profile.

I have also come to see assessment as a social process. It often feels like an ongoing conversation. One exchange is unlikely to contain all the information I need about a student. Sometimes when we exchange only monosyllables, I try out different responses and questions. A key question like, "Tell me about the movie in your head that you saw when you read this book," or, "Which author writes most like you?" may unlock a flood of images and responses.

As I gained more time to reflect on these issues, I understood that part of the challenge is that instruction had moved ahead of assessment. Curriculum and materials have shifted to using student-centered, constructivist definitions of learning, yet we are left with the same old tools of letter grades, skills checklists, reading-level tests, and norm-referenced test scores as indicators of progress in literacy. Assessment needs to follow the same path of experimentation and risk taking that we have followed with instruction. Good assessment needs the luxury of false starts, time for observation and reflection, and the creation of individual, rather than uniform, standards. The more we understand about authentic language use, the more sources of assessment data we are able to see. Assessment data also tend to become more idiosyncratic and context-rooted.

When I first tried to assess comprehension with a constructivist view of reading (Tierney, 1990), I had been fortunate enough to overhear a student talking to himself as he made a model of the ship in *The Voyage of the "Dawn Treader"* by C. S. Lewis (1952). John was lying on his stomach on the floor, carefully gluing craft sticks in place. As I walked by and asked him what he was working on, he replied in a low voice. It took me several seconds to recognize a voice that belonged to a character from the book. This character was telling me what the *inside of the ship* looked like. I had heard researchers (Tierney & Edmiston, 1988) use the metaphor "theater of the book" to describe what happens in reading with comprehension and reader engagement. I was astounded to find this spontaneous example in the middle of the floor in my classroom. I thought about the meaning of this ability to place oneself almost physically into a story. I realized that I could use this example to talk with John's parents about how he was able to enter the world of the book, had a verbal command of characterization, and could use materials to construct, literally, his own stage upon which the characters of the book came alive.

When reinventing assessment in the classroom, the tricky part is what use to make of such a special and individual demonstration of literacy like John's. It seems impossible and probably inappropriate to plan curriculum and assessment so that every child demonstrates understanding of story in precisely the way that John did. Not everyone needs or wants to build the *Dawn Treader* as a personal stage for comprehension and responses. However, I began to catalog this experience as a *type* of indicator for which to look in assessing reading. The power of John's behavior, his spontaneous demonstration of comprehension, encouraged me to develop a classroom policy that reading often would be determined by personal choice and that many avenues of expression (drama, artistic design and production, writing, conversation) would be considered as not only vehicles of learning but evidence of learning as well.

Tentative Design for Classroom Assessment

With John's demonstration as a point of departure, in the last three years I have developed assessments that respond respectfully to the learner's ideas, describe strengths, support and extend the child's level of literacy, provide focused feedback, and encourage self-assessment. The following three types of literacy assessment have evolved in my classroom and reflect the pragmatic decisions that practitioners are asked to make as they serve a number of different masters:

1. Monitoring Vital Signs: ongoing descriptive assessments that are sometimes recorded on a class grid sheet of big blocks with the students' names running down the left-hand column and the days of the week across the top—a no-frills recording device

2. Scoring Guides and Standards: more standardized classroom assessments that are connected to products or presentations and that typically feature a holistic or primary trait assessment scale (scoring guide) to which students have access

3. Community and Self: such as Authors' Circle, which is primarily a reading and peer response time, and portfolio activities

Type 1: Monitoring Classroom Vital Signs

Lehr (1988) notes responses to reading in literature-based classrooms occur in the context of "total reading events." Being aware of total reading events—that is, what has gone on before, during, and after the event and with whom it has occurred—is an important dimension of assessment. I try to assess consistently the following vital signs:

1. Are students choosing books and settling in with them for extended periods of time?

2. What happens when a student does not finish a book?

3. Can students get beyond plot summaries, retellings, or lists of

facts in order to tell what they think and feel about what they
have read?

4. Do students have literate conversations and reading/writing
   friendships?

5. Can students build a world by talking, constructing something
   physically, or writing from something they have read?

6. Can students look at how an author has crafted a selection and
   apply this to their own work?

7. Can students make connections among the books they have read,
   the experiences they have had, and the topics we are studying?

Making Deliberate Choices

I have observed differences in how students select books to read.
Many students read by series or by author. One year a number of
students were reading C. S. Lewis's books. They seemed to find great
comfort in Lewis's voice and continued to read these books to
sustain that relationship. Norman, a talented reader and writer,
made this comment in his reading log about Lewis's *Prince Caspian*
(1951):

> The middle of "prince Caspian" is great just like I say on all the
> reading logs that I've done on Narnia books. And I'm not just saying
> that either. I really mean that it's just wonderful. I've said how much
> I like C. S. Lewis already so that I don't even have to talk about him
> too much anymore except that I keep on reading his books and I
> never get tired of him.

I look for students to develop some way of finding a book that
will hold their attention. Students who have difficulty with the skills
and processes of reading also seem to have trouble choosing a good
book. It is as if they have few resources for discovering a story and
cannot find anything that is worth a risk. Until they click with a
special book, reading remains a school activity to be done for an
enforced period of time. Their responses to books are uneven, idiosyncratic, or forced. Such readers require great patience. Sometimes
in my enthusiasm to get them "on task" during a reading period, I
forget how frustrating it must be for them not to have dependable
strategies for locating good books. They need to hear many conversations about great books that other students are reading, to be told
or read the beginnings of books that might interest them, and to be
assisted in finding books that match their own interests and hobbies.
Patience and support for these students are usually rewarded.

Albert was a student who got off to a very slow start. He
brought *The Little House* by Virginia Lee Burton (1942) for an initial
book conference. It was not something he had actually read in class.
He explained that his mother had read it to him many times when he

was younger and that he loved the story. Every day during sustained silent reading, Albert had a new book, often nonfiction. Sometimes I would watch him staring into space. He was briefly captivated by *I, Houdini* by Lynne Reid Banks (1978), but it was only at the end of the year that he really connected with a book he loved. He read *My Side of the Mountain* by Jean Craighead George (1959) and identified so strongly with Sam Gribley that he actually ran away from the school playground for a brief period of time. Later he wrote George an enthusiastic letter about the book.

This ability to choose, to make a commitment to a book, strikes me as a critical literacy behavior. The mechanism that allows Norman to form a comfortable bond with C. S. Lewis and to want to open himself up to Lewis's thoughts is elusive. Norman came into my classroom with this disposition. Albert developed some of this ability over time.

Abandoned Books

What happens when a student does not finish a book relates to the previous issue of making choices and developing bonds with books. Almost everyone in my room has abandoned a book (often an award-winning children's literature title) at one time or another. It is something that I am usually quite aware of, although I usually do not comment on it. I look at how often this is happening and why a student quits a particular title. Norman, for example, stayed with *The Wind in the Willows* by Kenneth Grahame (1908) for about half the book. He commented when he dropped it:

> I've decided to quit reading this book because it's starting to get a little boring. All it is is talking. I start to not understand it because when all they do is talk, I start to loose my concentration on the book. The beginning of the book was okay, because it talks about how the mole and the rat became friends, and how they have mixed feelings about themselves. That's when I liked it.

Randy, a perplexing reader whose oral reading was garbled, read or started reading ten different books in the first two months of school. Randy did not finish *The Incredible Journey* by Sheila Burnford (1961), although he showed considerable enthusiasm for the book initially in his response log:

> I like this book because there is a lot of detail in it and it is like you fill like you are their. The Part that I like is the part when the two dogs and the cat run away and the people could not find them so the people who were watching them called the owner to tell him what happened meanwile the two dogs and a cat were on there way to find there owner and that is all I read.

Randy finished reading the book *Mustard* by Charlotte Graeber (1982), however. This is part of what he said about it:

> I like this book so far because it is almost like you are wright there with the characters there are so many details I like reading books about cats because I have a cat and I can compair the book to my real life. This book is good because it tells who takes care of the cat and how they take care of the cat.

Critical in this monitoring effort is separating the instances of someone displaying avoidance behaviors toward reading from the student who has just had it with a particular book. These really represent two different attitudes and require different responses. I tend to view the former instance as a serious problem. I have adjusted my thinking, however, to accept the latter as normal. Good readers can invest considerable time in a book and just let it go. Procedurally, I rarely question a student who is abandoning a particular book.

Emergence of Interpretation

When my students respond to something they have read, their initial reaction is often to write down everything that happened. It is difficult to show students what I mean when I say, "Tell me what you are thinking about or feeling as you read this story." Jim, a capable reader, had difficulty moving beyond plot summaries. His response to *The Return of the Indian* by Lynne Reid Banks (1986) is a typical response log entry:

> I am reading *Return of the Indian.* Omri brought a toy indian to life again named Little Bear. He was shot twice in the back. Omri's friend Patrick was visiting the school. Patrick and Omri took a toy nurse from Patrick's cousin so they could save Little Bear. If you want to know what happens read the book.

He was one of the students who responded to a question about the "movie" that he saw in his head while reading. I tried to get him to describe where he placed himself when he read by asking him through whose eyes he saw the story.

The movement from summary to interpretation and reflection is one that I look for and encourage constantly. The models I present and the pushing and probing I do in this area are probably the closest I come to the direct teaching of comprehension. I have the impression that this type of deeper, integrative thinking goes on constantly with readers, but that the students' sense of classroom expectations may keep these responses internalized. The quality of thinking that is exhibited in their written responses seems to be determined by what directions they give themselves internally. Betsy provides an illustration of this phenomenon in her reading log for *Charlotte's Web* by E. B. White (1952):

> I'm on the XXI chapter which is the last day. I read chapter the hour of triumph and in this chap. Wilber's name gets called on the loud-

speaker to come to the grandstand to be awarded when he gets there he feels happy but dizzy and as the guy goes on talking Wilber passes out Larvey goes to get a pail of water and Templeten bites Wilber's tail and Wilber gets up and when Lavey gets back he throws the water on Avrey and his Uncle on an accseden and then Avrey starts to act like a clown taking a shower with imaginary thing and his mother tells him to stop but all he hears is the crowed cheering.

This summary is in many ways typical of my students' initial efforts. I was surprised, however, to read another response that Betsy had written at almost the same time. What I had asked for in this instance was a description of what each student was proudest of having accomplished in reading and writing at that point of the year. Here is what Betsy said:

> I read Charlets Web. I thought that Charlets Web was the best out of all the books I've ever read because I could feel what is must of been like to live his life and how Charlet saved his life and how Charlet took the deepest part in of his heart and at the end of the book I was about to cry because Wilber said things about Charlet that made him cry and when I read it I cryed to. Because the book was so good that I had to buy it.

This is such a clear example of a response to literature—so connected to the central themes of the book—that I was baffled as to why Betsy did not write like this in her reading response log. Apparently I had one understanding of what a reader does in a response log and she had other assumptions. This intense relationship with the book was completely missed in the first log entry. It was from experiences like this that I began to think about the "sounding" metaphor for my assessment practices. It also strengthened the conversation metaphor as well by reminding me that I need to talk with and listen to my students and to be prepared to be surprised at any moment by some hidden insight. Missing the "total reading event"—that is, the depth and engagement of a student's response to reading—is easy to do.

Conversations about Books, Reading, and Writing

One element of these conversations is a teacher who reads books and writes alongside the children (Atwell, 1987). Norman, in one of his earliest logs, gave me an emphatic invitation to read *The Lion, the Witch and the Wardrobe* by C. S. Lewis (1950). Many children participated in an ongoing, casual conversation about how far we were in the book and what we thought about it. These talks about C. S. Lewis were largely unplanned and more like graceful pickup games on the basketball court. Students who were ahead of me in the series enjoyed telling me what I would be encountering in the sequels that they were already reading. There are differences between these conversations and the assessments that occur in our more formal book conferences. Conferences often feature retellings and some promptings from me to make connections with other books. These activities have their value, but there is a sharp contrast between them and the way we relate to each other and the types of things we say when a student and I are suddenly just talking about a book together.

I am also a shameless eavesdropper as I try to gauge how (or if) a culture of books, reading, and writing is developing in my classroom. I look for school experience to invade their play and casual discussions. A small group of us had chosen to eat lunch together in the room one day. Suddenly I heard an argument break out between two students who had been reading about Queen Elizabeth I. The argument was over the names of her various suitors and the sequence in which they had been favorites of the court. It was delightful to hear students using all the sources they had read to argue good-naturedly over who had the more accurate understanding of events.

Some of my students seem to have an intuitive understanding of the rules of collaboration. This note, yet another type of assessment artifact, was left in a writing journal:

> S1: I'm writing a story about a girl named Caryn and she goes to babysit for a family with a 2-year old and while she is doing this something happens (I don't know what yet)
>
> S2: Sounds neat. How long will it be?
>
> S1: 10 pg   100 pg   2 pg
>
> S2: Have you written your logs [reading logs for the week]?
>
> S1: 1 of them
>
> S2: Do you have your project done for library?
>
> S1: Nope!
>
> S2: If you have time now let's try to get something done on Lady Catherine [historical fiction story these two students had been working on for two months].
>
> S1: OK. I'll write my log tonight.

World Building

Bruner (1986, 1990) suggests that human beings have a fundamental urge to make sense of things by constructing narratives. Supporting this proclivity is a major goal of my teaching. I try to be alert to the world my students are constructing. John, an identified "gifted" student who struggled with putting ideas in writing, built the model of the *Dawn Treader* described earlier. This project absorbed his attention totally for several days. He literally could not rest until it was finished; I would notice him drifting off to work on it when he was supposed to be involved in other activities. It was not that I dismissed the project, but rather that I initially missed what must have been playing through his head as he was building it. It was not until he decided to share this model at a school assembly and began rehearsing what he would say that I understood how the model functioned as a tiny stage for dramatizations from the story. As he talked about which characters were inhabiting the various cabins and what scenes had taken place on board the ship, I was struck by how he was using this concrete object to make events from the story real. His talk revealed how close he was to this story; inner thoughts and images became public without formal probing or think-aloud protocols.

Randy, a student who did not do particularly well on norm-referenced measures of reading and language, ran out in the hall where I was working with another group of students one day to tell me what was going on in a book he was reading. A scene from *The Flunking of Joshua T. Bates* by Susan Richards Shreve (1984) was so vivid for him that he had to tell me what was happening. Randy re-created the scene for me. Later, he elected to develop a scene from the book that showed the main character, Joshua, being tutored by his teacher. The two figures were sitting at a table. Randy designed the figures so that Joshua's arm moved as he drank a glass of milk. He also informed me that this project actually showed two books he had read because he had read a children's carpentry book to get the design for the table.

Using Books as Writing Teachers

In my second year of teaching, I began to use texts as teachers in a conscious way. In a study of Jamestown, we used two read-alouds, *The Double Life of Pocahontas* by Jean Fritz (1983) and *The Serpent Never Sleeps* by Scott O'Dell (1987). I alternated between the two texts, which are set in the same time period and treat many of the same events. The books differ in point of view, style, and tone, however. I gave students background information to understand the time period and to develop the momentum to begin writing their own books.

The contrast in the two books had some unintended effects. Students became conscious of the different decisions that the authors had made. This gave the students license to experiment in construct-ing their own worlds. Authentic settings became important to them. They used nonfiction texts to gather the details of everyday life—food, furniture, houses. From an assessment perspective, I tracked how individual students were using texts as writing models and also as sources of information for their narratives and nonfiction works. The following reading log response written by a student while we were in the midst of these read-aloud and book-writing projects shows someone who is reading like a writer (Smith, 1988).

I think Scott O'Dell's book has more information in it. I also like Scott O'Dell's book better because it has more adventure in it. I think Scott O'Dell's book has more research because his book was written before Jean Fritz's book, and he had to look for stuff to research with. Plus his book is longer than Jean's and to make books longer you have to have more research.

Making Connections

The chief vital sign that I hope to see is students making connections across all the processes and content they are learning. I hope to see them use reading and writing in very purposeful ways. Karen was typical of students who used all the resources available to produce works that were personal breakthroughs in quality of writing and conceptual understanding. A writer who initially needed much support with the conventions of writing, Karen taught herself how to make substantive revisions in her writing and how to read expository texts in a purposeful way. She learned these things in the context of our extended Jamestown book project. As she listened to the two read-alouds, she got an idea for a story about an agent of King James who was sent to Jamestown to spy on Captain John Smith. From additional self-initiated readings, Karen learned about Captain Christopher Newport and the wooden trunk with sealed orders about the Jamestown mission given to him by King James.

After writing a first draft of a story outline, Karen was hit with an inspiration to begin the whole story in a classroom in King James's palace. Her story begins as a teacher is reading to the class from Captain Christopher Newport's diary. The world Karen created became so substantial that it took on a life of its own. Other students wanted to hear progress reports on her story and asked each day how many hours she had worked on the story at home and at school. On numerous occasions, Karen had to consult nonfiction texts to get details of the plot or setting just right. Her story, which ultimately ran about thirty pages, sounded like a curious hybrid of an eleven year old's voice and that of a mature author striving for authenticity and particular effects in her writing. Here is Karen's response to the story she had written:

> It felt really good when I started to write "Secrets." I enjoyed writing alot and, I like to get information from books then turn that into a story. With writing you can say stuff in your own words, and make up stuff [no] one has every did. When you write your in your own little world!

Karen and her classmates used texts and text worlds as resources to make important connections in their learning. My assessment role was to monitor and support this process for individuals. At one point Karen and I conferred to decide if the houses in Jamestown could possibly have had two floors. We tried to locate drawings in a nonfiction text. I used Karen's process for other students to see a model of how to make a decision about authenticity. These craft discussions were also opportunities to assess the conceptual and content understandings that were coming through a student's reading during his other writing.

Type 2: Setting Standards

I have wrestled for three years with my desire to communicate with students through non-evaluative responses and the need to make assessments for grading purposes. My decisions reflect a longtime involvement with holistic scoring practices used to study district writing samples (Myers, 1980). I use the idea of taking students' work samples or projects, sorting them into groups with similar characteristics, and making judgments about the relative quality of the work.

My procedure is simple. After collecting a sample of weekly reading logs, I read through them and sort them into four stacks. Each stack represents a level of quality, with level 4 containing the most fully developed ideas and interest explorations. I reexamine the papers and list the characteristics for each group of papers. Responses are handed back to the students with the scoring guide. I often leave the scale in handwritten form to convey to students that it is something I have developed in response to a particular assignment. (See Figure 26.1 for a sample scale in typeset format.) In practice, it should be noted, I rarely have responses turned in that I would judge to be level 1 papers.

After my description of the vital signs I try to monitor in my class, this nuts-and-bolts approach to assessment may be a shock. Here is what I have observed, however, about using scoring guides with students and scoring their work holistically:

- When I responded only to their reading logs, I was never able to coax some students beyond plot summaries. I would write an affirming comment each week and then try to find a new way to ask them to tell me what they were thinking.

- I had certain standards and types of responses in mind, but I was not being explicit about what they were. The scoring guides allowed students to see what my standards were from the outset.

- Once the concept of scoring guides was introduced, I was able to involve students in building scales to assess their major assignments. I would start the discussion by asking, "What do you think a level 4 would be like for this assignment?" Invariably they believed this level ought to show how hard they had tried, that they had been careful with craftsmanship, and that they had included detail in their work.

The more I work with these scales, the more confident I feel that they are a good compromise between pure response and the

Figure 26.1.
Holistic assessment scale for writing about reading.

4/4-	3+/3/3-	2+/2/2-	1+/1/1-
made general statements about the book/story *and* backed them up with examples and details	had good summary statements	had some basic ideas from the reading	didn't try at all
talked about main ideas or events and skipped little details (didn't tell *everything* that happened)	made good predictions	didn't expand or elaborate very much	
	showed interest and enthusiasm for book/story	didn't show what you were *thinking*	
sounded like someone talking (I could hear your own "voice")	were a little less focused on main ideas and didn't include quite as much information	may have told too many details from the story	
were interesting and honest	had some good clear thoughts	needed to do more "thinking out loud" on paper	
made *connections* to self or other readings	followed the directions	needed to stop and get the main ideas out of the reading	
had enthusiasm or energy (didn't sound bored)		couldn't hear your "voice" when you told about the story	
went beyond assignment			
showed real thinking			
followed the directions			

evaluative designations of our board-adopted grading scale, which uses letter grades and percentages. I build these holistic scales so that all students can be rewarded for their strengths. I also sense that I can assess complicated interdisciplinary projects with some degree of fairness. See Figure 26.2 for the scale we used to look at the book projects that came out of our Jamestown study.

The existence of a scale for reading logs also allows me to turn this assessment over to the students. My final version of the reading log scoring guide this year was set up as a checklist (shown in Figure 26.3) so that students could look for the elements in their own responses. The elements on this final version came from the students'

Figure 26.2.
Evaluation form for social studies/language arts projects.

Name _____

Project _____

Level 4

_____ Shows much time and effort

_____ Has voice

_____ Great details (tells enough to make people understand)

_____ Has lots of information

_____ Holds reader's interest

_____ Full descriptions; strong word pictures

_____ Time is right; dates are correct; realistic for the time period

_____ Shows much thinking

_____ Good paragraphs and chapters

_____ Sophisticated illustrations; pictures show effort

_____ Is complete

_____ Appropriate length

_____ Strong craftsmanship

_____ Neatly done

_____ Spelling almost pefect

_____ Good punctuation

Level 3

_____ Is complete

_____ Shows good effort

_____ Neatly done

_____ Has some good information

_____ Has historical details

_____ Has some voice

_____ Good spelling

_____ Good punctuation

_____ Good illustrations

_____ Has a sense of beginning, middle, and end

Level 2

_____ Might be incomplete

_____ Shows some effort

_____ Makes sense some of the time

_____ Not enough sentences on each page

_____ Has a few details

_____ Punctuation should be better

_____ Sentences have some run-ons or fragments

_____ Needed to explain things further

_____ Needed to edit for spelling

_____ Needed to edit for punctuation

_____ Uses "then" or "so" too often

Level 1

_____ Needs much improvement

_____ Little evidence of effort

_____ Confusing to try to read

_____ Major problems with spelling

_____ Major problems with punctuation

_____ Incomplete

Grades:

Social Studies _____

Writing _____

Presentation (spelling, punctuation, grammar, neatness) _____

Comments:

Excellent 4+/4/4-

_____ made general statements about the book/story *and* backed them up with examples and details

_____ talked about main ideas or events and skipped little details (didn't tell *everything*)

_____ wrote in your own voice; had a voice that sounded interested, lively, or enthusiastic

_____ gave your own ideas, questions, and impressions; told what the story made you think about

_____ made connections to your own experiences or other things you've read

_____ analyzed the way the author accomplished things

_____ thought about the theme of the book or the point it was trying to make

_____ made unusual observations about the book

_____ made predictions about what might happen

Very Good 3+/3/3-

_____ had good summary statements about the book

_____ gave a sense of who the characters were

_____ told the events that happened

_____ made some predictions

_____ showed interest and enthusiasm for the story

_____ told how you rated the book

_____ didn't include quite as much information

_____ needed to give more of your own thoughts

Good 2+/2/2-

_____ got down some good basic ideas from the story

_____ needed to expand ideas and tell more

_____ might have told too much about certain portions of the book; needed to concentrate more on main ideas

_____ showed interest and enthusiasm for the book

Needs More Work 1+/1/1-

_____ looks like it was dashed off

_____ didn't try at all

Name

Comments:

logs and from some ideas presented by Eeds & Wells (1989), who looked at the types of comments, generalizations, and analyses that children generated in open-ended discussions of literature. Although response logs rarely contain all the qualities listed under a level 4, using the scoring guide ideally encourages children to make more of these types of connections when the reading lends itself to such responses. Ultimately, when I used the ratings from the scoring guides as information for grading, I recorded three scores: the student's self-assessment, a score for completing the assignment (i.e., if three response logs were due and the student did all three, then this was recorded as an effort grade of 4), and my assessment of the logs. These three ratings were averaged, which left the student in control of two-thirds of this assessment.

Type 3: Authors' Circle and Portfolios

While I believe most students accept scoring guides as a tool to help me emphasize specific types of thinking and writing they should evince, an enduring and nurturing dimension of assessment develops in two classroom structures: Authors' Circle and portfolios. Authors' Circle is an hour we devote each week to sharing writing and projects with each other. More informal sharing goes on each day, but we pledge to each other that we will not allow this time to disappear from the schedule no matter what else happens. Students simply read their works aloud, and other students respond. I sit with my hand over my mouth and force myself not to evaluate the work and to wait until every student who wishes to respond has done so. I am certain that the most treasured part of this time for the authors is how closely their peers follow the development of their stories. The listeners often reiterate the writer's history, recall what else the student has been working on, and ask questions about plans for the story the student is currently writing or for future works. These are some of the most authentic and focused conversations we have during the year, plus they provide evaluation with a heavy emphasis on the "valuing" dimension.

For portfolio assessment, I have used the full discussion by Tierney, Desai, and Carter (1991) as my guide. I follow many of the basic procedures outlined by these authors. I am impressed by how strongly portfolios take hold when the children sense that they can use portfolios for their own purposes. Each quarter, students select what should go into the portfolio and write about how the work came into being and why they selected it. I also ask questions about whether they can hear a writer's "voice" developing in their work, because this is a special interest of mine. Notably, our portfolio experience has evolved outside the conventional grading system. In three years I have never put a grade or a holistic score (i.e., a number rating) on a portfolio activity. Some of the items students select to put in their portfolios may have grades or holistic scores on them, but these seem to be outside the criteria they use to select items.

Everyone in the class participates in these portfolio activities, particularly sharing the annotations that we write to go with each work selected. No one has ever asked me what grade he or she is getting on the portfolio, yet everyone completes the quarterly assignments. I caution myself and others, echoed by Tierney, Desai, and Carter's (1991) analysis of the uses of portfolios, to move carefully before we entertain the idea of standardized portfolios for accountability purposes. I have been able to see, rather serendipitously, how constructive this assessment can be when children remain in control of the process. Parental support has also been tremendous. Parents, too, forget about grades when presented with a showcase of work their child has selected and analyzed.

Conclusion

Even though I have thought about these issues a great deal, in day-to-day monitorings of the vital signs, setting standards, and participating in authors' conversations, I still lose my bearings at times. It is easy to lose sight of the nature of authentic involvement with texts and writing. Inertia, the tendency to keep doing things in systematic, sometimes nonsensical structures (taking weekly spelling tests or writing out definitions for vocabulary words, for example) is difficult to overcome. When two or three students will not read during sustained silent reading and write response logs that are flat and uninvolved and that resemble attempts to placate the teacher, panic ensues about how these students will be graded on their report cards in a few weeks. I am tempted to use low grades as leverage to get these students moving. School reporting schedules and teachers, too, wait impatiently for signs of progress. Parent conferences continue to evolve and require careful choices in language as we move parents from wanting evaluation of the child's "reading comprehension skills" to evaluating characteristics such as the child's willingness to enter a secondary world of text (Benton, 1983).

There is still the question of whether the vital signs I value are making any sense to students. Some children, especially at the beginning of the year, are puzzled by all the reading, writing, and talking we do. They want to know when we will be doing real "schoolwork." At one point, a student asked for a reading workbook. He seemed to be overwhelmed with the responsibility of making choices about how to use his time. "Doing school" (Green, Weade, & Graham, 1988)—participating in displays of procedural knowledge—is such a strong expectation in the school culture that resisting it is like being in the middle of a strong current, trying to stand up while the stream pushes on. Sometimes I think that I would feel more confident if I had students all reading the same book and answering my questions about the main ideas in the story. Then I become alarmed, like someone who jerks awake after having fallen asleep in class, as I realize what I am proposing to do. I force myself to rearticulate what the learning, attitudes, and dispositions are that I want to foster in my classroom. My goal is fairly simple: I want to increase the likelihood that these children will become adults who read and write. As we keep our theories of learning focused on such deceptively simple goals, however, I think the moments of discontinuity and personal reckoning will continue. I also believe that parallel systems of assessment (e.g., letter grades and portfolios) will characterize assessment in literature-based classrooms for some time to come.

References

Atwell, N. (1987). *In the middle: Writing, reading and learning with adolescents.* Portsmouth, NH: Heinemann.

Benton, M. (1983). Secondary worlds. *Journal of Research and Development in Education, 16*(3), 68–75.

Bruner, J. (1986). *Actual minds, possible worlds.* Cambridge, MA: Harvard University Press.

———. (1990). *Acts of meaning.* Cambridge, MA: Harvard University Press.

Eeds, M., & Wells, D. (1989). Grand conversation: An exploration of meaning construction in literature study groups. *Research in the Teaching of English, 23*(1), 4–29.

Gardner, H. (1991). *The unschooled mind: How children think and how schools should teach.* New York: Basic Books.

Green, J., Weade, R., & Graham, K. (1988). Lesson construction and student participation: A sociolinguistic analysis. In J. Green & J. Harker (Eds.), *Multiple perspective analyses of classroom discourse.* Norwood, NJ: Ablex.

John-Steiner, V. (1987). *Notebooks of the mind.* New York: Harper & Row.

Lehr, S. (1988). The child's developing sense of theme as a response to literature. *Reading Research Quarterly, 23*(3), 337–57.

Myers, M. (1980). *A procedure for writing assessment and holistic scoring.* Urbana, IL: National Council of Teachers of English.

Smith, F. (1988). *Joining the literacy club.* Portsmouth, NH: Heinemann.

Spiro, R. J., Vispoel, W. L., Schmitz, J. G., Samarapungavan, A., & Boerger, A. E. (1987). *Knowledge acquisition application: Cognitive flexibility and transfer in complex content domains* (Technical Report No. 409). Champaign: University of Illinois, Center for the Study of Reading.

Tierney, R. J. (1990). Redefining reading comprehension. *Educational Leadership, 47*(6), 37–42.

Tierney, R. J., Desai, L., & Carter, M. (1991). *Portfolio assessment in the reading-writing classroom.* Norwood, MA: Christopher-Gordon.

Tierney, R. J., & Edmiston, P. (1988). *The engagement factor: Understanding readers' multiple dimensions of experiences with text.* Paper presented at the National Reading Conference, Tucson, AZ.

Tierney, R. J. & McGinley, W. (1989). Traversing the topical landscape: Reading and writing as ways of knowing. *Written Communication, 6*(3), 243–69.

Wolf, D. P. (1989). Portfolio assessment: Sampling student work. *Educational Leadership, 46*(7), 4–10.

Children's Books Cited

Banks, Lynne Reid. (1978). *I, Houdini.* New York: Avon Books.

———. (1986). *Return of the Indian.* New York: Doubleday.

Bulla, Clyde Robert. (1971). *Pocahontas and the strangers.* New York: Scholastic.

Burnford, Sheila. (1961). *The incredible journey.* Illus. by Carl Burger. New York: Bantam Books.

Burton, Virginia Lee. (1942). *The little house.* Illus. by Author. Boston: Houghton Mifflin.

Fritz, Jean. (1983). *The double life of Pocahontas.* New York: G. P. Putnam's Sons.

George, Jean Craighead. (1959). *My side of the mountain.* New York: E. P. Dutton.

Graeber, Charlotte. (1982). *Mustard.* New York: Macmillan.

Grahame, Kenneth. (1908). *The wind in the willows.* New York: Charles Scribner's Sons.

Lewis, C. S. (1950). *The lion, the witch and the wardrobe.* New York: Macmillan.

———. (1951). *Prince Caspian.* New York: Macmillan.

———. (1952). *The voyage of the "Dawn Treader."* New York: Macmillan.

O'Dell, Scott. (1987). *The serpent never sleeps.* Illus. by Ted Lewin. Boston: Houghton Mifflin.

Shreve, Susan Richards. (1984). *The flunking of Joshua T. Bates.* Illus. by Diane de Groat. New York: Scholastic.

White, E. B. (1952). *Charlotte's web.* Illus. by Garth Williams. New York: Harper & Row.

VIII Supporting

27 Support Groups for Literature-Based Teaching

Marilou R. Sorensen
University of Utah

The shift to literature-based teaching is proving to be a strong thrust in curriculum planning. While advocates list the values of these practices in the classroom, one consideration is often overlooked: the needs of teachers themselves. Why do teachers need to discontinue practices that have been tried-and-true over time? How does someone whose background and training was based on the bottom-up theory commit to new strategies of literature teaching instead of skill-driven lessons? Where can teachers find support for literature-based teaching?

The answers to these questions center on three reasons why changes in philosophy and practice about literature-based teaching are needed. First is the alarming fact that teachers, unless given options, teach the same way (same questions, same stories) in which they were taught and learned. For many, that means merely assigning a familiar book with required assignments. It is basically a skill-and-drill approach, never considering the distance between the reader and the story.

Initially, these teachers who adhere to the tried-and-true need to be willing to give up the past—what Olson (1988) calls "authorized version of valid learning." This can happen only when they realize that closed goals and objectives in teaching relegate students to a level of "receiver of knowledge" rather than a "participant." Understanding the basic values of literature and its use as a pivot of curriculum is the next step. These two changes involve a major philosophical change. Seeing the verve and energy of teachers in literature-based classrooms may be a beginning. Also, sharing ideas and receiving encouragement in a support group will help.

The second need for instructional change is that there *are* better ways to motivate the lesson than closed techniques like writing synopses of the plot, extracting a treatment of the theme, or enumerating traits of a character that stultify the text and numb the real response to the literature.

Unfortunately, many of the teachers who do attempt a "change" in teaching end up following a set of guidelines prescribed by a book publisher, never realizing that the empowerment of effective teaching comes from their own observations, their own plans, and their own students' interests, needs, and questions.

The third reason for needed change in instruction is that teachers declare the lack of support for teaching literature from peers and administrators. They describe feelings of isolation and professional loneliness. I feel for new teachers and those changing from "traditional" instruction. So does Pace (1992), who suggests that "the dynamics of colleague hostility or support play a major role in school reform" (p. 461).

The remainder of this chapter describes suggestions for support and collaboration, ways to attain a network of "new idea" people.

Mentors for Teachers

Lilly was recently hired as a new teacher. Through conversation with other teachers in her school, she discovered that Grace had used novels with her fourth-grade students for years. Lilly approached the experienced teacher with some trepidation, afraid that Grace would think anyone *should* know how to incorporate literature into her teaching. Not only was Grace eager to help, but she was delighted that she finally had someone with whom she could collaborate. Together they approached the principal with a justification statement for a "needs list": more classroom sets of novels, an adjusted schedule of teaming, and the use of a volunteer for group facilitator. The principal readily agreed. In another school, the principal realized how much time and effort the mentor teacher would be contributing as a support to a new group of teachers and offered a stipend for the extra time.

Idealistic situations? Not really. Many teachers instruct "behind closed doors" because they feel the tension "as they pursued self-initiated changes in curriculum and instruction" (Pace, 1992, p. 461). Also real is the novice teacher who may have had a class in literature but who has limited practical application. Certainly we know of many new teachers whose student teaching did not offer exemplary practice in innovative literature-based instruction. The district or state reading supervisor may arrange for a substitute teacher and for released time for a novice teacher to visit a more experienced teacher who could demonstrate literature-based strategies. Or a mentor teacher may be given released time to assist teachers eager to try literature-based teaching (Colt, 1990; Herbert & Colt, 1989).

Often forgotten as a mentor is the media specialist or librarian who can introduce a new teacher to sets of novels that are in the school or ways to access them through interlibrary loan. Many librarians have lists of recommended titles and provide book talks for students as an introduction to thematic units or new books. They also gather books for a unit of study, update teachers on new books, and offer other ideas about how to use the library.

Support and Study Groups

Nan, Robert, and Beverly, who took a children's literature class together as part of their teacher preparation, wanted to continue their reading and development of literature lessons and units even though they work in separate schools. They meet every other Friday at a coffeehouse, bring a book they have all read, and share their notes about how to use the book in the classroom. They contribute ideas to teach the book, leaving space for the needs, interests, and questions for the individual classroom, and select another title for their next meeting.

A study group made up of dedicated literature-based teachers in one school district meets monthly, each inviting another teacher, librarian, or principal who wants insight into what they are trying in their classrooms. Some meetings feature films showing classroom practices. Consultants or visiting authors or artists also attend. Most often the teachers brainstorm ideas and share their own success stories. Their newsletter containing suggestions, titles, times and location of upcoming meetings, and notes from students in the classroom is distributed to other teachers through the district mail service.

Study groups within the school are another option. Sam, a sixth-grade teacher, paired his students with reading and writing buddies in Trudy's first grade. Every Friday the sixth graders share books with the first graders and then take dictation, helping the younger students with sequences in their stories and ultimately their final drafts. Sam is particularly pleased with those "reluctant" readers who find success with their first-grade buddies.

Betsy invites anyone interested in literature for young readers to her bookstore one Sunday a month for a discussion. Summer "junior scholar" groups are important to parents and eager readers. The program consists of invited speakers or discussion leaders. Announcements are made far enough in advance so that participants have time to read what is being discussed.

If there is an administrative mandate for changing to a literature-based approach, teachers have added reason to share their ideas with each other. Inservice training, money for materials, released time, and assistance with evaluation are all viable requests from teachers to the administration.

Volunteers as Support

One elementary school parent-teacher organization developed a series of book talks for students in the school. Each parent was assigned a title and a class and was given an outline for preparing a book talk. The parent volunteers became so excited about their reading and sharing that they have stayed together as a group, planning other volunteer projects. In addition, they meet as a study group to consider book titles and topics on literature and reading. There is a standing invitation for all parents in the school to attend the study group.

The Utah State Library Commission invites volunteers to review new books every month. Many teachers take the opportunity to bring home a bag of books, knowing that the next commission meeting will include their personal opinions and critiques of the books.

Developing a Network for Literature-Based Teaching

The following suggestions offer additional ideas for establishing a network for literature-based teaching:

1. Ask among your faculty about others who use literature-based teaching or who would like to begin. Do not overlook the media specialist or librarian, who can enhance a support group.

2. Put a note about your interest in literature-based teaching in a district newsletter or on professional bulletin boards. Notices in a reading room of a public library may attract someone who also is interested in studying together on classroom projects.

3. Begin an after-school group of students and parents. Consider topics such as new books, ways to help the discussion of books, and *Reading Rainbow* and other book-related television programs. (Sports functions have lots of after-school practice; why not literature reading?)

4. Contact a bookstore about sponsoring a literature study group. Remember the guidelines for success with such groups:

   - Have a clear agenda.
   - Set a time and place and stick to it. Consistency is a must even if only two or three attend—there will be more next time.
   - Review your goals periodically. There is nothing more revitalizing to a group than to note the progress that has been made and tasks accomplished.

5. Contact a state affiliate organization of NCTE or IRA. Find out about their meetings and workshops. Offer to begin a support group under their auspices.

6. Write to friends or former classmates. Set up a letter exchange to share ideas. (Remember that the fax machine and e-mail make everyone close at hand.)

7. Write to someone whose professional book or article you admired or was of special help. While this person may not be able to respond personally, writing the letter will give you confidence to think about innovative ideas that *you* are planning.

8. Team with a colleague on a small research grant or action research using literature. Check with local and regional humanities and arts councils. NCTE has a grant program for teachers, and other organizations may have similar programs.

9. Express your interest and needs to a university or college instructor and suggest the possibility of organizing a group with his or her help. (For two accounts of teachers who have done that, see chapter 16 by Patricia Cianciolo and chapter 25 by Charles Elster, Tammy Younts, Mary Lee Webeck, and Melissa Reed.)

"In many cases, the selection of what to study and how to study it is influenced by the kind of informal networking" (Hearne, 1988, p. 28). If you want to tread the path to literature-based teaching, there is likely someone to accompany you. Have a wonderful journey!

References

Colt, J. M. (1990). Support for new teachers in literature-based reading programs. *Journal of Reading, 34*(1), 64–66.

Hearne, B. (1988, August). Problems and possibilities: U.S. research in children's literature. *School Library Journal*, 27–31.

Herbert, E. H., & Colt, J. M. (1989). Patterns of literature-based reading instruction. *The Reading Teacher, 43*, 14–20.

Olson, D. (1988). On the language and authority of textbooks. In S. deCastell, A. Luke, & C. Luke (Eds.), *Language authority and criticism.* London: Falmer Press.

Pace, G. (1992). Stories of teacher-initiated change from traditional to whole-language literacy instruction. *The Elementary School Journal, 92*(4), 461–76.

Editors

Barbara A. Lehman is an associate professor at The Ohio State University at Mansfield, where she teaches courses in children's literature, language, and literacy. Previously, she was an elementary teacher for eight years in Virginia and New York City. Her research interests lie in the reading and criticism of children's literature and in literature-based literacy practices in elementary and middle school classrooms. She has presented on these topics at conferences of the National Council of Teachers of English, International Reading Association, and National Reading Conference and has published articles in *Language Arts, The Reading Teacher, Childhood Education,* and *Reading Horizons.* She is a member of NCTE's Children's Literature Assembly and served on its subcommittee on Literature in the Elementary Classroom and on the editorial board of (formerly) *The CLA Bulletin.* Within IRA, she has served as president of the Children's Literature and Reading Special Interest Group, as chair of the Arbuthnot Award Committee, and on the editorial board of *The Reading Teacher.*

Marilou R. Sorensen is an associate professor in Educational Studies, University of Utah, Salt Lake City, where she teaches courses in children's and adolescent literature, language development, and reading. Formerly, she was a classroom teacher and reading consultant for Encyclopaedia Britannica. She has presented at conferences and workshops sponsored by the National Council of Teachers of English, International Reading Association, and American Library Association; she has published in journals and has held committee assignments in each of these organizations. She is director of the Intermountain Conference on Children's Literature, held biannually at the University of Utah, and has written a weekly by-line column on books for young readers for fifteen years.

Contributors

Virginia G. Allen is professor of Language, Literature, and Reading at The Ohio State University at Marion. She is the coauthor (with Sharon Fox) of *The Language Arts: An Integrated Approach* and coeditor (with Pat Rigg) of *When They Don't All Speak English: Integrating the ESL Student into the Regular Classroom* (NCTE, 1989). She served as chair of the NCTE/TESOL Liaison Committee and was the first president of the NCTE English as a Second Language Assembly.

Joel D. Chaston is associate professor of English at Southwest Missouri State University, Springfield, where he teaches courses in both children's and young adult literature, as well as composition for elementary teachers. He is a former middle school teacher and is the coauthor of *Theme Exploration: A Voyage of Discovery* and a forthcoming study of children's writer Lois Lowry. He has published numerous articles on contemporary children's literature and serves on the board of directors of the Children's Literature Association.

Patricia J. Cianciolo is professor of Literature for Children and Adolescents at Michigan State University. She has been an elementary teacher in the Milwaukee, Wisconsin, public schools and has done research on children's and adolescents' response to book illustrations and to literature in translation and on the critical reading of literature by children in grades K-6. She is the author of numerous journal articles and book chapters, *Picture Books for Children,* and the 36-filmstrip series *Children's Literature: Using Literature to Develop Language Arts Skills in Grades K-2.* Currently she is director of a research study on the teaching and learning of literature-based literacy. She makes presentations regularly at NCTE conventions and conferences.

Patricia R. Crook is associate professor of Elementary Education at the University of Virginia, Charlottesville. She began her teaching career in an inner-city school, where she worked as both an elementary teacher and a reading instructor. She frequently presents at national conferences, has served on national committees, and works with school districts to help teachers turn theory into practice. She has published in several journals, including *Language Arts, The Reading Teacher,* and *The ALAN Review.*

Charles Elster is assistant professor of Literacy Education at Purdue University, West Lafayette, Indiana, where he teaches graduate and undergraduate courses and conducts research focusing on emergent literacy and literature-based programs. His articles have appeared, or will soon appear, in *The Reading Teacher, Young Children, Reading Research Quarterly,* and *Journal of Reading Behavior.* A former preschool teacher and a member of Teachers Encouraging a Love for Literature (TELL), he is a recent founder of a parent-run alternative school.

Linda Fenner is currently a fifth-grade teacher at Daniel Wright Elementary School in Dublin, Ohio. She began teaching in 1974 and has also worked as a reference librarian, school librarian, curriculum and library media coordinator, language arts consultant for the Ohio Department of Education, and coordinator of a literacy center. She returned to classroom teaching in 1990 and finds that working with children in a classroom setting continues to be a challenge for her.

Evelyn B. Freeman is associate professor and education coordinator at The Ohio State University at Newark, where she teaches courses in language arts and children's literature. A former preschool and elementary teacher, she conducts workshops for school districts and educational agencies. She is coeditor (with Diane Goetz Person) of *Using Nonfiction Trade Books in the Elementary Classroom: From Ants to Zeppelins* (NCTE, 1992) and has published in *Language Arts, Young Children, Phi Delta Kappan,* and *The Elementary School Journal.* She chairs the Orbis Pictus Award for Outstanding Nonfiction for Children Committee of NCTE, serves on the editorial board of *Language Arts,* and is the immediate past president of the Ohio Council of Teachers of English.

Mary Jo Fresch is a lecturer in the Faculty of Education at the Royal Melbourne Institute of Technology in Coburg, Victoria, Australia, where her research interests are literacy acquisition, spelling, and using children's literature in the classroom. A former elementary classroom teacher in the United States, she is now a teacher educator, specializing in reading, language, and literature. She reviews Australian children's literature for *The Dragon Lode,* the journal of the Children's Literature and Reading Special Interest Group of the International Reading Association, and has presented papers in the United States and internationally.

Gloria Kinsley Hoffman is currently a sixth-grade teacher at Eastern Elementary School in Lexington, Ohio. Prior to her three years teaching the sixth grade, she taught fourth grade for fifteen years, also at Eastern Elementary. She has taught as an adjunct professor at The Ohio State University–Mansfield Campus in the social studies, literature, and language arts areas, while also presenting at local and state conferences and in-services. Currently she is a doctoral student at The Ohio State University, a sixth-grade teacher, and a committee member on the state committee to develop the Ohio sixth grade writing proficiency test.

Sharon Kane is associate professor of Curriculum and Instruction at the State University of New York College at Oswego. She teaches courses and has published several chapters and articles on reading and whole language. She has presented at national, regional, and state conferences on literacy issues and teacher education topics.

Linda Leonard Lamme is professor of Instruction and Curriculum at the University of Florida, Gainesville, where she teaches language arts and children's literature. In addition to many articles in the professional literature, she is senior author of *Raising Readers* and *Learning to Love Literature* (both NCTE titles) and of *Growing Up Reading* and *Growing Up*

Writing. Her most recent book is *Literature-Based Moral Education,* an outgrowth of her work with teachers at Blackburn Elementary School in Manatee County, Florida. She attended Principia College and the University of Illinois and received her doctorate from Syracuse University.

Renee Leonard is a fifth-grade teacher in the Lansing, Michigan, public schools. As a teacher-researcher, she is also working in the Literacy Project and the Inclusion Project sponsored by the Michigan Partnership for a New Education/MSU. She has presented at national conventions of professional organizations.

Jill P. May is professor of Children's Literature at Purdue University, West Lafayette, Indiana. She has published over fifty articles in national professional journals of English, library science, and folklore and has served on the editorial boards of journals for the Children's Literature Assembly, Children's Literature Association, National Association for the Preservation and Perpetuation of Storytelling, and Indiana Library Association. Her current research interests include exploring the roles of the visual arts with young audiences, including children's illustrated books, theatrical experiences for children, and film adaptations of literature.

Jean McCabe is an elementary school principal and coordinator of language arts for the Grand Haven, Michigan, public schools, where she developed and implemented a whole language curriculum and a support group for teachers of whole language. She has also been instrumental in the support of process writing, including writing assessment and portfolios. She is coauthor of the state's speaking and listening curriculum and participated in the pilot of Michigan's new writing assessment. She has taught courses in language arts for local universities and makes presentations to various organizations. She is an active member of the Michigan Reading Association and NCTE.

Peggy Oxley teaches second grade at St. Paul School in Westerville, Ohio, where she has developed a literature reading and writing program that is integrated throughout her curriculum. She is coauthor of *Reading and Writing, Where It All Begins: Helping Your Children at Home,* president of The Literacy Connection, a teacher support group, and cochair of the NCTE Notable Children's Books in the Language Arts Committee. She makes frequent presentations at teacher conferences and workshops throughout central Ohio.

Donna Peters is a seventh-grade language arts and social studies teacher at Elida Middle School in Elida, Ohio. She has nine years of experience teaching at the middle school level and earned her master's degree in Language, Literature, and Reading from The Ohio State University.

Melissa Reed is a senior at Purdue University, West Lafayette, Indiana, from which she will graduate in May 1995 with a degree in Elementary Education, with a minor in Reading and a Kindergarten Endorsement. She currently is student teaching in the Indianapolis, Indiana, area. She is a member of Teachers Encouraging a Love for Literature (TELL) and aspires to teach in the early elementary grades.

Peter Roop teaches first and second grades at McKinley Elementary School in Appleton, Wisconsin. His enthusiasm for reading and writing were recognized when he was chosen Wisconsin State Teacher of the Year. The coauthor of twenty-five children's books, he also writes journal articles and book chapters and is coauthor of *Educational Psychology: A Partnership*. A founding member of NCTE's Outstanding Nonfiction Books Committee, he also served on the Notable Trade Books Committee and makes frequent appearances at reading and writing conferences.

Patricia L. Scharer is assistant professor of Education at The Ohio State University at Lima, where she teaches undergraduate and graduate courses in children's literature, reading methods, and language arts instruction and serves as coordinator of the educational department. She has been an elementary teacher and spent several years as a Reading Recovery teacher. Her research focuses on the use of children's literature in elementary and middle school classrooms and has been published in such journals as *Research in the Teaching of English, The Reading Teacher, Language Arts,* and the yearbooks of both the National Reading Conference and the College Reading Association. She was recently awarded an Elva Knight Research Grant from the International Reading Association to explore book discussions using narrative and expository texts in fourth- and fifth-grade classrooms.

Mary Jo Skillings is professor of Education in the Elementary/Bilingual Department at California State University, San Bernardino. She is coordinator of the Collaborative Learning Network and Project Learn, a partnership teacher education and support program with the Ontario-Montclair, California, school districts. A former classroom teacher, Chapter I reading specialist, and reading-language consultant, she has published in educational periodicals and has written several manuscripts for children. Professional activities include presentations at local, regional, and national conferences and workshops for local school districts on topics of literature-based reading instruction and portfolio assessment.

Glenna Davis Sloan, a graduate of Teachers College, Columbia University, is professor of Education and chair of the Department of Elementary and Early Childhood Education, Queens College, CUNY. A specialist in reading, language arts, and children's literature, she also has teaching and administrative experience in elementary and junior high schools. Her publications include *The Child as Critic,* a book on the teaching of reading and language arts; a series of three reading skills texts for junior high school; a sixth-grade language arts text; articles in professional journals; and novels for young people. She was author and consultant for the instructional series *Literature: Uses of the Imagination.* She is a member of the International Reading Association and NCTE and was elected to the Elementary Section Steering Committee of NCTE.

Gail E. Tompkins is professor of Reading/Language Arts at California State University, Fresno, and codirector of the San Joaquin Valley Writing Project. She is author of *Teaching Writing: Balancing Process and Product*, coauthor (with Kenneth Hoskisson) of *Language Arts: Content and Teaching Strategies*, and coauthor (with Lea M. McGee) of *Teaching Reading with Literature*. A former elementary teacher, she continues to work with elementary teachers across the United States through staff development programs.

Sylvia Mergeler Vardell is associate professor at the University of Texas at Arlington, where she teaches courses in literature-based teaching of reading, multicultural children's literature, and teaching the writing process. In addition to book chapters and articles in *Language Arts, English Journal, The Reading Teacher, The New Advocate, Young Children,* and *Horn Book,* she is coauthor of a chapter in *Using Nonfiction Trade Books in the Elementary Classroom* (NCTE, 1992). She also served on the NCTE committee which established the Orbis Pictus Award for Outstanding Nonfiction for Children. She has made numerous presentations at state, regional, national, and international conferences and has received grants from NCTE and the National Endowment for the Humanities. She taught at the University of Zimbabwe in Africa as a Fulbright scholar in 1989. She is currently editor of *The State of Reading,* a journal of the Texas State Reading Association.

Mary Lee Webeck is a sixth-grade language arts and reading teacher at Roosevelt Middle School in Monticello, Indiana, and a graduate student in the School of Education at Purdue University, West Lafayette, Indiana, where she is studying children's literature and critical literary theory. Her research interests also include intertextual and cultural influences in middle school students' discourse and writing. She is a member and active on the board of Teachers Encouraging a Love for Literature (TELL).

Karla Hawkins Wendelin is associate professor of Curriculum and Instruction at the University of Nebraska–Lincoln, where she teaches courses in emerging literacy, children's literature, and literature for adolescents. The author of journal articles and book chapters, she is also a regular presenter at national, state, and local literacy conferences. She is a former elementary classroom teacher and is currently on a sabbatical teaching second grade.

Tammy Younts is a visiting instructor in the Department of Curriculum and Instruction at Purdue University in West Lafayette, Indiana, and a teacher leader in the Indiana Reading Recovery Program, an early intervention program for first graders. She has taught a variety of undergraduate courses in language and literacy and currently trains teachers in public school settings to implement Reading Recovery. She is a member of Teachers Encouraging a Love for Literature (TELL).